Dr. Memory's™ *Picture Perfect Spanish* is th ___ook I have seen for learning Spanish.

Picture Perfect Spanish makes learning a foreign language fun. Dr. Memory™ specializes in making the intangible tangible. His students actually **see** a tangible picture of the vocabulary and grammar they are learning. His highly imaginative pictures make Spanish vocabulary acquisition an "unforgettable" experience. It works!

A student using *Picture Perfect Spanish* can create thousands of original Spanish sentences - far more than is expected of a typical first-year high school Spanish student. Language students usually cram vocabulary words for tests but then quickly forget them. Dr. Memory's™ highly imaginative pictures **burn** the vocabulary into their minds.

I can think of no other Spanish book that approaches the novelty of Dr. Memory's™ *Picture Perfect Spanish*. Nor do I know of any that promises a student more fun.

Michael Fawcett, Ph.D.
Hispanic Languages and Literature

PICTURE PERFECT SPANISH

A Survival Guide to Speaking Spanish

JERRY LUCAS — DR. MEMORY™

Doctor Memory ™

Learning That Lasts™

Lucas Educational Systems, Inc. – Dallas, Texas
www.doctormemory.com

Published by:

LUCAS EDUCATIONAL SYSTEMS, INC.
Post Office Box 794747
Dallas, Texas 75248 U.S.A.

Printed in the United States of America

Library of Congress Card Number: 00-104324
ISBN: 1-930853-00-9

Lucas, Jerry
Picture Perfect Spanish

Dedication

To all people everywhere who have struggled trying to learn Spanish.

Acknowledgements

I wish to express my gratitude to all of the people over the years who have helped me. Bill Murray, who has been my right arm for twenty years; Rolland Dingman, Mike Webster, Tony Price and Jon McIntosh who have brought the pictures in my mind to life in so many projects; Robert Wiley and Rodney McGuire, who assisted me in so many ways; and my wife, Cheri, who has always believed in me and with me. I also wish to acknowledge the help of Paul Smythe, and especially Michael Fawcett, Ph. D. Hispanic Languages and Literatures, who was my technical advisor.

Contents

About the Author

As a boy with a very active mind, NBA legend Jerry Lucas challenged himself by inventing mental games to test his memory. At an early age, Jerry realized that being a successful student in school took knowing not only HOW to learn but also HOW TO RETAIN that learned information. He became determined to develop ways to make the learning process EASY, FUN and LONG-LASTING.

Like a farmer who plants small seeds in the soil and carefully tends them so that they grow, Jerry has devoted his life to cultivating ideas and methods for fun and easy memory-retention methods. The resulting methods are now known as **The Lucas Learning System**™ and have earned him the title of **Doctor Memory**™.

Jerry graduated Phi Beta Kappa from Ohio State University. Not only a scholastic achiever, he excelled as an athlete as well. Jerry became the only basketball player in collegiate history to lead the nation in field goal percentage and rebounding for three years, thus becoming the only three-time recipient of the Big Ten player-of-the-year award. This achievement still has not been duplicated or surpassed. Chosen seven times as an All-Pro during his professional basketball career, Jerry was named one of the 50 most outstanding NBA players of all time. Being inducted into the NBA Hall of Fame in 1979 was perhaps his crowning achievement as an athlete.

Recently, Jerry was chosen as one of the five most outstanding college basketball players of the twentieth century by *Sports Illustrated* in its article entitled "Team of the Ages," which appeared in the November, 1999 College Basketball preview issue.

Although Mr. Lucas initially achieved fame and success by his impressive basketball accomplishments, he continues to score off the court as well. Through the years, Jerry has taught his memory-retention system to millions of people either in seminars or through sales of his books. Not only did he co-author the *New York Times* best-seller *The Memory Book*, he also has entertained countless television viewers with guest appearances on TV talk shows during which he dazzled large numbers of studio audience members by demonstrating his ability to meet and remember all of their names.

In total, Jerry Lucas has authored more than sixty books in the field of memory training and learning systems. **Doctor Memory**™ is now widely known and respected as an expert in developing the many methods that encompass his concept known as **Learning That Lasts**™.

Foreword
Cheri Lucas

I had the good fortune as a child to be raised in beautiful Latin America. My father's career in international banking allowed my sisters and me to become both bicultural and bilingual by living for many years in Honduras, Guatemala and Venezuela. Speaking fluent Spanish has been an asset for me ever since, both professionally and socially.

About twelve years ago Jerry asked me if I could teach him some Spanish words. When I was putting myself through college I briefly tutored a young girl in Spanish and found it to be very frustrating. I had images of struggling to teach Jerry as an adult, because it had been so frustrating with my young student.

A short time later we took a long trip. Jerry thought it would be a good use of our time to teach him a few Spanish words on the long drive. I began to tell him the meaning of many words: "ojo," "nariz," "casa," etc. As I pronounced a word he would pronounce it back a couple of times, then quietly reflect on the word for a moment, creating a picture to go with each word. Unbelievably, at the end of our five-hour drive, Jerry had learned well over 100 Spanish words. I was speechless.

Learning vocabulary is now far easier than I would have ever dreamed as a young girl. Jerry's learning pictures make the process both easy and fun. When the words are learned his unique drills enable you to use your new vocabulary in interesting and fun applications to fully understand how to use the words you have learned.

The boring, repetitive, traditional learning method is a thing of the past. I found myself laughing out loud at many of Jerry's learning pictures and had a tough time putting the book down to move on to my other duties. Throughout the day, Jerry's pictures automatically entered my thought process, words in pictures that made them impossible to forget.

What I would have given during my college years to have had the advantage of this system for the student I tutored. Not only would it have been far easier for me to teach her, but she would have actually looked forward to her Spanish lessons. You are about to embark on one of the great adventures of your life. I know you will appreciate the years of work my husband has done to change the way Spanish is learned forever.

CHAPTER 1

The Present Day Educational Dilemma

When a child enters school he or she is normally very excited and full of anticipation for this new learning experience in his or her life. Far too quickly almost every student begins to make comments like, "I don't like this," or "This is no fun." Unfortunately, a young mind full of unlimited imagination and potential begins to turn off and tune out. Worst of all, children are not generally taught **How to Learn**, even though that is the proposed reason for going to school in the first place. Since a student is not taught **How to Learn**, he or she has to rely on boring repetition while trying to remember the necessary information to pass tests and become educated. It is not the fault of the many wonderful and dedicated teachers. They were never taught **How to Learn** either, so they can't teach what they in turn don't know.

The child, the child's parents and the child's teachers are not generally aware that the basic method of learning employed prior to entering school is altered forever after entering school. The method of learning in the home prior to school and the method of learning after entering school are diametrically opposed to one another. The "**learning battle**" doesn't really begin until a child enters school, and tragically, it doesn't have to be a battle at all. What began with such great expectations far too soon turns into a dull, lifeless routine. Can this process be changed? Yes! **Learning really can be fun**. Learning and laughing at the same time or laughing during the process of learning are not unnatural. It will happen more and more in schools, homes, churches and places of business when **The Lucas Learning System**™ is applied.

There are only three steps in the educational process. They are:
1) Getting information
2) Learning the information
3) Using the information that has been learned

Unfortunately there is a great chasm or abyss in our present day educational system between steps 1 and 3. **Getting information** is no problem. From textbooks to the internet information is readily available. **Learning the information**, since we are not taught how to learn, becomes the boring, repetitive, non-productive process that we have become all too familiar with. The rote process may enable us to remember the information long enough to pass a test, but it leaves our minds in short order, and we can't really **use the information**, because it hasn't really been learned. **You can't use what you lose**. Unfortunately, students try to learn and relearn the same information, such as the rules of capitalization, year after year. Not only do they forget most of it shortly after taking a test, but they graduate from high school, if indeed they do graduate, having forgotten or lost most of it. Students keep falling back into the chasm or abyss of unlearned information as shown in the drawing below. Eventually they get tired of crawling out of this hole time and time again.

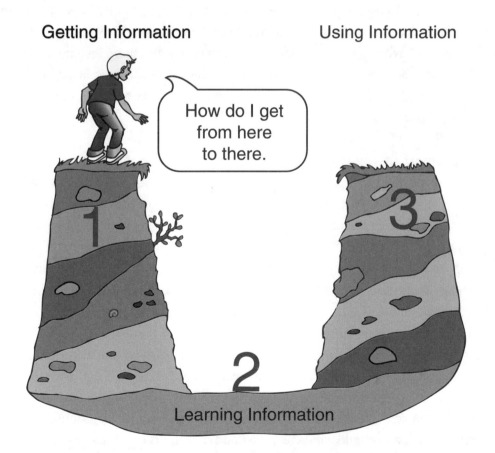

What they hoped to have learned was only crammed into their minds for a very short period of time. It didn't become knowledge. Students fall back into the chasm or abyss and have to climb back out time and time again. After a period of time and repeated failures, many of them simply give up and mentally drop out, which causes an alarming number to literally and physically drop out of school. When that happens the results are often disastrous.

Our prisons and welfare rolls are testaments to our failure in this area. If students don't give up but keep fighting this uphill battle, they take their learning frustrations into their adult lives and careers. Business and industry then spends billions of dollars trying to accomplish what wasn't accomplished in school. Unfortunately, the same repetitive processes continue to be used in business and industry, and the results are less than satisfactory. That is why you have a problem remembering such things as foreign vocabulary.

Everyone is attracted to what is enjoyable and rewarding in his or her life. It is my contention that we can and will change one of the most difficult and discouraging dilemmas facing America today. I believe you will agree with this statement after reading and applying the principles and learning systems taught in this book. We can make learning fun and rewarding. We can change young lives and give them hope instead of despair. We can teach students how to face, attack and solve learning problems effectively and efficiently. Even though this book is not about our total educational needs but about remembering Spanish, you will see a few examples and get some insight into why I believe this is true.

For example, if you have a mechanical problem with your automobile, you need to take it to a qualified mechanic who possesses the knowledge and has the proper tools with which to find and repair problems in your car. One problem may require a simple tool like a screwdriver or a wrench. Other problems may require much more sophisticated and perhaps even electronic tools. The correct tool or tools are selected from his toolbox to solve or repair each problem. You will feel much more at ease if you can find a **master mechanic**, because he certainly will not only have the tools for the job, but he will possess extraordinary skill with which to use them.

In education and in our social and business lives there are a variety of learning problems that need to be solved or fixed, if you will, like mechanical problems in a car. They include learning how to read and write, how to spell, grammar and punctuation rules, English and foreign vocabulary, definitions, formulas, the periodic table in chemistry, lists, numbers, muscle location, graphs, speeches, magazines or manuals, names and faces, **foreign languages**, dates and calendars and much more. Of course, the list goes on and on. Which learning tool did you use to learn definitions? Which learning tool did you use to learn formulas? Which learning tool did you use to learn vocabulary? For the subject matter of this book, which learning tool did you use to remember foreign vocabulary? The **tool** you used for each and every learning problem in the past is **a Stone Age tool** at best. It is the **Stone Age axe of repetition**. If we were **auto mechanics** we would be out of business in a hurry if we had only Stone Age tools, because we wouldn't possess the up-to-date tools to correct problems and be able to compete with more qualified mechanics, especially **Master Mechanics**. We approach every learning problem, even after years of school, by using repetition. This boring, rote-type process dulls the senses and defeats the user. Unfortunately your basic ability to learn and your knowledge of how to learn haven't changed much since you entered school. Yes, you have slugged it out with repetition over the years, but you are still using the Stone Age axe of repetition to try to learn. You have a very limited **mental toolbox**. Fortunately, there are **legitimate tools of learning** to select for various learning problems much like an auto mechanic selects the proper tool from his toolbox for his various needs. These **learning tools** enable the user to analyze, attack and solve any learning problem effectively, efficiently and with confidence. Most importantly, the user will experience rewarding, satisfying results as he or she selects the appropriate tool from a complete array of tools in his or her **mental toolbox**. My goal with this book is to make you a **Master Mind Mechanic** who knows how to easily remember **Spanish**, not with the **Stone Age axe of repetition** but with **sophisticated, modern, high-tech learning tools**. It is time for a much needed, refreshing and life-changing reformation.

In reality, we are still in the Stone Age as far as learning is concerned. So many incredible advances have occurred in other areas, but we still attempt to learn with repetition. Yes, we do have better repetition equipment like computers, but they still haven't changed the basic problem. It is time to **get out of the Stone Age** as far as learning is concerned and move into **high tech, up-to-date learning** methods available with **The Lucas Learning System**™.

I admire America's teachers. They are interested in the youth of America, wield considerable influence on their lives, and most of them are highly dedicated, underpaid in my opinion, and do the best job possible under the circumstances. Unfortunately they cannot teach what they have not been taught. Teachers, like the rest of us, were not taught learning systems when they were in school. They had to use the Stone Age axe of repetition to pass tests like everyone else. A teacher cannot teach what he or she has not been taught. As a result, students have to try to learn by boring repetition. Such attempted learning is no fun and becomes stressful for the teacher, the student and the parent who tries to help. This process develops a lack of confidence, a lack of self-esteem and causes people to grow into adulthood making statements like, "I can't seem to remember anything," or "I have a terrible memory." People don't have bad memories, just untrained ones.

This book will teach you how to learn Spanish with applications that go way beyond what was taught in *The Memory Book*. Many new applications have been developed since *The Memory Book* was published in 1973.

How It All Began for Me

As a boy I had a very active mind like most children, but the release of my mental energies began to be a little bit different than most people. I began to invent mental games to keep me occupied when I was bored, especially during long automobile trips. On one particular long vacation trip with nothing to do, I saw a word on a billboard and got an idea. I wondered what the word would look like if I mentally rearranged the letters in the word and put them in alphabetical order. So with my little grade school mind, I began to mentally rearrange the letters in alphabetical order. I did it, saw another word on a billboard and rearranged the letters alphabetically in that word as well. I continued to do it with other words I saw the rest of that trip. Some words were too long and complicated for me to even attempt at first, but I got hooked after that day and continued to do it every day of my life without anyone knowing it. Neither my parents nor my brother knew I was doing it. It was something to do to relieve boredom.

That mental game lead to many others in time. Suffice it to say that my mind was always active with some mental game or activity. As a matter of fact, I got so good that I could spell words alphabetically faster than others could regularly. I could spell them so fast that the letters blurred together and others couldn't decipher the letters I was calling out. I had to deliberately slow down so I could be understood. I will explain later how others began to discover that I spelled alphabetically.

I say all of this to let you understand that my mind was very active and looking for activity to keep it occupied. I began to realize that memory and learning was becoming more and more important to me as a student in grade school. I also began to realize that I was not being taught **How to Learn**. My teachers weren't saying things like, "Here is what you have to learn for your next test and here is how to learn it." They were saying things like, "Here is what you have to learn for your next test. The test will be on Friday."

No further help was forthcoming, except maybe some repetitive drills in class. Learning the material was being left up to me. I was on my own. What did that mean? Repetition - repetition - repetition. I didn't like it and neither did my classmates, but what could we possibly do? I didn't know, but I sure didn't like what I had to do to pass my tests. I was doing well on tests because I was diligent, but eventually I said to myself, "There has to be an easier, more fun and long-lasting way of learning than repetition," and the greatest adventure of my life began. I was determined to think of ways to make the learning process easy, fun and long-lasting. That meant experimentation and lots of trial and error. Now my active mind had a real adventure to explore, a real challenge. That simple beginning, that small seed has grown into **The Lucas Learning System**™.

At first, since I was so good at alphabetical spelling, I began to take the first letters of words in lists I had to remember and alphabetize them. I remembered the alphabetical list, and it was a memory aid that helped lead me to the actual list, because the alphabetized letters triggered the information in the list. I wouldn't know for years that I was using a very basic **anagram** device. An **anagram** learning device is a word or phrase developed by rearranging the beginning letters of a word, phrase or list. As a young boy I began to use that idea without realizing what it was. Since this idea was limited in its application, I began to experiment with other ideas, be involved in trial and error, and eventually began to research memory training. Through the years, **The Lucas Learning System**™ began to take form and become reality.

Several people have taught general applications using memory aids of one kind or another that have been helpful, but I believe my contribution to learning has been the development of unique, in-depth systems and applications that not only solve learning problems but also specific educational needs. I have even written several, detailed curricula for educational needs that I believe will forever change the way we teach and learn.

It is vitally important that you start all over again with the learning process. I am going to take you back to the place where all of the trouble really began, when you entered school. You had no real learning problems before then, because your parents, your first and best teachers, were using the best method of learning, but they really didn't know it. You will soon learn what your parents did to teach you and why it was so successful. You didn't have to worry about trying to learn intangible letters, numbers, words and symbols before entering school. You also had a great imagination as a child. You invented playmates and situations to keep your mind and your time occupied. As children, we get bored very easily and develop all kinds of make-believe situations to stay active and occupied.

School, unfortunately, dulls that great imagination. We don't like what we have to do and subconsciously click off our imaginations and similar skills to try and find something more enjoyable and fascinating. Unfortunately, this leads to far too much television, too many video games and passive activities instead of active applications. What differed in my development was that I didn't click off my imagination. I turned up the imaginative and creative juices even more by trying to develop tools of learning. As a result, Dr. Richard Watson, a good friend of mine who has tested some of my learning curricula, has said to me, "Jerry, you're different from the rest of us teachers because you think like a child." I consider that to be one of the greatest compliments I have ever received, and he meant it that way. You need to start thinking once again like you did when you were a child. I will teach you how to stoke the childish fires of your imagination and how to have the wide-eyed anticipation you once had toward learning before school altered it.

A Beginning for You

There are several points I want to discuss and have you understand before actually beginning to teach you. It is vitally important that you understand the principles behind **The Lucas Learning System**™ before any instruction starts.

The very best way to begin is with a test. Isn't that wonderful? I will be able to predict how you will do on this short test. All I want you to do is mentally answer yes or no to the following questions. Here they are:

1) _____ Yes _____ No   Can you describe what a giraffe looks like?

2) _____ Yes _____ No   Can you name the 23 uses of a hyphen in grammar and punctuation? You might be thinking, "I had no idea there were 23 uses of a hyphen." I find that English teachers even make that comment.

3) _____ Yes _____ No   Can you list the furniture in your living room in order from left to right around the room without being in the room?

4) _____ Yes _____ No   Can you name 30 of the 48 rules of capitalization from grammar and punctuation? You might be thinking the same kind of thoughts you did when I asked you about the

uses of a hyphen, "I had no idea there were 48 rules of capitalization." In my research when writing curriculum for grammar and punctuation, I found that many rules were grouped together instead of separated for clarity and better understanding.

5) _____ Yes _____ No   Can you name the basic parts of the outside of an automobile from front to back? This does not mean that you would have to name any working parts in the engine or drive chain.

6) _____ Yes _____ No   Can you write the formula for the quadratic equation?

7) _____ Yes _____ No   Can you describe the appearances of most of the houses on the street where you live?

8) _____ Yes _____ No   Can you list the rules for using an apostrophe?

9) _____ Yes _____ No   Can you describe the basic contents and location of the items in your chest of drawers?

10) _____ Yes _____ No   Can you name elements number 10, 30, 9, 41, 16 and 5 from the periodic table in chemistry?

I would say that you answered a yes to questions 1, 3, 5, 7 and 9. Why am I so sure? Because those were all tangible items that you have seen with your eyes. They are not intangibles that conjure up no picture in your mind. To understand the importance of that last statement, I must talk about the learning process of a young child. This child could have been you or me.

When a child reaches the age when he or she is able to communicate with his or her parents, the first learning experiences begin. Parents are normally very eager to begin teaching their children and, in fact, become the first and best teachers the child ever has as I have already stated. You will understand why I believe parents are the best teachers a child ever has as this discussion continues. A parent begins to teach a child the only normal and natural way he or she can. Since the child can't read and doesn't know numbers, printed material certainly can't be used. All a parent can do is point to and identify tangible objects in the home and environment. In this process the following is typical. A parent will point to an object, perhaps a chair and say, "This is a chair. Look at it. This is a chair. Say chair." The child then looks at the chair, says what it is and is rewarded by the parent with a hug, smile or similar pleasantry. The child may not actually learn what a chair is with this initial exposure, but after a few other exposures and similar incidents the child will learn what a chair is. How does this learning take place? What actually happens can be explained in the following sequence. The child **sees** the chair, **recognizes** what it is and **registers** a picture of it in his or her mind. A miracle has just occurred, but the greatest miracle is yet to occur. What is really exciting is that the next time and every time that child ever thinks of a chair again, a picture of a chair automatically appears in the child's mind. The child **retrieves** a mental picture of a chair effortlessly and automatically. The knowledge of a chair has forever been locked into that child's mind. It can never be lost or forgotten for the rest of the child's life. The information has become **knowledge** which is **the goal of all education**. This is the first and most important miracle of learning. It will be repeated thousands and thousands of times during that child's life. It is what I have come to call **Automatic Learning**™, because the information is retrieved automatically.

I want to lead you through a typical sequential learning experience in the life of a child. A parent will typically do the following when beginning to teach a child to recognize animals, for instance. The parent could point to a picture of a cow and say something like this, "This animal is called a cow. Look at this picture. This is a cow. This animal has four legs. Do you see the four legs? We get milk from cows. Say cow. Look at this picture again and say cow again. What is this animal called? Cow, that is correct. Look at the picture and say cow one more time." This procedure will continue until the child learns what a cow is. What happens during this process? Once again the child must **see** the cow and **recognize** the cow, so he or she can **register** a picture of a cow in his or her mind. At the instant the child understands the identity of a cow a picture of a cow is automatically registered in the mind. Once the picture has been registered in the mind, the child can **retrieve** a mental picture of a cow by just thinking of it, because now the child knows what it looks like. Another miracle has taken place. The cow has become **knowledge** that the child can use. The bold words are **see**, **recognize**, **register**, **retrieve** and **knowledge**. These five words make up the process of learning that I call **Automatic Learning**™.

In the next learning session the teaching might continue like this. Let's assume that the parent then shows the child a picture of a horse and asks what it is. I think that we would agree that the child would call a horse a cow if asked to identify the animal without any explanation, because the child has never seen a horse before. The only animal the child knows is a cow. It is the only animal the child has **seen** and **registered** in the mind. The parent could then point to the picture of the horse and say something like this, "This animal is called a horse. Look at this picture. This is not a cow but it is a horse. This animal also has four legs like a cow, but it is different from a cow as I will **show** you. We don't get milk from a horse. I also want you to see that a horse has a longer neck and a different shaped head and tail. People ride on horses to get from one place to another. They were used to get from one place to another before we had cars. Say horse. Look at this picture again and say horse again. What is this animal called? Horse, that is correct. Look at the picture and say horse one more time." The parent will probably point to a cow and a horse one at a time and ask the child to identify it. When the parent is assured that the child has recognized the difference between a cow and a horse, the lesson will probably end. Once again the child must **see** the horse and **recognize** it, so he or she can **register** a picture of a horse in his or her mind. Once the picture has been registered in the mind, the child can **retrieve** a mental picture of a horse by just thinking of it, because now the child knows what it looks like. Another miracle has taken place. The horse has now become **additional knowledge** that the child can use. Now the child knows the difference between a cow and a horse, because he or she has **seen** the difference and **registered** the differences in his or her mind.

I want to go through only one more potential lesson in this series. I will make the assumption that next, the parent will teach the child what a giraffe is. The parent would point to a picture of the giraffe. If the parent asked the child what the animal was, he or she would most likely say a horse; of course, because it looks most like that animal he or she has already learned. At that time, the mental retrieval storage mechanism, the mind, only has two animals stored in it to call upon to compare with the giraffe. The parent would probably say, "This animal is called a giraffe. It is not a horse. Look at this picture, and I will **show** you the differences. This animal also has four legs like a cow and a horse, but it is different from both of them as you will **see**. We don't get milk from a horse or a giraffe, only from a cow. I also want you to see that a giraffe has a much longer neck and a different shaped head and tail." The parent would probably point out other differences that the child could **see**. The parent then might say, "Look at this picture again and say giraffe. What is this animal called? A giraffe, that is correct. Look at the picture and say giraffe one more time." The parent will probably point to each animal one at a time and ask the child to identify it. When the parent is assured that the child has recognized the differences between a cow, a horse and a giraffe, this lesson may end. Once again the child must **see** the giraffe and **recognize** it, so he or she can **register** a picture of a giraffe in his or her mind. Once the picture has been registered in the mind, the child can **retrieve** a mental picture of a giraffe by just thinking of it, because now the child knows what it looks like. Another miracle has taken place. The giraffe has now become **additional knowledge** that the child can use. Now the child knows the difference between a cow, a horse and a giraffe, because he or she has **seen** the differences and **registered** the differences in his or her mind. The mental retrieval storage mechanism has added another picture to **retrieve** at any time. The **knowledge** that the child possesses has grown by one more tangible item. There is no limit to the amount of information that can be registered in the mind with pictures, because each tangible item is different from other tangible items, and each item has its own specific identity that conjures up its identity when it is thought about. It should be very comforting to realize that there is no limit to the amount of information that can be registered in the mind using your **photographic mental ability**. The only limit is the amount of time you are willing to spend developing and inputting information. You will be very excited when you learn how easy it is to do this.

What does this mean? It means that we have been blessed with the God-given ability to see pictures in our minds, and it is the only way for us to learn as children. As children we learn by the following already mentioned procedure. We **see, recognize, register** and **retrieve** information that becomes usable **knowledge** by **storing pictures in our mind**. We all have what I have come to call a **photographic mind**. Notice that I didn't say a photographic memory but a photographic mind. My definition of a **photographic mind** is simply the innate ability that we all possess to store and retrieve pictures of tangible items we have seen, recognized and registered in our minds. We actually possess an **automatic photographic mind**, because the retrieval mechanism works automatically. This is what I now call **Automatic Learning**™. Once a tangible item has been learned, a picture of that item automatically appears on the **mental screen** in our mind when we think of it. Even blind people see pictures in their minds. My first blind student had been blind from birth, and I told him that I didn't think my systems would help him, because **The Lucas Learning System**™ was dependent on our innate ability to see pictures in our minds. His reply was, "I don't have any problem seeing pictures in my mind. I may not see exactly the same thing in my mind as you do when I think of an elephant, for instance, but I know what an elephant looks like to me from having one described to me and having felt a statue of an elephant. I have no difficulty seeing pictures and distinguishing one thing from another in my mind." I was pleasantly surprised, and he turned out to be an exceptional student.

Your photographic mind will enable you to learn faster and better than you ever dreamed possible. It is the only way we can possibly learn as a child and is, and always will be, the best way of learning anything. That is why our parents are our best teachers, in my opinion, because they teach us by using our very best learning gift. What they teach us in this photographic style is never lost or forgotten. It becomes **knowledge** that we can use throughout our lifetime. I will teach you how to use your photographic mind in remembering Spanish. Be encouraged, you have far more ability to learn than you ever imagined. I have far more confidence in you than you have in yourself, and you will learn that my confidence in you is warranted as you proceed through this book.

I haven't yet discussed the definition of a photographic memory. The two words actually define themselves. They mean to photograph and remember. Someone with a pure photographic memory would have the ability to photograph and remember everything the eyes saw. That person could look at page after page of printed material, for instance, photograph the information from the pages on his or her mind, and be able to recreate or retrieve that information by reproducing the printed pages on the mental screen in his or her mind. I don't believe anyone has that ability. I know I don't, but I have come closer and closer to that ability by learning how to use my photographic mind. Now it's your turn.

Observation

Before teaching you the **tool of learning** you will use to remember Spanish, some further explanatory discussion is warranted. Observation is very important in learning. Observation is defined in the dictionary as the act of noting, perceiving or seeing. It is my contention that there is much more to true observation than this dictionary definition. I think information must be registered on the mind before it is truly observed. Let me prove it by taking you through a few of the observation drills that I use in my seminars.

You may be wearing a watch. If so, don't look at it until after I ask you a question and then ask you to look at it. Since you own the watch, you have seen it hundreds or even thousands of times. Try to answer this question about the number six on your watch without looking at it. Do you think the number six on your watch is a Roman numeral or the regular Arabic number six that we use in our number system? Please don't cop out and say, "I'm not really sure." If you aren't sure, guess. After you have decided which of the two you believe the number six to be, look at your watch to see if you were correct. Typically about 20% of you will have missed. Most of the people who miss realize for the first time that they don't even have a number six on their watch but just a dot, dash or some kind of mark in the place where the number six should be. You may have been one of them. Certainly the people who miss have seen their watches many times, but true observation didn't occur, because **the information didn't register on their minds**.

I also ask people in my seminars to try to remember who is pictured on five, ten and twenty dollar bills. When I ask the audience to respond in unison by calling out the last names of the men pictured on those bills, it is amazing the names that are called out. But I do ask everyone to participate in the drill by calling out a name even if they aren't sure. I ask them to at least guess "Smith" if no other name comes to mind. You may not know who is pictured on these three bills. Certainly the people in my seminars have seen a myriad of these bills before, but many can't remember because the **information didn't register on their minds**. Their response is normally, "I haven't seen enough money to be sure. I guess I need to see a lot more of it." A pretty greedy excuse at best.

Let me ask you about a phone dial as I do the students in my seminars. Please don't look at a phone dial if one is near you. I want you to try to remember which letters of the alphabet are on the number one on a phone dial. In my seminars, I ask for a show of hands of the people who think the letters A, B and C are on the number one, and about two-thirds of the hands go up. Do you agree with them? If you do, you all are wrong, because there are no letters on the number one of a phone dial. The letters begin on the number two. There are also no letters on the zero, and two letters are missing. Do you know which ones? Most people can't answer these questions even though they see and use a phone almost daily. True observation doesn't really take place, because the **information isn't registered in the mind**, and the information isn't remembered. Are you beginning to agree that there is more to observation than the act of noting, perceiving or seeing?

One more observation drill should suffice to drive home my point. In a moment, I want you to advance to the next page and read the few large, bold words at the top of the page. Here are my instructions before turning to the next page. When you read the large, bold words don't speed read them and don't drag through them slowly. Just read them at a normal rate of speed to yourself. Don't read them out loud. Then after you read the words only once, I want you to continue reading the rest of the information on the page without looking back at the large, bold words. Do it now.

PARIS IN THE THE SPRING

How many of the words "the" did you read? Almost 100% of the people in my seminars answer one "the," but they are wrong. I would imagine that you might have had the same answer.

Now look at the words again, and you will notice that there are actually two "the's" among those few words. What happened? Yes, you saw both "the's" with your eyes, because you looked at the words, and they were there, but one of them didn't register in your mind. True observation didn't take place. **To retain information it must register in your mind**. To learn better you need a better "registerer." You already possess the necessary talent to have that happen. Your photographic mind will allow you to accomplish that task, but you need the proper **learning tools** to make it happen with Spanish.

What Is Learning

Before discussing learning tools, I want to spend a little time discussing the actual process of learning. Learning is simply the process of connecting items of information together. Most learning requires the connection of **one** piece of information to **one** other piece of information. Examples of this would include a state to its capital, a product to its price, a name to a face, a word to its definition, a number in the periodic table to the element at that number, or **an English word to its foreign equivalent when learning languages, including Spanish**. I call this **One-On-One Learning**. I played basketball for many years at all levels of competition and played the well known **One-On-One** game countless times when practicing. That simply means **that one player plays against one other player**, and the best and most accomplished player wins the game. It would be far more difficult for a player to win if he or she had to play **Two-On-One**, **Three-On-One**, **Four-On-One** or even **Five-On-One**. When I was young, I used to be the One in Two-On-One and even Three-On-One games. I felt I would have to work harder and improve faster if I had to play against two or even three players at a time. You won't be faced with these kinds of odds when learning Spanish vocabulary. It will be a simple **One-On-One** learning opportunity. You will be associating one English word to one Spanish word, and you will soon find out that I have done all of the work for you. My practice sessions will pay off for you.

The Tools of Learning

There are **eight basic tools of learning** with some of them having adaptations or variations that the **Master Mind Mechanic** must understand and have at his or her disposal in his or her **mental toolbox**. He or she must also know which tool or tools to select for which learning problem or problems. You only need to know one of these tools to have success remembering Spanish. That tool is **The Sound-Alike Word System**. This tool is used to make intangible words tangible so they can be seen as easily as a cow or any other tangible object. Since I have done all of the work for you in learning Spanish you don't really need to know how to apply it. However, I do want you to fully understand its use and application. The basic purpose of all of these tools is to make the intangible tangible so it can be seen and easily registered in the mind. There is nothing more intangible than a foreign word when you don't know the language.

I also want you to become an **ODD person**. I became a very **ODD** person. What do I mean by that? I mean that I was very Organized, Disciplined and Diligent. The three letters in the word **ODD** stand for Organized, Disciplined and Diligent. I will talk about organization, discipline and diligence throughout this book. A student in college, for instance, should return to his or her residence after a lecture and briefly organize lecture notes and class instruction to determine what needs to be learned. As a college student I was **organized** and **disciplined** because, being an athlete in a major sport, I didn't have as much time as other students did. I was also **diligent** to review the learning aids I had developed. I always arranged for interviews with my professors to learn how they conducted their classes. I asked if they tested from lectures or the textbook. If he or she said, "I test from my lectures only," I wouldn't even buy a textbook. I simply made sure I attended every class, took good notes and **organize**d my notes on a regular basis. As a result I was a straight "A" student my freshman year at Ohio State University. The important thing for me was to be **disciplined** to do a little each day so I wouldn't get way behind and have to stay up long hours when mid-term and final tests were given. I was also **diligent** to review on weekends. Since I have done all of the major learning work for you for Spanish vocabulary I'm not talking about something that requires hours of application on a daily basis. I'm just talking about a little here and a little there on a regular basis. On a regular basis is the most important point. Learn to be an **ODD** person.

I will tell you many times when you begin to learn Spanish vocabulary that you need **a little bit of discipline** to be successful. In almost anything you do in life it only takes **a little bit of discipline** to be successful.

During my names and faces seminars I always hold my index finger and thumb together and say in a shrill, high voice, "I was able to learn how to picture names, because I had **a little bit of discipline.**" I then ask those in attendance to do and say the same thing. Several hundred people hold their index finger and thumb together and repeat in a shrill, high voice, "**A little bit of discipline**." I want them to begin to understand, as I do you, that all it takes to be successful in remembering anything is to have **a little bit of discipline**.

You see an artist's picture of me below holding my fingers together in this same fashion reminding you that you only need to have **a little bit of discipline** to be successful. In the picture I am going fishing to try to hook a few more Spanish words.

CHAPTER 2

The Sound-Alike Word System

You have already read that the **Sound-Alike Word System** is a **tool** that is used to make intangible words tangible, so they can be pictured in the mind. Most of what we are called upon to learn is in word form. What could be more intangible than foreign vocabulary, so this tool is very important. Of course there are many words that are already tangible and automatically conjure up a picture in the mind in English for an English speaking person. Those are the kinds of words that your parents and others began to teach you prior to entering school. Our problem is not with these words because they can be seen in our mind. Our problem is with intangible words. They are abstract or intangible and don't conjure up a comfortable picture in the mind. If you think of an elephant you can easily see an image of an elephant in your mind, but what about a **pronoun**? If a pronoun came to your front door do you think you would say, "Well, there's a pronoun. I haven't seen one of those in three or four days." I would think it is safe to say you have never seen a pronoun and wouldn't know how to go about seeing one. In that sense a pronoun is a **nothing**. By being a **nothing** I mean it has no tangible identity and conjures up no tangible picture in your mind. It isn't a something like a cat, horse, dog or tree that you can easily see in your mind.

It is difficult to learn that kind of intangible information in school. You had no idea what a pronoun was or looked like, so you attempted to go over and over the words that defined a pronoun until hopefully you learned the definition. To complicate matters, the words that defined it were also intangible. They were also a **nothing**. I say to people in my seminars, "So then, what were we trying to learn in school? **Nothing!**" The information was a nothing, since it had no tangible identity. My goal as a boy was to try to make intangible information tangible so I could see it. If I could **make a nothing a something** learning it would be easy.

A pronoun isn't a particularly hard problem, because it is defined with only a few words. When you had twenty or thirty rules in grammar to learn and had nothing to look at but intangible words, frustration set in quickly, and the joy of learning vanished in a hurry. The **Sound-Alike Word System** will give you the ability to make intangible words tangible, so you can see them like a cat, horse, cow or dog. Then they will be easy to learn.

The idea behind this system is to develop a new word that will be tangible in place of the original word that can't be pictured. We know what a squirrel or a fox looks like. Each has its individual identifiable picture, so we can't confuse it with anything else. We can do the same thing with a **pronoun** or any other intangible word using the **Sound-Alike Word System**. We simply say the original word slowly and think of something that it sounds like that can be pictured, thus the **Sound-Alike Word System**. It doesn't have to necessarily sound exactly like the original word, but the closer we can come to the actual pronunciation the better. Look at this picture.

You see a picture of a **nun**, a catholic nun. She is swinging a golf club. She is a very good golfer. As a matter of fact she is a **pro** golfer. That makes her a **pro-nun** or a **pronoun**. Now you have seen your first pronoun. That picture does not teach you what a pronoun is. It is not intended to. It is simply intended to show you that you can see an intangible that to this point never had a tangible identity in your mind. If you saw a nun walking toward you swinging a golf club you could now point to her and say, "There is a pronoun. I have seen one of those before."

When my children were young I wanted to make the learning process fun for them, so I developed a learning picture for the basics that they had to learn in school. I changed what was previously intangible and had no identity to tangible pictures that had an identity and had artists draw the tangible learning pictures, so my children could easily **see**, **recognize**, **register** and **retrieve** the information from their minds. The ultimate goal was to make learning so much fun that they would be eager to learn more. They were, and in time I began to teach them my sophisticated learning systems and tools so they could become **Master Mind Mechanics** themselves. When they needed to learn the states and capitals, I developed and showed them pictures of the states and capitals that connected a state to its capital in a tangible picture. They were learning that each state and capital had its own identifiable picture like a cow, horse or giraffe.

In the picture above you see a picture on an **ark**, like Noah's Ark, with a **can** in front of it. The ark is holding a **saw**. An **ark**, a **can** and a **saw** are my sound-alike words for the state of **Arkansas**. The word Arkansas is no longer an intangible nothing. It has now become a something with a tangible identity. To learn the capital it is necessary to see it pictured with the picture of the state. Look at the picture again, and you will see that the can is being used as a holding place, so the ark can saw a **little rock** in half. This pictures not only teaches that the capital of **Arkansas** is **Little Rock**, it also allows the student to see it in a tangible picture. **What was a nothing has been changed to a something that can never be forgotten**. The reason it can't be forgotten is that every time the student thinks of Arkansas after seeing and studying this picture, the picture will automatically appear in the mind. It is impossible for that not to happen. That is the way God has made our minds work. It is out of our control. Let me prove it more conclusively by asking you not to do something. It is easy not to do things. Doing something is often hard for many people, but doing nothing is easy. Here is my request. Please do not see a zebra in your mind. That's right, do not see a zebra. You saw a zebra didn't you. It is impossible not to see any tangible item in your mind when you think of it. It's how the mind functions. It is out of our control. Like it or not, for the rest of your life, every time you think of Arkansas the picture of an Arkansas you just saw will pop into your mind. You can't forget it now because you have seen it.

I developed pictures for all of the states and capitals to make it easy for my children to learn them. Other parents asked me to help their children learn the states and capitals with the same pictures, so I eventually published a book of the states and capitals so others could learn them as quickly and efficiently as my children had. Something that had been such a problem in the past had become fun to learn. I continued to create more and more and more educational material to make the learning process for everything else as easy as learning Arkansas and Little Rock.

If you are interested in making learning fun and easy for you and your family, you will find a listing of a wide variety of books covering many subject matters listed at the back of this book. All of these books use The Lucas Learning System™ and are full of full color pictures to make the process of learning other material as easy as it was for Arkansas and Little Rock. Dr. Memory™ has done all of the work for you. There is no reason that you and your family shouldn't have fun when you learn. You can laugh and learn at the same time.

I must get on a soapbox at this point. If I had the attention of a million grade school children by satellite hookup and asked this question, "How many of you know what a cow is? Raise your hand if you know. How many of you know what a horse is? Raise your hand if you know. How many of you know what a bear is? Raise your hand if you know." What do you think the response would be? I don't think there is any doubt that every child would raise his or her hand on every everyday tangible object I would mention, because they all would have seen them. What if I asked this question, "How

many of you know the capital of the state of Arkansas? Raise your hand if you know."
Or what if I asked, "How many of you know the twenty-three uses of a hyphen? Raise
your hand if you know." What percentage of the hands do you think might be raised in
response to those questions? It is anybody's guess, but I think we could agree that the
response probably would be 100% would not know the twenty-three uses of a hyphen.
Why? Because they had never seen them tangibly like a cow or a horse. Their photographic minds easily retrieved a cow and other tangible items, but they had never even
seen an Arkansas or the rules of using a hyphen. Hopefully school children all over
America will learn the states and capitals and much, much more from Dr. Memory's™ fun
learning materials.

Let's make another assumption. What if I showed the picture of Arkansas and
Little Rock to those same children and taught it to them? If I had the same satellite
hookup with the same one million children one week later and once again asked this question, "How many of you know what a cow is? Raise your hand if you know." As the week
before, I think that every child would raise his or her hand, because they all would still
know what a cow was. What if I asked this question again, "How many of you know the
capital of the state of Arkansas? Raise your hand if you know." I think that we could
probably agree that practically all of the children would raise their hands, because they
had the opportunity to **see**, **recognize**, **register** and now **retrieve** a picture of an Arkansas.
What a difference a picture makes! You have heard the cliché, "A picture is worth a thousand words." It certainly is when it comes to learning. It is my contention that every child
in every school should have the opportunity to learn with these kinds of pictures. They
would have more fun, look forward to the process more eagerly, and certainly have more
confidence and self-esteem, and they would learn.

The long-range goal would be to teach them to use learning systems to be able to
create their own learning aids and become **Master Mind Mechanics** themselves. What
if we fell somewhat short of that goal with every child? Motivation enters into each life
and its activity. At least they would learn the basics of what have become known as the
three R's. They would learn how to read, write and many other skills by pictures and
could become a functioning member of society instead of a ward of society who ends up
in prison or on welfare, because they didn't learn basic skills in school with which to
become gainfully employed. This is not a pipe dream. It is what has consumed me for
the last thirty years. Enough soap boxing, back to the job at hand.

You need to learn how to remember Spanish words as easily as you just learned
Arkansas and Little Rock. You will soon find out that you can.

I'm sure you have said many times to many people, "I'm sorry, I remember your face, but I just can't remember your name." This statement is repeated thousands, if not millions, of times daily around the world. Have you ever wondered why people don't say, "Sir, I remember your name, but I'm sorry I just can't seem to remember your face." The answer to this question is rather obvious. We all remember faces much better than names, because we see faces and only hear names.

If we are called upon to learn, or want to learn, a foreign language, it becomes frustrating because every word in the foreign language is intangible. Learning vocabulary is always the most difficult part of learning a foreign language. Some Spanish learning courses would like people to think that there is no memory work involved in learning a new language. They advertise that the student just needs to listen to a set of audio cassettes and the language will be learned. I beg to differ. Students who listen to audio foreign language courses continually struggle with the vocabulary as all students of a foreign language do.

In Spanish, for example, a **house** is not a house but a **casa**. It is a totally intangible word to the beginning student. However, you are fortunate. This course is the most unique and revolutionary foreign language course ever created. You will tangibly **see** every Spanish word you learn as easily as you have seen a horse, a cow or a dog. You will **see** the Spanish word pictured with its English counterpart in a tangible format. You will also **see** the exact and perfect pronunciation of the Spanish word tangibly. There will never be a doubt as to how the Spanish word should be pronounced. This has never been done before, for any language, to my knowledge. It took many, many years of research, writing and artwork, but now it is completed. You will **see** all Spanish words tangibly, not just nouns, but all of them. Congratulations on the start of a great and natural learning adventure.

We start to learn tangible items in our native tongue as our parents point out tangible items to us. These words, or nouns, are automatically learned through this process. Learning other parts of speech, such as verbs, adverbs, adjectives, pronouns, prepositions, conjunctions and interjections is more difficult; because most of them are not tangible and don't conger up comfortable pictures in the mind. This is why people struggle while trying to increase their vocabulary knowledge. Luckily, because of how this course is structured, acquiring a good Spanish vocabulary won't be that frustrating.

To begin this course, you will learn the basic sounds made by the letters of the Spanish alphabet. Incidentally, there are far fewer sounds in the Spanish language than there are in the English language even though the Spanish alphabet contains more letters.

CHAPTER 3

The Spanish Alphabet

The Spanish alphabet has thirty (30) letters, four more than the English alphabet. If you know the English alphabet, you will know the Spanish alphabet except for the four new letters. Three of the additional letters are actually two letters that represent single sounds. They are treated as one letter, because they are never divided. These three sounds are "ch," "ll," and "rr." The fourth is a letter "ñ" with a mark called an **en-yeah** over it. The **"yeah"** sound here is as though you were cheering at a sporting event. The letter "ch" in Spanish sounds like a "ch" in English, but it is considered to be one letter. The pronunciations of these four sounds will be pictured along with the sounds of the entire Spanish alphabet when necessary. In reality the Spanish alphabet only has twenty-nine (29) letters, because the letter "w" is used in foreign words only.

a	f	l	p	u
b	g	ll	q	v
c	h	m	r	w
ch	i	ñ	rr	x
d	j	n	s	y
e	k	o	t	z

A complete listing of the Spanish alphabet and the pronunciation of each letter is on our web site for review purposes.

Just as there are regional differences in pronunciation of English words in the United States, there are also regional or global differences in pronunciation of Spanish words. Since more Americans use Spanish in the United States itself or in Latin America for business purposes or pleasure, this course will use the Latin American pronunciation and not the Castilian pronunciation of Central and Northern Spain. There are, however, minor differences in pronunciation among some Latin American countries just as there are different pronunciations in various regions of the United States.

Since this course is based on **seeing** the sounds made by Spanish words, **the sounds made by the letters of the Spanish alphabet must be pictured** and learned tangibly. We will start with the vowels, which are the most important sounds in any language.

This course teaches conversational Spanish and is not an advanced Spanish course. You will learn all of the basics, an extensive vocabulary, some Spanish grammar and some verb conjugations. You will also learn how to communicate easily and freely in basic phrases and sentences. You will learn how to make statements, both affirmative and negative, and how to ask and answer questions.

It is imperative to be able to **see** the sound or sounds made by letters to be able to **see** the exact pronunciations of Spanish words. All Spanish sounds will be pictured for you, but you should have a basic understanding of the sounds made by the letters in the Spanish alphabet for your own knowledge.

Some letters are **reliable**: that is, they make only **one sound** all of the time. They can be depended upon! Other letters are **unreliable**, that is, they can and do make **more than one sound** when used in different words. Strangely enough, there are far more unreliable letters in English than there are in Spanish.

Big Boss Vowels

All words are made up of syllables or a single syllable, and the vowel in each syllable determines the basic sound of the syllable. In the how to read and write course which contains two components, *Dr. Memory's*™ *Alphabet Friends* and *Dr. Memory's*™ *See and Know Picture Words*, vowels are the **Big Bosses** of every **syllable**. That simply means that the vowel forces the rest of the letters in its syllable to take on its sound. If the vowel is long, the syllable is a long syllable. If the vowel is short, the syllable is a short syllable. This is why vowels are so important.

Each Spanish vowel is clearly pronounced and not slurred over as happens sometimes in English. All letters in the Spanish alphabet are not pronounced the same way as in English, so they will be pictured for you as they are pronounced in English, since you don't yet know Spanish. You will not need a picture for all Spanish letters, since many of them are pronounced the same way in English and Spanish.

      A - An Ape in the exact same shape of a capital letter "**A**" to picture a letter "**A**." All of the alphabet letter pictures not only **look exactly like the letter**, but they also **sound exactly like the letter** as it is said when saying the alphabet.

      The letter "**A**" in the English language makes four sounds, **long** "**a**" as in the word **ape**, **short** "**a**" as in the word **apple**, the sound of "**uh**" as in the word **aquarium** and the sound "**ah**" as in the word Amish. The Letter "**A**" is the second most unreliable letter in the English alphabet. It can and does make four sounds. The Spanish alphabet has far fewer sounds than the English alphabet.

      The letter "**A**" in Spanish only makes one sound, and it is the sound of "**Ah**" as in Amish. It is the sound a doctor asks you to say when he places a tongue depressor in your mouth. The doctor says, "Say ah." Therefore, it is reliable. The picture of the ape below will teach you that Spanish sound. As you can see the Ape looks exactly like a letter **A**. You will also notice that the Ape has a **tongue depressor** in its mouth as if it is saying "**Ah**." A **tongue depressor** is a way of picturing the "**Ah**" sound. In the future when you think of the letter "**A**" this is the picture your mind will conjure up, and you will know the only sound ever made be the letter "**A**" in Spanish is the "**Ah**" sound.

E – Dr. Memory™ pictures a letter "**E**" by seeing an **E**agle in the shape of a capital letter "**E**." It looks like and sounds like the letter "**E**." You can see this picture below. In English the letter "**E**" makes a **long** "**e**" sound as in **e**agle, and a **short** "**e**" sound as in **e**gg. The Spanish letter "**e**" sounds like a **long** "**a**" in English as in the word **a**pe when it comes at **the end of a syllable or word**. This long "a" sound isn't drawn out as much as the English long "a" but is cut off more sharply. However, if a letter "e" appears at the **beginning or in the middle of a syllable** in Spanish it is pronounced like the **short** "**e**" in **e**gg. As a result, you see the **E**agle below laying an **e**gg at the **middle** of a **big inning**, **beginning**, on a baseball scoreboard to represent the short "e" sound as heard in the word **e**gg. This will show you that a Spanish letter "e" makes the short "e" sound as heard in the word "egg" when it appears at the beginning or in the middle of a syllable.

You also see a movie screen with the words **The End** on it. The eagle had been watching a movie. An Ape, representing the **long "a"** sound as heard in the word **ape** is on the screen as well to show you that the **long "a"** sound is heard when a letter "**e**" appears at **the end of a Spanish syllable or word**. Later when you think of the letter "e" this **E**agle will pop into your mind, and you will know the two sounds made by the Spanish letter "e," and where they occur.

I - The letter "**I**" is pictured by seeing blocks of Ice in the shape of a letter "**I**." You can see the Ice below. You will notice that an Eagle is pecking on the ice. This will teach you that the Spanish letter "**I**" **always** makes the **long "e"** sound as heard at the beginning of the English word **E**agle. There will never be any controversy with this letter. That is the only sound the letter "**I**" ever makes in Spanish.

O - The letter "o" is pictured by seeing a pair of Overalls with a large letter "O" stitched on them as their logo or trademark. This is a made-up brand of overalls, but it works. You don't need a picture, since the Spanish letter "o" **always** makes the **long "o"** sound as in Overalls. There will never be any controversy with this letter. That is the only sound the letter "o" ever makes in Spanish. Overalls will be used in Dr. Memory's™ pictures to picture the "o" sound.

U - The letter "U" is pictured by seeing a U-bolt that looks exactly like a capital letter "U." You see it below. The Spanish letter "u" always makes the **double "o"** sound as heard in the English word "sh**oo**t." That is why the U-bolt pictured below is "shooting" a slingshot. Examine the picture for a while, and you will know that the Spanish letter "u" always makes the **double "o"** sound as heard in the word "sh**oo**t."

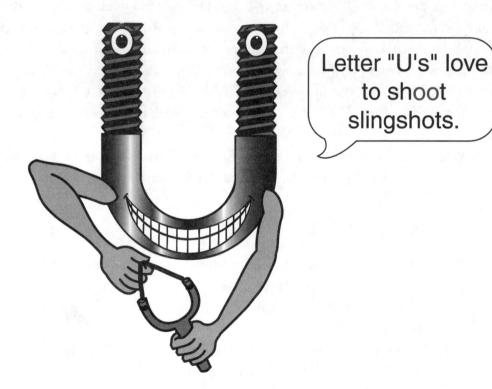

Letter "U's" love to shoot slingshots.

Vowel Victory Review

Before continuing with other letter sounds you should make sure you have remembered the sounds for the **Big Boss Vowel** sounds.

We picture the letter "**A**" by seeing an **A**pe. Do you remember what was in the ape's mouth? It pictures the only sound ever made by the Spanish letter "A." If you have difficulty remembering, look back and lock the picture and sound into your mind.

We picture the letter "**E**" by seeing an **E**agle. Do you remember the eagle picture? You should "see" the two sounds made by the letter "e." You should remember that one sound is made by an "e" at the beginning or middle of a Spanish word or syllable, and a different sound is made at the end of a Spanish syllable or word. If you have difficulty remembering, look back and lock the picture and sound into your mind.

We picture the letter "**i**" by seeing **I**ce. Do you remember what was pecking on the blocks of **I**ce? It pictures the only sound ever made by the Spanish letter "**i**." It is reliable. If you have difficulty remembering, look back and lock the picture and sound into your mind.

We picture the letter "**O**" by seeing **O**-brand **O**veralls. Do you remember the letter "o's" only sound? It always makes only one sound. It is reliable. If you have difficulty remembering, look back and lock the picture and sound into your mind.

We picture the letter "**U**" by seeing a **U**-bolt. Do you remember what the **U**-bolt was doing? It pictures the only sound ever made by the Spanish letter "**u**." It is also reliable. If you have difficulty remembering, look back and lock the picture and sound into your mind.

Now you should be the **Big Boss** of the **Big Boss Spanish Vowels**, because you know the sound or sounds each vowel can make in the Spanish language.

Other Vowel Sounds

Y - The letter "**Y**" is considered to be a vowel in many words in English and Spanish. In the English word "fly" the letter "y" sounds exactly like a long "i" and is the vowel in that word. In the English word "baby" the letter "y" sounds exactly like a long "e" and is a vowel in that word as well.

The letter "**Y**" when used **alone** or at **the end of a word** in Spanish sounds like a long "e" as in **e**agle. The letter "**Y**" is pictured by seeing a "**Y**" in a road. In the picture on the next page you see a "**Y**" in a road. On the left, an eagle is getting **a loan** at a bank. On the right, a movie screen reads **The End**. An eagle is also on the screen. This will teach you that the letter "**Y**" when used **alone** or at **the end of a word** in Spanish sounds like a long "**e**" as in **e**agle.

In all other instances when the letter "**Y**" comes **before a vowel** it sounds like "**yuh**" as in the word "**yu**ck." That is why you also see the "**yu**cky" stuff flowing down at the bottom of the "**Y**" in the road. The letter "**y**" makes this same basic sound in English as well. This "**yuh**" sound is the consonant sound of the letter "**y**." We have not begun to discuss consonants yet, but since the letter "**y**" was discussed for its vowel sound, the consonant sound was made part of the same picture.

There are several other vowel sounds in the Spanish language when various vowels appear next to each other such as "ai," "au," "ei," "ia," "ie," "io," "oi," "ua," "ue," ui," "uo" and others. These sounds will not be discussed specifically in this section, but will be fully pictured in the words where they may appear. The letter "y" was discussed specifically, because it is considered to be a vowel just like the five main vowels in many words.

Conceiving Consonants

B - The letter "**B**" is pictured by seeing two **B**ees clinging to a post. The post and the **B**ees look exactly like a capital letter **B** as you can see in the picture on the next page. In Spanish the letter "**b**" is pronounced two ways. At the beginning of a word it is pronounced much like the "b" in "balloon." Inside a word it is softer and sounds like a cross between an English "b" and "v." You can listen for the "b" on our web site where Spanish words are pronounced.

It is important to remember that the letters "b" and "v" sound the same in Spanish. Since they are identical, Spanish-speaking people sometimes ask for a clarification if words are being spelled out. A "b" is called "b" grande which means big "b." A "v" is called "v" chica which means little "v."

C - The letter "C" is pictured by seeing a **C-clamp**. The C-clamp pictured on the next page looks like and sounds like the letter "C." The Spanish letter "**c**" makes two sounds, and they are the same as the two sounds made by the English letter "**c**." The C-clamp on the next page has a **soft marshmallow** in its clamping device to represent the **soft "c" sound** as heard in the English words "**cent**" and "**century**." A **soft** letter "c" in Spanish always sounds like the English letter "s." You will also notice that some "**ice**," representing the letter "**i**", and an "**eagle**," representing the letter "**e**," are standing on **soft marshmallows** to the right of the C-clamp. This will teach you that the letter "**c**" makes the **soft** letter "**c**" sound as in "**cent**" when it comes before a letter "**i**" or a letter "**e**."

Below you see another **C**-clamp with a **hard rock** in its clamping device to represent the **hard "c" sound** as heard in the English words "**c**ar" and "**c**andle." A **hard** letter "**c**" in Spanish always sounds like an English letter "**k**." You will notice that an **a**pe, representing the letter "**a**", some **o**veralls, representing the letter "**o**," and a **u**-bolt, representing the letter "**u**," are on **hard rocks** to the right of the **C**-clamp. This will teach you that the letter "**c**" makes the **hard** letter "**c**" sound as in "**c**ar" when it comes before the letters "**a**," "**o**," or "**u**." It also makes the hard sound when it comes before a consonant. Once again, the vowels determine how this letter will be pronounced. The Big Bosses strike again.

Ch - The two letters "**ch**" are considered to be one letter with one sound in Spanish. They are pronounced exactly like the "**ch**" letters in English. They make the "**ch**" sound as in the words "**church**" and "**chi**cken." No picture is needed for this sound since it is so easy and the same as heard in English.

D - The letter "**D**" is pictured by seeing a **D**eep pocket. This particular pocket looks like a letter "**D**" on its side. It sounds like and looks like the letter "**D**." The most common sound the letter "**D**" makes is the "**D**" sound heard in the English word "**d**uck." No picture is needed for this sound since it is so easy and almost the same as heard in English. There is a slight difference. Your tongue is behind your front teeth when you speak a "d" in Spanish. A letter "d" also sounds something like a "th" when it is between two vowels, but all "d's" will be pictured as the "d" sound in "duck."

F - The letter "**F**" in the Spanish language makes the same sound as it does in English. The letter "**F**" is pictured by seeing what we will refer to as an "**F**" pole in the shape of a letter "**F**". That is simply a way of saying a **f**lag pole, so a letter "**F**" can be pictured tangibly. It is reliable and always makes the "**f**" sound as heard in the word "**f**lag." No picture is needed for this sound since it is so easy and the same as heard in English.

Consonant Sound Review

Think of the following five consonants and try to recreate the sound pictures in your mind for each one in the Spanish language. When you see the pictures in your mind you will know the sound or sounds made by the letter. Since some consonants make the same sound in English and Spanish no pictures were developed for those consonants. The five consonants are "B - C - CH - D - F." If you have a problem with any of them go back to the teaching section for a quick sound review until you know them well.

Conceiving More Consonants

G - The letter "**G**" is not reliable in Spanish or English. It is pictured by seeing a **G**enie and its lamp in the shape of a letter "**G**." It makes a **soft** and a **hard** sound like the letter "c." In the picture below you see a **G**enie in **soft marshmallows**. An "**e**agle," for the letter "**e**," and some "**i**ce," for the letter "**i**" are coming out of that Genie's lamp. The soft "**g**" **sound** is heard in Spanish when a letter "**g**" comes before a letter "**e**" or a letter "**i**." The **soft** "**g**" sound in English sounds like a letter "**j**," but a **soft** "**g**" in Spanish sounds like the English letter "**h**" as in the word "**h**oot," but it is a stronger rasping type sound like you make when you clear your throat. That is why the **G**enie is "**h**ooting" like an owl. Study this picture to know this sound.

Below you see another **G**enie lamp with **rocks** around it. The rocks will represent the **hard** "**g**" **sound** as heard in the English word "**g**ift." You will notice that the **hard G**enie lamp has an **a**pe, the letter "**a**", some **o**veralls, the letter "**o**," and a **u**-bolt, the letter "**u**," coming out of it. This will teach you that the letter "**g**" makes the **hard** "**g**" **sound** as in "**g**ift" when it comes before the letters "**a**," "**o**," or "**u**." That is why the "**g**ift" package is pictured with this **G**enie lamp. Study this picture to know these Spanish sounds.

H - The letter "**H**" is **always silent** in Spanish. You can picture the letter "**H**" by seeing a trailer "**H**itch". The word "**H**itch" sounds very much like the letter "**H**," and this "**H**itch" looks very much like the letter "**H**." You will notice the gag around the hitch's mouth on the right to show that it is silent. You can't speak a sound with a gag around your mouth. It is **reliable** in that it **never makes a sound** in the Spanish language.

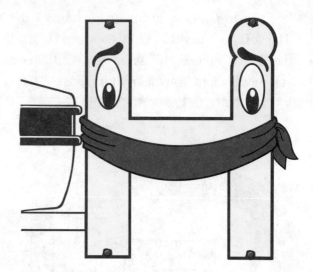

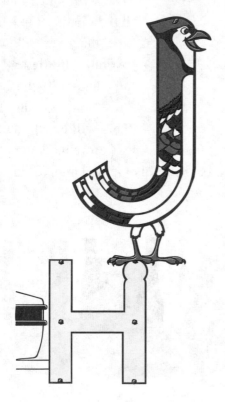

J - The letter "**J**" is pictured by seeing a "**J**aybird" in the shape of a letter "**J**." As you can see in the picture to the left it is perched on a trailer "**h**itch." It is on the trailer "**h**itch," because the Spanish letter "**j**" always makes the "**h**" sound. This sound is also a **strong rasping** "**h**". Study this picture to know the sound.

K - The letter "**K**" is pictured by seeing "**K**ay" the cheerleader in the shape of a letter "**K**". The letter "**k**" is reliable in Spanish and makes the same sound as the letter "**k**" in English. The word "**k**ick" is the sample word used in English to highlight the "**k**" sound. No picture is needed for this sound since it is so easy and the same in Spanish as heard in English.

L - The letter "**L**" is pictured by seeing an "**E**lbow" in the shape of a letter "**L**." A bent "**E**lbow" looks like a letter "**L**." No picture is needed, since it makes the same sound in English and Spanish. It makes the "**L**" sound heard in the word "**l**emon."

Consonant Sound Review

Think of the following five consonants and try to recreate the sounds in your mind for each one. When you see the pictures in your mind you will know the sound or sounds made by the letter. The five consonants are "G - H - J - K - L." Since some consonants make the same sound in English and Spanish no pictures were developed for those consonants. If you have a problem with any of them go back to the sound teaching section for a quick sound review until you know them well.

Conceiving More Consonants

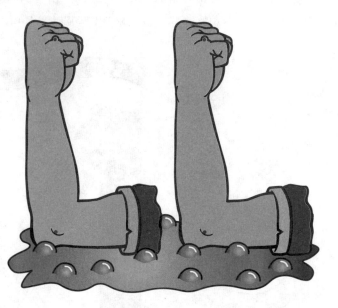

LL - The double letter "**LL**" is pictured by seeing two "**El**bows." As you can see in the picture to the right they are in some "**yu**cky" substance to show that they make the "**yuh**" sound as heard in the word "**yu**ck." This sound is also heard in the words "**y**es" and "**y**ellow."

M - The letter "**M**" is pictured by seeing four "**Em**ory" boards in the shape of a letter "**M**." The "**Em**ory" boards looks like a letter "**M**." No picture is needed, since it makes the same sound in English and Spanish. It makes the "**M**" sound heard in the word "**m**oon."

N - The letter "**N**" is pictured by seeing an acrobatic "**In**dian" in the shape of a letter "**N**." The acrobatic "**In**dian" looks like a letter "**N**." The "**In**dian" has a big **n**ose to represent the only sound made by the letter "**n**" in English and Spanish. A letter "**n**" in

Spanish always sounds like the letter "**n**" in the English word "**n**ose." No picture is needed, since it makes the same sound in English and Spanish.

     Ñ – This Spanish letter is called an **eñe**, pronounced **ehn-yeah**. You just learned that the letter "**N**" is pictured by seeing an acrobatic "**In**dian" in the shape of a letter "**N**." The Indian pictured below has an odd looking boomerang above his head. The boomerang represents the symbol above this letter, which is called an **eñe**, pronounced **ehn-yeah**. This acrobatic "**In**dian" has "onions" next to him to show the sound this letter makes, which is the "yuh" sound heard in the word "onion." This sound is also heard in the English words "million" and "canyon." In Spanish this sound is an "**n**" sound followed by the "**y**" consonant sound, or "**ny**" which then takes on the following Big Boss vowel sound. In "onion," "million," and "canyon" it is "**nyuh**," because the vowels following the "**ny**" sound in each of these three words make the "**uh**" sound. In other instances it will take on the following vowel sound, whatever it might be.

     Each time this sound appears in a Spanish word Dr. Memory's™ special **eñe onion** will be in the picture. The onion will always have the letters "**ny**" on it to represent this **eñe onion** sound. You see two of those onions pictured above. There will always be something else accompanying the **eñe onion** that illustrates the following Big Boss vowel sound. For instance, if the vowel "a" follows the **eñe onion** sound, the onion will wear a tongue depressor headdress to denote the "**ah**" sound which all letter "a's" make in the

Spanish language. Doctors ask you to say "ah" when they place a tongue depressor in your mouth. You see a **nyah eñe onion** pictured with the regular **eñe onion**. You will always be able to see this **eñe onion** sound tangibly when it appears in Spanish words.

The Big Boss vowel following this sound can and does influence a blended vowel sound. So then, this letter really is reliable, in that, there is always the "**ny**" sound, but it is strongly influenced by the Big Boss vowel that follows to make a blended vowel sound.

P - The letter "**P**" is pictured by seeing a "**Peacock**" in the shape of a letter "**P**." The letter "**P**" in Spanish is pronounced like the letter "**P**" in English. It always makes the sound heard in the word "**peck**." No picture is needed for this sound since it is so easy and is almost the same as heard in English. There is a slight difference. The Spanish "p" has no puff of air accompanying it.

Consonant Sound Review

Think of the following five consonants and try to recreate the sound pictures in your mind for each one. When you see the pictures in your mind you will know the sound or sounds made by the letter. The five consonants are "ll - m - n - ñ - p." Since some consonants make the same sound in English and Spanish, no pictures were developed for those consonants. If you have a problem with any of them go back to the sound teaching section for a quick sound review until you know them well.

Conceiving More Consonants

Q - The letter "**Q**" is pictured by seeing a "**Q-tip**" in the shape of a letter "**Q**." You see it pictured on the next page. You also see that "Kay" the cheerleader is going to pull some cotton away from the "Q-tip" to show that the Spanish letter "**Q**" always sounds like the English letter "**K**." This picture will help you remember this sound. The letter "**Q**" in Spanish is always followed by a letter "**U**" as it is in English. The English letter "**Q**" sounds like "kw" with a "w" sound following the "k" sound, but that isn't so in Spanish. The Spanish "**Q**" only, and always, makes the "**k**" sound as heard in the English word "kick." The letters "qu" in Spanish are always followed by a letter "e" or "i." The "que" letter combination is pronounced "kay," because a letter "e" at the end of a Spanish syllable makes the long "a" English sound. The "qui" letter combination is pronounced "key," because a letter "i" at the end of a Spanish syllable makes the long "e" English sound.

R - The letter "**R**" is pictured by seeing an "**AR**cher" in the shape of a letter "**R**." It makes the "**r**" sound as heard at the beginning of the word "**r**ain" in Spanish as it also does in English, so no picture is needed. The Spanish "R" is trilled or flapped like the "R" sound heard in "ladder."

RR - The double letter "**RR**" is pictured by seeing two "**AR**chers" side by side in the shape of two letter "**R**'s." You see them pictured on the next page. You see a **roller skate** with two letter "**R**'s" on it **rolling** away from these archers. This is to show that the double letter "R's" make what Dr. Memory™ refers to as the **Rolling "R"** sound. This sound lasts longer than a single letter "R," and **rolls** out of the mouth for a longer time. You will hear this sound later when you click on the words that contain this sound in Dr. Memory's™ Internet site. You also see a letter "R" above the roller skate that looks like it has been rolling. One of the archers appears to be aiming at it. You will see a roller skate and/or this rolling letter "R" in the Spanish pictures where this sound is heard.

S - The letter "S" is pictured by seeing an "ESkimo" in the shape of a letter "S." The "S" sound heard in the word "Snake" is the only sound the letter "S" ever makes in Spanish. The letter "s" is not reliable in English. The "z" sound heard in the English word "rose" proves it is not reliable in English. No picture is needed for this sound since it is so easy and the same as heard in most English words.

T - The letter "T" is pictured by seeing a "T-square" in the shape of a letter "T." The "T" sound heard in the word "Top" is the only sound ever made by the Spanish letter "T." No picture is needed for this sound since it is so easy and the same as heard in English. Place your tongue behind your front teeth as you did with the letter "D."

Consonant Sound Review

Think of the following five consonants and try to recreate the sound pictures in your mind for each one. When you see the pictures in your mind you will know the sound or sounds made by the letter. The five consonants are "Q - R - RR - S - T." Since some consonants make the same sound in English and Spanish no pictures were developed for those consonants. If you have a problem with any of them go back to the sound teaching section for a quick sound review until you know them well.

Conceiving More Consonants

V - The letter "**V**" is pictured by seeing a "**V**-neck" sweater in the shape of a letter "**V**." Spanish-speaking people pronounce a "b" and a "v" exactly the same, but the sound is much **softer in Spanish**. For reasons of clarity, Dr. Memory™ will have you pronounce the Spanish "v" like the English "v" when you first learn vocabulary words. Then listen to the Spanish-speaking speaker pronounce "v" words and try to imitate her.

W - The letter "**W**" is pictured by seeing a special brand of bubble gum. Four sticks of the gum are shaped exactly like a letter "w." It is called "Dubba-Ya Bubbles" brand bubble gum. Of course, "Dubba-Ya" sounds very close to the actual pronunciation of the English letter "**W.**" In Spanish this letter only appears in foreign words and not Spanish words, so technically, it isn't used in the Spanish language.

X - The letter "**X**" is pictured by seeing an "**E**xerciser" in the shape of a letter "**X**." You see him pictured below. As you can see he is doing jumping jacks and looks just like the letter "**X**." The letter "**X**" in English is the most unreliable letter of all, because it makes six different sounds in various words. The letter "**X**" is also unreliable in Spanish, but it only makes two sounds.

On the left of the "**E**xerciser" you see a small "Eagle" and a "con-sun-ant" keeping its eye on a "snake." An "ant" with "convict" stripes and a "sun" is how to picture the word "consonant." **Con-sun-ant = Consonant**. This shows that the letter "x" is pro-

nounced like the letter "s" in "snake" when a letter "e" comes before it, and when it is followed by a consonant. You will remember that we used the sample word "snake" for the
"s" sound when the letter "s" was discussed. The Spanish words "experto" and "exteri-
or" contain this "s" sound because of this rule.

In other cases the Spanish letter "x" makes two sounds like some words in English.
It is usually between two vowels in these instances. In the English and Spanish word
"taxi" the letter "x" makes two sounds, a "k" and an "s" sound. Say it out loud now, and
you will hear these two sounds. That is why you see a "taxi" pulling away from the
"Exerciser." Notice that the "taxi" has the letters "K" and "S" on it to point out this sound.

Make sure you spend a little extra time with these two sounds to lock them into
your mind securely. Even though you need to learn every sound the letters of the Spanish
alphabet make, every sound in all the words you will be learning will be pictured tangibly, so you can actually "see" the pronunciation of each word. These sound pictures will
help you in the future if you want to learn other Spanish words and increase your vocabulary. The comprehensive Spanish course will teach you well over an additional thousand
words as well as Spanish grammar, conjugation of verbs and much, much more.

Y - This sound was discussed earlier. You will remember that a letter "**Y**" in
Spanish makes the "**yuh**" sound as in "**yu**ck" when used as a consonant. You will remember that a letter "**Y**" is pictured by seeing a "**Y**" in a road. You see the "**yu**cky" substance
at the bottom of the road below to picture this sound. You will remember that the letter
"**Y**" in Spanish sounds like a long "e" as in **e**agle when used **alone** or at **the end of a**

word. This is the vowel usage of this letter.

Z - The letter "**Z**" is pictured by seeing a "**Zebra**" in the shape of a letter "**Z**." You see him pictured below. You also can see that the "**Zebra**" seems to be frightened by a "**snake**." This illustrates you that the sound made by the Spanish letter "**z**" is the "**s**" sound as heard in "**snake**."

Consonant Sound Review

Think of the following five consonants and try to recreate the sound pictures in your mind for each. When you see the pictures in your mind you will know the sound or sounds made by the letter. The five consonants are "V - W - X - Y - Z." Since the letter "w" is not used in Spanish no picture was developed for it. If you have a problem with any of these go back to the sound teaching section for a quick sound review until you know them well.

Complete Consonant Sound Review

Think of all of the Spanish consonants and try to recreate the sound pictures in your mind for each. When you see the pictures in your mind you will know the sound or sounds made by the letter. The twenty-four (24) consonants are "b - c - ch - d - f - g - h - j - k - l - ll - m - n - ñ - p - q - r - rr - s - t - v - w - x - z." Since some consonants make the same sound in English and Spanish no pictures were developed for those consonants. If you have a problem with any of these go back to the sound teaching sections for a quick sound review until you know them well.

CHAPTER 4

Phonetic Sound Standards

Before discussing phonetic sound standards you need to understand how this course is constructed, so you will understand how it will benefit you. There are over 600 words taught in this survival Spanish course. A 600 word vocabulary is quite a large vocabulary. There are 220 **sight words** in the English language. They are called **sight words**, because teachers want students to **recognize them by sight**. These words make up 75% of all reading a student will do in the elementary grades and over 50% of all the reading we all do during our lifetime. Most people find this fact almost impossible to believe, but test after test has proven it to be true. So then, by just learning these 220 words any student would have a pretty good grasp of any language, but you will learn more than 600 words.

All of the Spanish words in this course have been categorized to make them easier to learn. Some categories are so broad that they have sub-categories within them. For instance, the category headed "body parts" has three sub-categories. Sub-categories include: body parts from the neck up, body parts from the neck down, and internal body parts. Some categories have up to eight sub-categories in the comprehensive Spanish course. You might notice that meals aren't exactly food, but they are so closely related to food that they were placed in this category. Most categories contain words with the same part of speech, but sometimes a word is included because it fits, even though it may be another part of speech.

Other categories include eight different kinds of action words, food, clothing, shopping, money, travel and many, many more. You will enjoy learning Spanish words in these categories and feel fully rewarded by knowing them before going on to the next category or learning instruction. Just as children begin to learn their native language by learning nouns and tangible items first, this course will also follow that same "natural" process, however, when other words are learned they will also be tangible, so they can be seen as easily as nouns.

The English words used to represent the Spanish syllable sounds will match the Spanish syllable sounds exactly, so there will never be any doubt about how the Spanish words should be pronounced. Sometimes only parts of English words will be used to make sure that only the exact Spanish sound is being represented. For instance, the Spanish word for **embassy** is **embajada**, and it has a "**dah**" syllable sound at the end of it. There is no one English word to represent this exact sound, but the beginning sound in "**do**t" or "**do**ctor" represent it perfectly. The letter "o" in both of these English words makes the "ah" sound, so with the letter "**d**" in front of the "**ah**" sound "**dah**" is heard. This concept of using only a part of a word will be frequently used to assure exact pronunciations, although entire English words are used whenever possible.

Sometimes a letter will be used along with a word or part of a word to represent the exact Spanish pronunciation. The Spanish word for **groceries**, for example, is **comestibles**, and the last syllable is pronounced "**blace**." Remember that a Spanish syllable ending in the letter "e" makes a "long a" sound. The letter "s" at the end of this word simply changes a singular word to a plural word. Dr. Memory™ put a letter "**b**" or a "bee sound" with a shoe "**lace**" to picture and match the exact syllable sound. Since there are no rules, so to speak, about methods of teaching these exact pronunciations, in order to make the learning process practically automatic, Dr. Memory™ creates the rules as needed.

Sometimes more than one word will be employed to develop the exact phonetic sound for the Spanish syllable being learned. For instance, there is a "**chehn**" sound in the Spanish word for "eighty." Dr. Memory™ couldn't find an English word that has that exact sound in it, so he chose to use the beginning sounds in two English words. Those two words are "**ch**ain" and "**en**gineer." You can see a **ch**ain, and you can see a railroad **en**gineer, and the beginning sounds in these two words when blended together produce the "**chehn**" sound as heard in Spanish. It is very seldom that this course has to use two words to represent a single Spanish syllable sound, but when necessary it has been done to make it easier for you to see and understand the pronunciation. It causes no learning problem, since the exact phonetic Spanish sound is being represented and pictured.

You will also find that Dr. Memory™ has created some very special characters to make some very intangible words tangible. The word **when**, for instance becomes a letter "**W**" that looks like a **hen**. The word **what** becomes a letter "**W**" that is very **hot**. You will be introduced to many of these characters throughout this course.

You also need to understand that if an object or thing is used to represent itself when the Spanish word is being learned it will be very large and dominate the picture. That same object or thing may be used in other pictures to represent a particular sound but it won't dominate the picture. For instance, when the word "ear" is being learned in Spanish the man in the picture has very large and dominant ears, but when the "ear" sound is needed and used in other pictures the ear will be normal size and may even be part of something else. This will not cause you any problem at all. The difference is obvious when the pictures are studied.

Sample Word Picture

The main purpose of the course is to teach you Spanish vocabulary, so you can easily know Spanish words and their exact pronunciation when you think of the English equivalent. This, of course, will be accomplished with pictures, since that is the easiest and best way to learn. You will learn Spanish words the same way you learned Arkansas and Little Rock earlier. The English word and its Spanish equivalent will be pictured together in the same way. The picture will contain the exact pronunciation of the Spanish word so it can be seen tangibly. As a result, there will never be any doubt of how the Spanish word is to be pronounced. You can also hear the exact Spanish pronunciation on the Dr. Memory™ web site. A complete explanation will accompany each learning picture, so you will fully understand the connection between the English and Spanish words.

The best way for you to understand the procedure is with a sample word. The Spanish word for the English word **mouth** is **boca**, which is pronounced **bow-cah**. In the picture on the opposite page you see a big open mouth to picture the English word. A **bow** tie is worn by the **cah**ing crow that is flying out of the mouth. The English word **mouth** and the Spanish pronunciation of **boca** are both pictured so you can see them together. Above the picture you see the English word **mouth** in green type. The English word will always be in green type. The Spanish word **boca** is in **black**. The Spanish word will always be in **black** type. Below these two words you see the correct phonetic pronunciation of the Spanish word in red type. These phonetic sounds will always be red. In the explanation of the picture, which will always be under the picture, the English word will once again be green, and the phonetic pronunciation will be red. This pattern will be used in each vocabulary picture.

To learn that **mouth** means **boca** in Spanish all you have to do is follow the procedure listed below the picture as you study it.

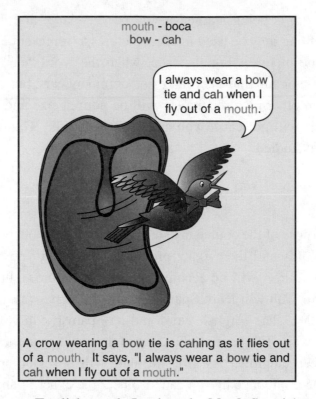

Look at the green English word. Look at the **black** Spanish word. Look at the red phonetic pronunciation of the Spanish word. Even though the exact Spanish pronunciation is reproduced phonetically, you may want to click on the word on the web site in order to hear the word pronounced by a Spanish-speaking person. You will hear the proper pronunciation as well as the proper accent. Say the Spanish word several times.

Read the explanation below the picture and look at the picture to make sure you understand the explanation. Remember that the English word will be green, and the phonetic Spanish pronunciation will be red in each explanation.

Study the picture until you are sure you know it. Then look away from the picture and think of the English word. The picture should pop into your mind, and you will see a mental picture of the Spanish word and its phonetic pronunciation. If for some reason the picture does not come fully to mind, look back at the picture and its explanation until you know it before continuing.

A short review will be conducted after you have learned several words to reinforce the picture and full understanding of the word. Longer reviews will be suggested as you learn more and more words.

You will learn words in categories. Some of the categories were mentioned earlier. You will learn these Spanish words the way you began to learn English. You first learned nouns that your parents pointed out and identified. You saw them, learned their identity and never forgot them, because they were tangible and easily reappeared in your mind when you thought of them. After learning tangible items you began to learn intangible words that had no picture identity. These kinds of words became harder and harder to learn because they conjured up no comfortable image or picture in your mind. That is why many people do not develop extensive vocabularies. You will not have that problem in this course, because you will see every Spanish word and its pronunciation in a tangible picture.

After you have learned several categories of words you will learn how to put them together to be able to speak Spanish phrases and sentences. You will have learned parts of speech other than nouns before this occurs. The whole process will be easy, fun and painless.

CHAPTER 5

Masculine and Feminine

Before starting the learning pictures you must understand the difference between **masculine** and **feminine** words in the Spanish language. In the English language nouns that refer to people and animals are either **masculine** or **feminine**. Most of them are obvious such as man, boy and bull for **masculine**; and woman, girl and cow for **feminine**. Sometimes things and even ideas and places are given personification. A ship or a city may be referred to as "she."

In Spanish all nouns are considered to be either **masculine** or **feminine** for grammatical purposes. The grammatical gender of people and animals can also be determined by their natural gender in Spanish, such as **cow** being **feminine** and **bull** being **masculine**. In Spanish the grammatical gender of ideas and places can often be determined by the noun ending. Most nouns ending in the letter "**o**" are **masculine**, and most nouns ending in the letter "**a**" are **feminine**. Dr. Memory™ has developed pictures, as usual, to help you understand this gender concept as well as all other **masculine** and **feminine** concepts.

Since the colors **blue** and **pink** are often used to refer to **masculine** and **feminine** with babies, these colors will be used to help you understand the **masculine** and **feminine** endings in Spanish as well as other **masculine** and **feminine** concepts.

The Definite Article

The word "**the**" is known as the "**definite article**" in English. In Spanish the definite article "the" can be either **masculine** or **feminine**. The **masculine** definite article "the" is expressed as "**el**" in Spanish, and the **feminine** definite article "the" is expressed as "**la**" in Spanish depending on the gender of the noun it precedes. "**El**" is used before a **masculine** noun, and "**la**" is used before a **feminine** noun.

In the picture on the next page you see a man, **masculine**, dressed in **blue** overalls. The **overalls** are **blue** to represent the standard color for the **masculine** gender, and the word **overalls** begins with the letter "**o**" to depict the ending of **masculine** words. He says, "**Masculine** men wear **blue** overalls to show that **masculine** words end in the letter "**o**." His elbow is bent in the shape of a letter "L" to remind you that the **masculine** definite article "**the**" is expressed as "**el**" in Spanish. The sign in the picture reads, "The **masculine** "**the**" in Spanish is "**el**." Study this picture until you know these two **masculine** characteristics.

At the top of the next page you see a woman, **feminine**, dressed in **pink** with a pink apron. The **apron** is **pink** to represent the standard color for the **feminine** gender, and the word **apron** begins with the letter "**a**" to depict the ending of **feminine** words. She says, "**Feminine** women wear **pink** aprons to show you that **feminine** words end in the letter "**a**." She is singing several "**la**" syllables to remind you that the **feminine** definite article "**the**" is expressed as "**la**" in Spanish. Study this picture to know these two **feminine** characteristics.

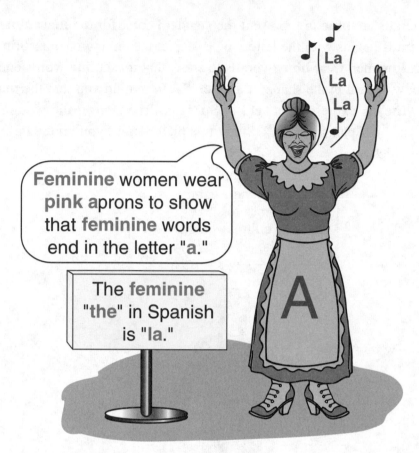

The sign in the picture reads, "The **feminine** "'the'" in Spanish is '" **la.**'" Study this picture until you know these two **feminine** characteristics.

Masculine – "**El**" precedes **masculine** nouns. Notice the masculine letter "**o**" endings in the sample words below.

        el burr**o**   **el** sombrer**o**   **el** tor**o**

Feminine – "**La**" precedes **feminine** nouns. Notice the feminine letter "**a**" endings in the sample words below.

        la banan**a**   **la** tortill**a**   **la** verand**a**

All Spanish nouns do not end in a letter "**o**" or a letter "**a**," but most of them do. The **blue** and **pink** colors will be used for **masculine** and **feminine** whether or not the noun ends in these letters.

When you learn enough Spanish words to have a fairly extensive vocabulary you will begin to use the definite articles "**el**" and "**la**" in sentences. This principle is taught before you begin to learn Spanish vocabulary, so you will be aware of it as you study and say **masculine** and **feminine** words. You will notice that the color of the nouns you will be learning will be either **blue** or **pink** in the review lists. This will indicate whether the noun is **masculine** or **feminine**. It will be indicated when you should practice using "**el**" and "**la**" in the study process.

The Indefinite Article

The word "**a**" is known as the **"indefinite article"** in English. You have already learned the definite article "the," which is "el" or "la" in Spanish. The indefinite article is also either **masculine** or **feminine** depending on the gender of the noun it precedes. The **masculine** indefinite article "a" is expressed as "**un**" in Spanish, and the **feminine** definite article "a" is expressed as "**una**" in Spanish depending on the gender of the noun it precedes. "**Un**" is used before a **masculine** noun, and "**una**" is used before a **feminine** noun.

In the picture at the top of the next page you will notice that something has been added to the **masculine** picture that was used earlier to teach the definite article "the." This time the picture for the indefinite article "a" has been added. This picture will continue to grow as more **masculine** principles are added to it. **Blue** will continue to be used for the **masculine** indefinite article "a." A **blue** clock that registers the time of **noon** has been added to the picture to show that "**un**," which is pronounced "**oon**," is the **masculine indefinite article** for "a" in Spanish." The clock says, "Noon is **a** good time." Both the word "**a**" and the letters "**oon**" in "noon" are **blue** to remind you of this **indefinite article** principle. Study this picture to know this **masculine** principle.

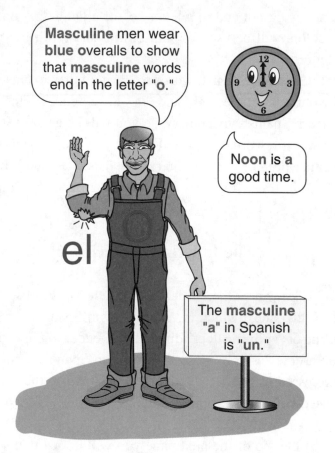

In the picture at the top of the next page something has been added to the **feminine** picture used earlier to teach the definite article "the." This time the picture for the **indefinite article** "a" has been added. This picture will continue to grow as more **feminine** principles are added to it. **Pink** will continue to be used for the **feminine indefinite article** "a." A **pink** tuna fish has been added to show that "**una**," which is pronounced "**oonah**," is the **feminine indefinite article** for "a" in Spanish." The tuna says, "**A tunah** is **a** good fish." The words "**A**," "**a**" and the letters "**unah**" in "**tunah**" are **pink** to remind you of this **indefinite article** principle. The word "tuna" has a slightly different pronunciation in English than the one portrayed here. So, to lock in this sound, the tuna spelled its own name as "**tunah**." The "**ah**" sound at the end of the word is what is important and needs to be remembered. Study this picture to know this **feminine** principle.

In addition to the masculine and feminine discussion, the **eñe onion** sound concept will be repeated before you begin to learn Spanish vocabulary. One of the words in the first group of words you will learn contains this sound. You will recall that the **eñe** was pictured by seeing an acrobatic "**In**dian" in the shape of a letter "**N**." The Indian had an odd looking boomerang above his head. The boomerang represents the symbol above this letter, which is called an **eñe**, pronounced **ehn-yeah**. This acrobatic "**In**dian" was pictured with **onions** to show the sound this letter makes, which is the "ny" sound heard in the word "onion." This sound is also heard in the English words "million" and "canyon." In Spanish this sound is an "**n**" sound followed by the "**y**" consonant sound, or "**ny**" which then takes on the following Big Boss vowel sound. In "onion," "million," and "canyon" it is "**nyuh**," because the vowels following the "**ny**" sound in each of these three words make the "**uh**" sound. In the first word you will be learning that has this sound the "ny" sound is followed by the vowel "a" which always makes the "ah" sound in Spanish. As a result, the sound in the word will be "nyah."

Accent Rules

Before learning and beginning to speak Spanish words the accent rules must be learned. When you speak Spanish, more stress is given to some syllables than others. In the following simple rules you will be instructed as to which syllable to stress in a Spanish word. As usual, Dr. Memory™ has developed pictures to teach these accent rules.

Accent Rule Number One - When a **word end**s in a **vowel** or an "**n**" or "**s**," the **accent** is **generally on the next to last syllable**. The bold words in the rule are pictured at the top of the next page. You see a book named the "**Word** Finder." Consider it a dictionary where you "find words." Below the book there is a movie screen which shows the "**end**" of a movie. The owl on the screen is wearing a V-neck sweater. A **V**-neck on an **owl** is Dr. Memory's™ picture for a **vowel**. The five vowels are on the owl's sweater. In addition, the letters "**n**" and "**s**" are on the end of the movie. General Lee, for the word "**generally**," is to the left of the book. Three "silly bulls" representing a "syllable" are standing on the Word Finder book. Each silly bull is holding an **axe** with a **cent** on it to picture the word "**accent**." The **next to last silly bull** accents himself by hitting himself on the head with his "axe cent." Read the rule on the sign in the picture a few more times while examining the picture and you will have no problem remembering this **vowel accent rule**.

Accent Rule Number Two - When a **word end**s in a **consonant** other than an "**n**" or an "**s**," the **accent** is **generally on the last syllable**. The bold words in the rule are pictured at the bottom of the next page. This picture is very similar to the last picture. You see another "**Word** Finder." The movie screen which is below the book shows the "**end**" of a movie. On the screen with "the end" on it, you see a **con**vict with a **sun** as part of its body that is an **ant**. A **con-sun-ant** is Dr. Memory's™ picture for a **consonant**. The letters "**n**" and "**s**" have been crossed out to represent other than "n" or "s." General Lee, for the word "**generally**," is to the left of the book. Three "silly bulls" representing a "syllable" are also standing on this Word Finder book. Each silly bull is holding an **axe** with a **cent** on it to picture the word "**accent**." The **last silly bull** accents himself by hitting himself on the head with his "axe cent." Read the rule on the sign in the picture a few more times while examining the picture and you will have no problem remembering this **consonant accent rule**.

There are exceptions to these two rules, but in those cases an **accent mark** indicates where the stress falls no matter how the word ends.

CHAPTER 6

It's Time to Learn Spanish - Body Parts

Now that you have been properly introduced to Dr. Memory's™ method of teaching it is time for you to learn Spanish. You will learn far more vocabulary in this book than a first year Spanish student is required to learn, and you will retain it while most of them won't. When several Spanish teachers were asked to give lists of words they expected a first year Spanish student to learn, the most words received from any of them was 375 to 400. That list has been considerably expanded for this survival guide for speaking Spanish. You will actually learn more than 600 words, and they will become knowledge. Most first year Spanish students learn Spanish words to pass a test, but, unfortunately, the words are forgotten fairly quickly by most of them, and the words do not become knowledge. It is also very difficult for instructors, because their students don't have a reservoir of vocabulary knowledge to call upon. They teach knowing this limitation, but Dr. Memory™ won't have that limitation. His learning pictures will allow you to have a reservoir of vocabulary knowledge that students have not been able to enjoy.

The first category of words you will learn is **body parts**. This category has three sub-categories within it. They are body parts from the neck up, body parts from the neck down, and skin and internal body parts.

As a child we first begin to learn our own body parts as our parents begin to point to and identify them. They point to a body part and say things like, "Do you see this? This is your nose. This is your eye." This is how we begin to learn everything as a child. This course will teach you Spanish in the same way.

There will normally be four words pictured and taught per page. Some pages will have more than four words if some words have two different meanings. Some pages will have fewer than four words if there are fewer than four words to finish a category. After you have studied several words a brief review will be conducted to make sure you can see the picture words in your mind and remember the Spanish words. Even though each Spanish word will have its exact phonetic pronunciation in words and pictures, it is suggested that you listen to the words on the Internet web site. Dr. Memory's™ web site address and special code to allow you to enter the *Picture Perfect Spanish* pronunciation section are printed on page 362 of this book. Each time you click on the English word you will hear the Spanish equivalent pronounced by a Spanish-speaking person. You can click on words as many times as you like to hear the pronunciation over and over again if you so desire. All words within the categories will be learned in alphabetical order.

Bad grammar will be used sometimes to accommodate the sound that is needed in the learning picture. Dr. Memory™ knows proper grammar, but sometimes he bends the rules to help you.

Sometimes a different version of the phonetic sound that is used in the explanation below the picture will be used in speaking bubbles in the picture. This will give you more than one aid for the phonetic sound of the Spanish word.

Study the words on the next two pages and then follow the instructions. Make sure to study each vocabulary word picture until you can easily recreate it in your mind and say the Spanish equivalent when thinking of the English word before going to the next word. You have already learned the first word in the category of **body parts from the neck up** when you learned that the Spanish word for "**mouth**" is "**boca**."

You will find a fun drill on our web site that will help you learn which nouns are **masculine** and which are **feminine**.

beard & chin - barba
bahr - bah

A barbed wire beard on a boxer's chin is no problem for our razor.

Barbed wire is growing as a beard on the chin of a boxer. A razor company spokesman says, "A barbed wire beard on a boxer's chin is no problem for our razor."

ear - oreja
o - ray -ha

When I wear overalls, and ray guns fly out of my ears, it is funny, Ha-ha!

HA-HA

A man wearing a pair of overalls has ray guns flying out of his big ears. He is laughing and saying, "Ha-Ha."

eye - ojo
oh - hoe

Oh, this eye can see very well to hoe.

Feast your eyes on this.

Two large eyes wearing overalls are using hoes to work in their garden. The sign reads, "Feast your eyes on this." One eye says, "Oh, this eye can see very well to hoe."

eyebrow - ceja
say - ha

Don't use your eyebrow pencil here.

This sailor has to say Ha-Ha, because of this raised eyebrow.

Eyebrow counter

A female sailor raises an eyebrow, laughs and says, "Ha-ha." The sign reads, "Don't use your eyebrow pencil here!"

eyelash - pestaña
pehs - tah - nyah

This pesticide's tomahawk will trim your "Nyah" as well as your eyelash.

Eyelash trimming $5

Ny

PESTICIDE

A bottle of pesticide uses a tomahawk to trim the eyelashes of a female Indian onion (ny) wearing a tongue depressor (ah) headdress. The sign reads, "Eyelash trimming $5."

face - cara
cah - rah

Say cah and rah all you want. We have to face the music.

Cah - Rah

Face the wall.

A cahing crow is a cheerleader. She is cheering and saying, "Rah," as she jumps around in front of a big face. Spectators are standing with their faces to the wall, because the sign reads, "Face the wall."

forehead - frente
frehn - tay

Friends always put tape on your forehead.

A person stands in front of his friend and sticks several pieces of masking tape to his forehead. The sign reads, "I have a noble forehead."

hair - pelo
pay - low

Payday hair rollers are a locust's best hair aid.

A Payday candy bar is being rolled up in some hair as a hair roller by a locust. Notice that other Payday candy bar rollers are below the hair.

You have now studied and should know ten Spanish words, since some of the words had dual meanings. Here is a listing of those ten words. If the word in Spanish is **masculine**, the English word is **blue**. If the word in Spanish is **feminine**, the English word is **pink**. Practice saying these words in Spanish out loud as you look at each English word listed below. After you are sure you know the words well precede each word with either "**el**" or "**la**" depending on whether it is a **masculine** or **feminine** word as you practice saying the word in Spanish. This is good practice for getting used to the **masculine** and **feminine** expressions in Spanish. You should do this with every review you participate in as you learn more and more Spanish nouns.

Beard	Chin	Ear	Eye	Eyebrow
Eyelash	Face	Forehead	Hair	Mouth

If for some reason you can't see the picture in your mind for each English word and be able to speak the Spanish word, go back and study the picture until you know it. When you lock the picture into your mind you will know its Spanish equivalent.

Let us now discuss using **a little bit of discipline**. As you learn these Spanish words you should review them every time you have a chance. Most people waste far more time then they realize. They simply throw away time that could be used quite constructively. Suggestions will be made to will allow you to redeem much of the time that you normally throw away.

A complete list of the Spanish words you learn in the order that you learn them is printed in the back of this book for review purposes. As you learn more and more words, it wouldn't make sense to update the list after every few words you learn. That would take up far too much space in this book. As you learn more and more words, you will be instructed to turn to the list in the back of the book for a quick review of all the words you have learned. You can review several hundred words in just a few minutes, as you will find out. You will know the words so well after studying the vocabulary pictures that you will breeze through this review process.

This same complete review list will also be made available on the Internet web site, and you can download this handy review aid without having to take your book with you everyplace you go.

As for now simply make sure you know these first ten words thoroughly before continuing to the next group of words. You will find that you will get better and better at learning these words after you get used to these learning pictures. You probably already have a smile on your face, because you learned these first eleven words so quickly. On the next two pages you will continue to learn body parts from the neck up. The word "mouth" is pictured in its appropriate alphabetical place even though you have already learned it.

Before you study the next few words you need to learn another sound principle that Dr. Memory™ has developed. He calls it the **running sound**. This sound involves the vowel "u" when it is followed by another vowel in Spanish. A sound seems to **run in** from oblivion to make a new sound in these instances. Dr. Memory™ wants you to imagine that another letter "u" **runs in** to squeeze itself in next to the original letter "u" in the word. As a result a **double "u**,**"** or a "**w**" is formed. The new sound that is created is a slight "w" sound that will be influenced by the trailing Big Boss vowel. If the vowel "a" follows the letter "u," the sound that will be blended with the slight "w" sound will be the "ah" sound, which is the only sound a letter "a" ever makes in Spanish. The "w" sound in these words is not a hard sounding "w" but a soft "w" sound. You will hear it when you go to Dr. Memory's Internet web site to hear all of these words pronounced.

One other principle also occurs with this **running sound**. The consonant letter that precedes this "**u-vowel**" combination is also spoken much softer than it normally would be spoken, and in many instances Spanish-speaking people totally discard it and don't even pronounce it. The Spanish word for **water**, which is **agua**, is a good example of this principle. Technically speaking, if each vowel sound were spoken separately, the Spanish word **agua** should be pronounced **ah-goo-ah**, since the initial letter "a" must make the "ah" sound. The letter "g" should blend with the trailing vowel "u" to make a "goo" sound, since the vowel "u" in Spanish always makes the "oo" sound as in the English word "shoot." The final vowel "a" in the word must be pronounced "ah." Thus, technically you get **ah-goo-ah**, but a sound in these "**u-vowel**" combinations runs in from oblivion to influence the original letter "u" to join itself with another letter "u" to form the slight double "u," or "w" sound.

Consequently, the new sound actually sounds like **ah-gwah**. The new double "u" sound becomes a slight "w" sound blended with the trailing "ah" sound to form the new **gwah** sound. When this **gwah** sound is spoken the new "w" sound is very soft, and the preceding consonant is also spoken more softly than normal. As was mentioned earlier, in many instances Spanish-speaking people totally discard the consonant that precedes this double "u" **running sound**. Many Spanish-speaking people pronounce "agua" as "ah-wah" instead of "ah-gwah" with a slight "w" sound following the "g" sound. How these kinds of words are pronounced depends upon the region of the world in which people live. On Dr. Memory's™ web site you will hear the consonant that precedes this special sound spoken softly. An English word that produces this exact sound is "**igua**na." The "**gua**" letter combination in "**igua**na" is a perfect sound example of this concept. It is pronounced "**gwah**."

In the word "agua" you can see that the letter "u" is followed by the vowel "a." Dr. Memory's™ **running sound** principle says that another letter "u" runs in to join the original letter "u" to form a double "u." As a result, that new **running sound** word could be written like this "aguua." In the picture below you see that a letter "u" is forcing itself in the place after the original letter "u" in the word "agua." You will also see a little **running figure** in the picture below. That running figure represents this special "**running sound**." That running figure will appear in every vocabulary picture where this sound occurs. You will become familiar with this **running figure** as you proceed through this course. In the picture below the sound "**gwah**" is below the running figure, because the **running sound** in the word "agua" is "**gwah**."

Now you can learn the group of words on the next two pages.

head - cabeza
cah - bay - sah

"I love to cah in this bay and do my sock head paintings."

A cahing crow in a bay is painting by dipping its sock into paint. As you can see, it has painted a head. The crow is a master artist. It must be a headmaster. It says, "I love to cah in this bay and do my sock head paintings."

lip - labio
lah - bee - oh

"Mr. Llama, bee nice with your lips on this old lip lover."

A llama with very big lips caught a bee in its lips. The llama is wearing bib overalls. The bee says, "Mr. Llama, bee nice with your lips on this old lip lover."

mouth - boca
bow - cah

"I always wear a bow tie and cah when I fly out of a mouth."

A crow wearing a bow tie is cahing as it flies out of a mouth. It says, "I always wear a bow tie and cah when I fly out of a mouth."

neck - cuello
coo - ay - yoh

kway

"Coo, Mr. Ape, please don't play yo-yo with my neck."

Don't stick your neck out.

A cooing dove's neck was stretched by an ape sitting on egg yolks. The dove says, "Coo, Mr. Ape, please don't play yo-yo with my neck." The sign reads, "Don't stick your neck out." This word also means "collar."

nose - nariz
nah - reese

A doorknob is always difficult for a nose when it is covered with grease.

A large nose reaches for a doorknob to try to open it. It can't open it because it is covered with grease. It says, "A doorknob is always difficult for a nose when it is covered with grease."

teeth - dientes
dee - ehn - tace

Decoy ducks love endive. We taste it with our teeth.

A decoy duck holds some endive lettuce and tastes it with its very big teeth. It also says, "Decoy ducks love endive. We taste it with our teeth."

throat - garganta
gahr - gahn - tah

Don't cut your own throat.

A garter snake and a gondola propelled by a tomahawk. It gets you in the throat.

A garter snake is wrapped around the throat of the man riding in the gondola. A tomahawk giving the man a ride says, "A garter snake and a gondola propelled by a tomahawk. It gets you in the throat. The sign reads, "Don't cut your own throat."

tongue - lengua
lehn - goo - ah

I'm running towards Lynn, because that iguana's tongue is too long.

gwah

Hold your tongue.

A girl named Lynn stuck her tongue out at an iguana, and it stuck its long tongue out back at her. The sign reads, "Hold your tongue."

You have now studied and should know 17 Spanish words. You will soon see a listing of those 17 words. As mentioned earlier an ongoing list of all of the words you have learned each time you learn additional words will not be included. It will be present for the first category until you get used to the process. Then you can turn to the list in the back of the book for your ongoing reviews. This brief review process is vital for you to be successful. As mentioned before, you need to become an **ODD** person. That means you need to be **O**rganized, **D**isciplined and **D**iligent. The three letters in the word **ODD** stand for **O**rganized, **D**isciplined and **D**iligent. If you just have **a little bit of discipline** to review these words on a regular basis you will be thrilled with your building vocabulary knowledge.

You should practice saying these words in Spanish out loud as you look at each English word listed below. After you are sure you know the words well you need to precede each word with either "**el**" or "**la**" depending on whether it is a **masculine** or **feminine** word as you practice saying the word in Spanish.

Beard	Chin	Ear	Eye	Eyebrow
Eyelash	Face	Forehead	Hair	Head
Lip	Mouth	Neck	Nose	Teeth
Throat	Tongue			

If for some reason you can't see the picture in your mind for each English word and aren't able to speak the Spanish word, go back and study the picture until you know it and can speak the Spanish word. When you lock the picture into your mind you will know its Spanish equivalent.

The next sub-category in the body parts section that you will study is **body parts from the neck down**. Study the next two pages as you learn more words in the body parts category.

ankle - tobillo
toe - bee - yo

A toe and a bee sure can yo-yo an ankle.

yo-yo

A toe and a bee are wrapping a yo-yo string around an ankle as though it was an ankle bracelet. The bee says, "A toe and a bee sure can yo-yo an ankle."

arm - brazo
brah - sew

A bra is sewn onto an arm.

back - espalda
ehs - pahl - dah

Mr. Eskimo, this policy on your back can't be read by this domino.

Policy

Watch your back.

An Eskimo has an insurance policy stuck on its back. A domino is trying to read the policy. The sign reads, "Watch your back."

biceps - bíceps
bee - sehps

This bee has biceps that are separators.

The World's only Biceps Wood Splitter

A bee uses its big biceps muscles and separates a two by four piece of wood. What a strong bee. The bee says, "This bee has biceps that are separators." The sign reads, "The world's only biceps wood splitter."

body - **cuerpo**
coo - air - poe

kwair

Coo

Cooing doves fly into the air when they see a body, but a polar bear always catches them.

AIR

Don't step over my dead body.

Body

A cooing dove flies into the air and is caught by a polar bear. It flew because it was frightened when it saw a dead body. The sign reads, "Don't step over my dead body."

breast & chest - **pecho**
pay - cho

I would pay to pull the choke chain from your chest.

A rooster is beating on its breast, and an ape is beating on its chest. The chicken has a Payday candy bar peg leg, and the ape has a choke chain around its neck. The rooster says, "I would pay to pull the choke chain from your chest.

elbow - **codo**
co - doe

An elbow can crack this coconut if the donut holds it still.

An elbow is trying to crack a coconut that was placed in a donut to keep it from rolling away. The elbow says, "An elbow can crack this coconut if the donut holds it still.

finger - **dedo**
day - doe

A daisy uses a donut to play ring around the finger.

A daisy places a donut around a big finger. It says, "A daisy uses a donut to play ring around the finger."

You have now studied and should know 26 Spanish words. Here is a listing of those 26 words. Once again, you should practice saying these words in Spanish out loud as you look at each English word listed below. After you are sure you know the words well you need to precede each word with either "**el**" or "**la**" depending on whether it is a **masculine** or **feminine** word as you practice saying the word in Spanish.

Beard	Chin	Ear	**Eye**	Eyebrow
Eyelash	Face	Forehead	**Hair**	Head
Lip	Mouth	**Neck**	Nose	**Teeth**
Throat	Tongue			

Ankle	Arm	Back	Biceps	Body
Breast	Chest	Elbow	Finger	

If for some reason you can't see the picture in your mind for each English word and aren't able to speak the Spanish word, go back and study the picture until you know it and can speak the Spanish word.

The next few words you study will complete the **body parts from the neck down** sub-category. The word for hand in Spanish is "mano." This word is an exception to the masculine and feminine endings. Even though "mano" ends with a letter "o," it is feminine in gender. As a result, you will notice that it is pink in the review list.

fingernail - uña
ooh - nyah

Ooh, my nyah headdress isn't nearly as snazzy as my fingernails.

Fingernail Polish

Ny

Ooze

Fingernail polish is oozing out of the tipped over bottle of fingernail polish. A female onion (ny) wearing a tongue depressor (ah) headdress admires her freshly painted fingernail.

fist - puño
poo - nyoh

Mr. Poodle, this nyoh onion has a heavy fist.

Never shake your fist at anyone.

The poodle was knocked down by the large fist of the onion (ny) wearing overalls (oh). The onion says, "Mr. Poodle, this nyoh onion has a heavy fist." The sign reads, "Never shake your fist at anyone."

foot - pie
pea - ay

Bigfoot can use its big foot to kick peas through an ape's arms with no trouble.

Peas

A Bigfoot, a Sasquatch, with one foot much larger than the other one is kicking a can of peas through an apes uplifted arms as an extra point in football.

forearm - antebrazo
ahn - tay - brah - sew

It's on, and tape will help this bra sew the switch to the forearm.

ON

An on and off light switch is taped to a forearm to steady it, so a bra can sew the switch on the forearm. You have learned that "arm" means brah sew. The ahn and tay sounds simply precede these sounds for the word forearm.

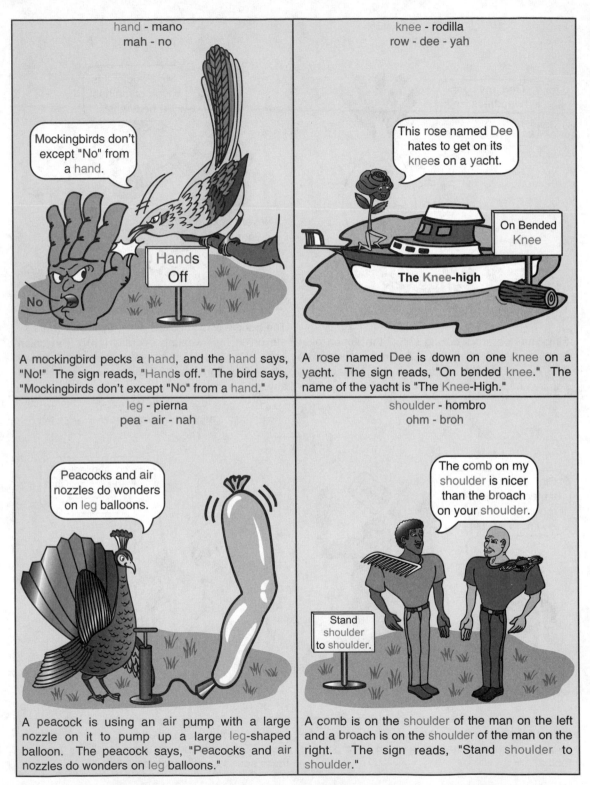

hand - mano
mah - no

Mockingbirds don't except "No" from a hand.

No

Hands Off

A mockingbird pecks a hand, and the hand says, "No!" The sign reads, "Hands off." The bird says, "Mockingbirds don't except "No" from a hand."

knee - rodilla
row - dee - yah

This rose named Dee hates to get on its knees on a yacht.

On Bended Knee

The Knee-high

A rose named Dee is down on one knee on a yacht. The sign reads, "On bended knee." The name of the yacht is "The Knee-High."

leg - pierna
pea - air - nah

Peacocks and air nozzles do wonders on leg balloons.

A peacock is using an air pump with a large nozzle on it to pump up a large leg-shaped balloon. The peacock says, "Peacocks and air nozzles do wonders on leg balloons."

shoulder - hombro
ohm - broh

The comb on my shoulder is nicer than the broach on your shoulder.

Stand shoulder to shoulder.

A comb is on the shoulder of the man on the left and a broach is on the shoulder of the man on the right. The sign reads, "Stand shoulder to shoulder."

The Spanish word for toe literally means the finger of the foot. You have already learned "finger" and "foot." All you have to do is put the Spanish word for "of the," which is "del," in between them. (day - doe - dell - pea - ay)

A mooing cow and an onion (ny) are preparing to compete in a wrist wrestling contest. The toy, stuffed ape is the onion's good luck charm. The cahing crow judge says, "Moo and nyeah all you want. I'll cah the wrist winner."

You have now studied and should know 36 Spanish words. Here is a listing of those 36 words. As before, you should practice saying these words in Spanish out loud as you look at each English word listed below. After you are sure you know the words well you need to precede each word with either "**el**" or "**la**" depending on whether it is a **masculine** or **feminine** word as you practice saying the word in Spanish.

Beard	Chin	Ear	Eye	Eyebrow
Eyelash	Face	Forehead	Hair	Head
Lip	Mouth	Neck	Nose	Teeth
Throat	Tongue			
Ankle	Arm	Back	Biceps	Body

Breast	Chest	Elbow	Finger	Fingernail
Fist	Foot	Forearm	Hand	Knee
Leg	Shoulder	Toe	Wrist	

If for some reason you can't see the picture in your mind for each English word and aren't able to speak the Spanish word, go back and study the picture until you know it and can speak the Spanish word.

The picture below and on the next page will complete the body parts category. The last body parts sub-category is **internal** and **skin body parts**.

blood - sangre
sahn - gray

This sauna causes my blood to turn a grape color.

Blood is thicker than water.

A sauna bath has a bunch of grapes in it. Blood is flowing out from under the sauna bath door. The sign reads, "Blood is thicker than water."

bone - hueso
ooh - ay - sew

weigh

Ooh

I'll wait on your aching bones while you're on this sofa.

A bone says, "Ooh," as it soaks its bony feet. An Ape pours warm water while the bone is seated on a sofa. Notice the other bones throughout the picture. The ape comments.

heart - corazón
core - ah - sewn

This apple core's heart needed to be, ah, sewn up.

We put your heart at rest.

An apple core just got a heart operation. The tongue depressor (ah) surgeon has just sewn it up. The sign reads, "We put your heart at rest."

muscle - músculo
moose - coo - low

Mr. Moose, this cooing dove and locust love to ride you on this big muscle.

Don't move a muscle.

Muscle

A moose is being ridden by a cooing dove and a locust. They are riding along a muscular leg muscle. The sign reads, "Don't move a muscle."

skin - piel
pea - ehl

This can of peas studies elephant skin at the university.

Peas

It's a good thing I have thick skin.

Beauty is only skin deep.

A can of peas is riding an elephant. It said, "This can of peas studies elephant skin at the university." The elephant said, "It's a good thing I have thick skin." The sign reads, "Beauty is only skin deep."

stomach - estómago
ehs - toe - mah - go

This Eskimo hit the toad's stomach, and that mop is a go-getter.

Go pick on someone your own size.

For an upset stomach take Stomach Ease.

An Eskimo hit a toad in its stomach. The mop said, "Go pick on someone your own size." The advertising sign reads, "For an upset stomach take Stomach Ease."

You have now studied and should know 42 Spanish words relating to the body. Here is a listing of those 42 words. When you learn how to put these words together with other parts of speech later, you will be able to discuss your body with a doctor if you have a problem and need attention. You could survive such a meeting and be able to communicate. That is what survival Spanish is all about. This knowledge might allow you to survive in a literal sense.

As before, you should practice saying these words in Spanish out loud as you look at each English word listed below. After you are sure you know the words well you need to precede each word with either "**el**" or "**la**" depending on whether it is a **masculine** or **feminine** word as you practice saying the word in Spanish.

Beard	Chin	Ear	Eye	Eyebrow
Eyelash	Face	Forehead	Hair	Head
Lip	Mouth	Neck	Nose	Teeth
Throat	Tongue			

Ankle	Arm	Back	Biceps	Body
Breast	Chest	Elbow	Finger	Fingernail
Fist	Foot	Forearm	Hand	Knee
Leg	Shoulder	Toe	Wrist	

Blood	Bone	Heart	Muscle	Skin
Stomach				

If for some reason you can't remember the Spanish word, go back and study the picture until you know it and can speak the Spanish word.

CHAPTER 7

Plural Rules for Nouns

Nouns are either singular or plural in Spanish just as in English. Of course, singular means one of something, while plural means more than one of something. Dr. Memory™ has created pictures for the most important rules for making singular nouns plural. Only these three rules will be taught in this survival Spanish book. There are other rules that are used far less and they aren't needed for survival Spanish.

Plural Rule Number One - **Add** an "s" to a **noun** that **ends with a vowel**. The bold words in the rule are pictured below. A **add**ing machine with a letter "s" on the paper is held by a **nun**. A **nun** is used by Dr. Memory™ to picture a **noun**. The **end** of the paper is next to a V-owl, a **vowel**, that is holding it up. The V-owl says, "Add an "s" to a noun that ends with a vowel." Read the rule at the beginning of this paragraph a few more times while examining the picture and you will be able to remember this plural rule.

Below you will see some examples of some nouns that you have already learned and others you haven't learned displaying this plural rule.

mano + s = manos   radio + s = radios

dedo + s = dedos   café + s = cafés

ojo + s = ojos   cobra + s = cobras

Plural Rule Number Two - **Add "es" to a noun that ends with a consonant.** The bold words in the rule are pictured below. An **add**ing machine with the letters "**es**" on the paper is held by a **nun**. The **end** of the paper is next to a con-sun-ant, a **consonant**, that is holding it up. The con-sun-ant says, "Add an "es" to a noun that ends with a consonant." Read the rule at the beginning of this paragraph a few more times while examining the picture and you will have no problem remembering this plural rule.

Below you will see an example of a noun that you have already learned and another you haven't learned displaying this plural rule. There is no accent in the plural form of these words.

corazón + es = corazones   melón + es = melones

Plural Rule Number Three - **Noun**s that **end with a letter "z" change** the "z" to "**c**" and **add** "**es**." The bold words in the rule are pictured below. A **nun** is holding the adding machine. The paper **end**s **with a letter "z."** **Change** is flying out of the mouth of a zebra in the shape of a letter "**z**." The change is falling on a C-clamp in the shape of a letter "**c**." The **add**ing machine paper has the letters "**es**" on it. The nun says, "Nouns that end with a letter "z" change the "z" to "c" and add "es."" Read the rule at the beginning of this paragraph a few more times while examining the picture and you will be able to remember this plural rule.

Below you will see an example of a noun that displays this plural rule. "Lápiz" means "pencil" in English. You will have a learning picture for this word in another category. The accent remains in the plural form of this word.

lápiz + es = lápices

Look back at the final review list of all of the words you have just learned and determine how they would be made plural when applying the rules you just learned. Remembering these rules and how to apply them should be no problem due to Dr. Memory's™ plural learning pictures. Each time you learn a new noun you should make it a practice to think of the plural for the noun by applying these rules.

Definite and Indefinite Article Plurals

You have already learned that "el" and "la" are the masculine and feminine definite articles in Spanish, and that "un" and "una" are the indefinite articles in Spanish. Since you have just learned plural rules for nouns you should also learn the plurals for these articles.

The **definite feminine article** "la" simply becomes "**las**" when used before a plural noun. You simply add a letter "s" to "la." The **definite masculine article** "el" has a more drastic change, but it follows the lead of the feminine "las." You have learned that most feminine nouns end in a letter "a," and most masculine nouns end in a letter "o." As a result, understanding the **masculine plural definite article** is simple. The **masculine plural definite article** is "**los**." The feminine letter "a" in "las" is simply changed to the masculine letter "o" to arrive at "**los**." "**Los**" or "**las**" must be used to match the **masculine** or **feminine** gender of the nouns they precede.

The **indefinite feminine article** "una" simply becomes "**unas**" when used before a plural noun. You simply add a letter "s" to "una." The **indefinite masculine article** "un" has a more drastic change, but it also follows the lead of the feminine "unas." The **masculine plural indefinite article** is "**unos**." The feminine letter "a" in "unas" is simply changed to the masculine letter "o" to arrive at "**unos**." "**Unos**" or "**unas**" must be used to match the **masculine** or **feminine** gender of the nouns they precede.

Singular and plural definite and indefinite articles are used below with some of the body part words you have learned as examples of the singular and plural uses of the definite and indefinite articles.

el ojo - **los** ojos	**un** ojo - **unos** ojos
el corazón - **los** corazones	**un** corazón - **unos** corazones
la boca - **las** bocas	**una** boca - **unas** bocas
la nariz - **las** narices	**una** nariz - **unas** narices

CHAPTER 8

Animals and Insects

The second and third categories of words you will learn are **animals** and **insects**. The animal category is probably the second set of words you began to learn as a child when your parents first began to teach you. As with all categories, these words will be taught in alphabetical order.

We will now review the **Rolling "R"** sound before you study this next group of words, because this sound first appears in one of these words. The **Rolling "R"** sound occurs when double letter "R's" occur next to each other in Spanish words. As was stated when the Spanish alphabet was discussed, this sound lasts longer than a single letter "R," and **rolls** out of the mouth for a longer time. You will hear this sound when you click on the words that contain this sound in Dr. Memory's™ Internet web site. You will see a roller skate and/or rolling letter "R's" in the Spanish pictures where this sound is heard.

Since the review lists will not be used any longer you need to have **a little bit of discipline** to participate in a regular review process. All of the learning pictures for the entire animal and insect categories will be shown without any interruptions for review. You should still review the animal and insect's categories as well as all of the words you have already mastered after learning eight new words. You will not be as successful as you want to be without these brief but important reviews.

As before, you should practice saying these words in Spanish out loud as you look at each English word during the review process. After you are sure you know the words well, precede each word with either "**el**" or "**la**" if you select the definite article depending on whether it is a **masculine** or **feminine** noun as you practice saying the word in Spanish. If you choose to use the indefinite article use either "**un**" or "**una**" depending on whether it is a **masculine** or **feminine** noun.

animal - animal
ah - knee - maul

Ah, I'm on my knees. Please don't maul me, Mr. Animal.

What an animal.

Animal Crackers

A tongue depressor (ah) is on its knees in a shopping mall. A wild animal got loose from the wild animal zoo and approached the tongue depressor. It said, "Ah, I'm on my knees. Please don't maul me, Mr. Animal." This animal shouldn't look like a real animal or it might be confusing.

bear - oso
oh - sew

Bear's overalls always need to be sewn up.

It's a bear market.

A bear wearing overalls is sewing up a hole in its overalls. It says, "Bear's overalls always need to be sewn up." The sign reads, "It's a bear market." A female bear is "osa."

bird - pájaro
pah - ha - row

Pots are, Ha-Ha, hard to row for a bird.

Bird Ahoy

A bird in a cooking pot laughs and says, "Ha-Ha," as it rows the pot like a boat. The floating sign reads, "Bird Ahoy."

bull - toro
tore - oh

That bull tore my old sleeve.

That bull tore my overalls clean off.

Take the bull by the horns.

The bull tore the overalls off the cowboy who is running away from the bull. The farmer says, "That bull tore my old sleeve." The cowboy says, "That bull tore my overalls clean off." The sign reads, "Take the bull by the horns."

cat - gato
gah - toe

Cats with goggles love to scratch toes.

He's a real cool cat.

A cat wearing goggles is using a big toe as a scratching post. It says, "Cats with goggles love to scratch toes. The sign reads, "He's a real cool cat."

chicken & hen - gallina
gah - yee - nah

Goggles help chickens see better to hold yeast between our knock-knees.

This is chicken feed.

Knock Knock

Yeast

A chicken wearing goggles is holding a package of yeast between its knock-knees. The sign reads, "This is chicken feed." This term refers to a live chicken in this example.

cow - vaca
vah - cah

Vaudeville is great for cows and cahing crows.

The Vaudeville Cow

When will all the cows come home?

Cah

A cow is performing a vaudeville act with a cahing crow. The cow comments on the performance. The sign reads, "When will all the cows come home?

deer - ciervo
sea - air - boh

Deer me, this cedar chest is airy, but my bow tie helps.

Air

Cedar

A deer is standing in a cedar chest under an air conditioner while wearing a bow tie. The deer says, "Deer me, this cedar chest is airy, but my bow tie helps."

dog - perro
pay - rrow

Payday the rolling dog is rope bound.

He's top dog.

A Payday candy bar wrapper is worn by a dog on roller skates (rolling "R's") as it heads for a rope at the finish line of a skating race. The sign reads, "He's top dog."

duck - pato
pah - toe

Ducks love popcorn at toga parties.

I'm no lame duck.

A duck is popping popcorn at an outdoor party while wearing a toga. It says, "Ducks love popcorn at toga parties." The sign reads, "I'm no lame duck." Another duck waits for popcorn.

elephant - elefante
ehl - ay - fahn - tay

That elf doesn't want this ape and fawn to tape measure the elephant's tusks without the elephant having water.

An elf gives water to an elephant as an ape and a fawn use a tape measure to measure the elephant's tusks. The ape comments on what is happening in the picture.

fish - pez
pehs

That pesticide looks fishy to me.

PESTICIDE

Live fish are jumping up out of the water, because a container of pesticide is pouring into the water. One fish says, "That pesticide looks fishy to me." There is another word for "fish" when it is not a live fish, but a fish to be eaten. That word is taught in the "food" category.

fox - zorro
zoh - rroh

A fox dressed like Zorro is in a no-row zone but is still rowing the boat. It says, "This no-row zone where I row will fox them out." Even though the word "Zorro" isn't pronounced in English the same way it is in Spanish, it will still help.

goat - cabra
cah - brah

A cahing crow encourages a brahma bull that has a lasso around a goat. The brahma bull is pulling back, but it can't budge the obstinate goat. The goat says, "I'm a goat of a different color."

horse - caballo
cah - bah - yo

A cahing crow watches a boxer use a yo-yo to punch a horse. The sign reads, "Get off of your high horse." The crow says, "Cah, that boxer with the yo-yo glove doesn't horse around."

lamb - cordero
core - dare - oh

An apple core daredevil just jumped over an overpass on a lamb. It says, "This apple core is a daredevil that jumps overpasses on a lamb." The sign reads, "He's taking it on the lamb."

lion - léon
lay - own

Quit laying down on the job. I own you, Mr. Lion.

Be lion hearted.

A lion trainer points at his lion and says, "Quit laying down on the job. I own you, Mr. Lion." The sign reads, "Be lion hearted." Please excuse the bad grammar. It was used to create the correct sound.

monkey - mono
moe - no

Two of you monkeys can leave this mobile home and come with Noah.

No Monkey Business

Monkeys are in front of a mobile home. Noah invites two of them to get on his ark. He says, "Two of you monkeys can leave this mobile home and come with Noah." The sign reads, "No monkey business." The monkeys think hard.

pig - puerco
poo - air - co

pwair

That poodle is arrogant. It and the cobra are going to toss this pig in that poke.

Pig out.

A poodle tossed a pig up in the air with the help of a cobra. The pig says, "That poodle is arrogant. It and that cobra are going to toss this pig in that poke." The sign reads, "Pig out."

rabbit & turtle - conejo & tortuga
co - nay - hoe & tore - two - gah

The rabbit tripped on a coconut that I neighed in with a hoe.

This turtle ran so fast I tore two sets of goggles off.

A rabbit and a turtle are in a race. The rabbit turned around backwards to cross the finish line, but it tripped on a coconut that a neighing horse pushed with a hoe. As the turtle slowly crossed the finish line it said, "This turtle ran so fast I tore two sets of goggles off."

rooster - gallo
gah - yoh

Goggles help a rooster **see** how to yo-yo better.

A Rooster Booster

A rooster wearing goggles is playing with a yo-yo. The rooster **says**, "Goggles help a rooster **see** how to yo-yo better." The sign reads, " A rooster booster."

sheep - oveja
oh - vay - ha

That old vase counts modern sheep to try to sleep, Ha-ha. It ought to count this sheep.

Ha-ha

An overall skirt is worn by the sheep being counted by the vase trying to go to sleep. The sheep is saying, "Ha-ha," as it jumps in the vase's dream. A sheep at the foot of the bed says, "That old vase, counts modern sheep to try to sleep, Ha-ha. It ought to count this sheep."

snake - culebra
coo - lay - brah

This snake will cool them down when I lay down by that brahma bull.

A snake was awakened by a party. The snake sees a coot and laces on a brahma bull. They don't know the snake is there. The snake says, "This snake will cool them down when I lay down by that brahma bull."

tiger - tigre
tea - gray

Having tiger tea with a gray squirrel is a tiger's highest joy.

TEA

A tiger is having tiger tea with a gray squirrel. It says, "Having tiger tea with a gray squirrel is a tiger's highest joy."

turkey - pavo
pah - voh

This turkey reads this pocket book over and over to try to learn Spanish vocabulary.

Pocket
Vocab

Pocketbook
Turkey
Vocabulary

A turkey is reading a pocket book about Spanish vocabulary. He is doing it the hard way, what a turkey. He needs to talk turkey with Dr. Memory".

wolf - lobo
low - bow

This locust offers this bow tie as a peace offering, Mr. Wolf.

A locust offers a bow tie to a wolf that frightened it. The locust says, "This locust offers this bow tie as a peace offering, Mr. Wolf." The sign reads, "This is no wolf in sheep's clothing."

ant - hormiga
oar - me - gah

Using an oar to hit meteors makes ants gah-gah.

Don't get ants in your pants.

An ant uses an oar to knock a meteor back into the sky. It is wearing goggles to protect its eyes. The ant says, "Using an oar to hit meteors makes ants gah-gah. The sign reads, "Don't get ants in your pants."

bee - abeja
ah - bay - ha

Ah, baseball and bees make you holler.

Ha-Ha!

Ah-Bay

Bee careful.

A tongue depressor bat, ah, is used in a baseball game against bees. A bee caught the ball as the batter said, "Ha-Ha." Another bee runs to pull the ball off of the stinger. The sign reads, "Bee careful."

bug - bicho
bee - choh

This bee is going to choke you, Mr. Bug.

Mr. Bee, please don't choke this bug in anger.

I have the travel bug.

A bee is going to choke the bug. The bee says, "This bee is going to choke you, Mr. Bug." The bug says, "Mr. Bee, please don't choke this bug in anger." The sign reads, "I have the travel bug."

fly - mosca
mohs - cah

Moses can cause fly plagues.

Most cahing crows love a fly or two.

There's a fly in the ointment.

Moses extends his rod and brings on a plague of flies (fly). Cahing crows are eating the flies (fly). The sign reads, "There's a fly in the ointment." The sound in Moses is not exactly "mohs," but it will work.

insect - insecto
een - seck - toe

I'm a teenage, insect secretary, but I do a good job for Mr. Toe.

An insect that is a teenager is a secretary for a big toe. She is ready to type what he is about to dictate. She says, "I'm a teenage, insect secretary, but I do a good job for Mr. Toe."

spider - araña
ah - rah - nyah

My spider friend is, ah, a rock solid pal that is nyaht what he appears to be.

A spider is reaching to eat a fly given to it by its friend. The fly is held on a tongue depressor (ah). The spider's onion friend is rocking in a rocking chair. The onion (ny) is wearing a tongue depressor (ah) headdress. The onion says, "My spider friend is, ah, a rock solid friend that is nyaht what he appears to be."

You have now studied and should know 76 words, 43 words relating to the body and 34 animal and insect words. Make sure to review all of the words regularly. Having **a little bit of discipline** in this fashion will pay big rewards. The reward far surpasses the small investment of time required for these reviews.

You should also know that the gender of most Spanish nouns can be changed by simply changing the last letter of the word. As an example, the word for bear is either "oso" or "osa." Obviously, "oso" is a **masculine** bear, and "osa" is a **feminine** bear. Likewise, the word for dog is either "perro" or "perra." Obviously, "perro" is a **masculine** dog, and "perra" is a **feminine** dog.

CHAPTER 9

Sentence Practice

The first verb that will be discussed with sentences is the verb "is," which is "es" in Spanish. The word "my," which is "mi" in Spanish, will also be used in one of the first example sentences. These two words are simple to learn, since only one letter changes in each of them. The picture below shows these two English words changing to their Spanish counterparts. "Es" is pronounced "ehs" as though you were saying the letter "s" when saying the English alphabet. "Mi" is pronounced "me," since the letter "i" always makes the long "e" English sound in Spanish.

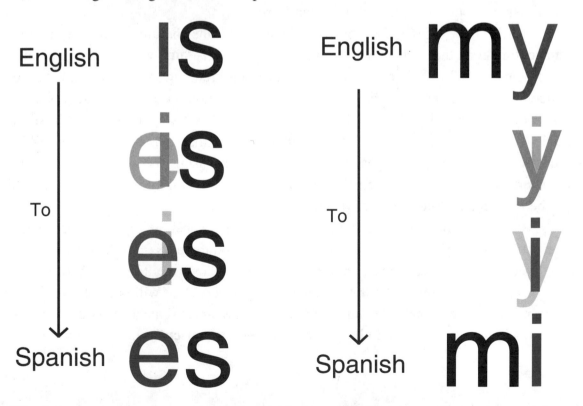

Affirmative Statements

The order of affirmative statements is the same in English and Spanish. Five example English statements using the verb "is" can be seen below.

It is the dog.   It is a dog.   It is my dog.   It is the cow.   It is a cow.

When saying these sentences in Spanish, the words "it is" are understood in the Spanish verb "es," so only the word "es" is used. The English and corresponding Spanish statements can be seen in the example sentences below. The definite and indefinite articles have been used in these sample sentences.

It is the dog.   It is a dog.   It is my dog.   It is the cow.   It is a cow.
Es **el** perro.   Es **un** perro.   Es mi perro.   Es **la** vaca.   Es **una** vaca.

When making affirmative statements in Spanish, the intonation or vocal pattern is downward. When the intonation or speaking pattern is raised, Spanish-speaking people aren't making a statement, as you will soon learn.

Notice that "**el**" was used for the definite article "the" before "perr**o**," because it is a **masculine** noun that ends in a letter "**o**." Also notice that "**un**" was used for the indefinite article "a" before "perr**o**," because it is a **masculine** noun that ends in a letter "**o**." Notice that "**la**" was used for the definite article "the" before "vaca," because it is a **feminine** noun that ends in a letter "**a**." Also notice that "**una**" was used for the indefinite article "a" before "vaca," because it is a **feminine** noun that ends in a letter "**a**." When you practice making up and speaking Spanish sentences using "is," "the," "a" and "my" in a short time, you will have to remember to use the correct definite and indefinite articles before a **masculine** or **feminine** noun.

It is now time for you to begin to make up and speak affirmative Spanish sentences. Dr. Memory™ has created a unique way for you to do this. At the top of the next page you see a clown standing at a mirror putting his clown **make-up** on before a performance. He is standing next to his **make-up** wardrobe. You will use the doors of his **make-up** wardrobe to **make-up**, and speak your own Spanish sentences. Notice that parts of the doors have been painted **blue** and **pink** to refer to **masculine** and **feminine**.

At the top of the next page you see that the doors of the make-up wardrobe have been opened to reveal that there are actually multiple doors. You will also notice that a drill is inside the wardrobe. This will help remind you that the clown's make-up wardrobe doors will be used in **sentence make-up drills**.

Dr. Memory™ uses the clown's doors in various ways to allow you to practice making-up and speaking Spanish sentences of various kinds. He has also created multiple colored doors to help in this process. You will start with simple sentences using "is," "my" and "the" along with the Spanish vocabulary you have learned to this point. On the next page, you will see two doors. The words "it is" are to the left of the first door. You will notice that the first door is **blue**, brown and **pink**. The word "the" is on the **blue** and **pink** sections, and the word "my" is on the middle, brown section. You also see ten English words on the door to the right. These words include some "body parts" and "animals" that you should have already learned. All you had to do to learn them was to have **a little bit of discipline**. If you haven't learned them you will have to go back and review them, as well as all of the other words in those two categories, or you won't be able to take part in Dr. Memory's™ sentence make-up drills. You also see the rest of the words in the "body parts" and "animal" categories above, below and to the right of these doors.

The purpose of this drill is to have you **make-up affirmative statements** that all begin with "it is," which is "es" in Spanish. Then you can use "the," "a" or "my" before one of the English words you choose to use to make-up a Spanish sentence. Of course all of this will be done in Spanish. That is why you can't participate in this drill without knowing the Spanish words in these two categories. When you choose to use the word "the" in a sentence you make-up, you will have to use the appropriate form of the definite article "the" in Spanish. If it is used before a **masculine** noun the usage must be "**el**," and if it is used before a **feminine** noun the usage must be "la." When you choose to use the word "a" in a sentence you make-up, you will have to use the appropriate form of the indefinite article "a" in Spanish. If it is used before a **masculine** noun the usage must be "**un**," and if it is used before a **feminine** noun the usage must be "**una**.-

As an example, if you made up the sentence "It is **the** dog," you would have to use "**el**," since "perro" is a **masculine** noun. If you made up the sentence "It is **the** cow," you would have to use "la," since "vaca" is a **feminine** noun. These were two of the sample sentences used earlier. When you use the word "my" you will not be concerned with the masculine or feminine gender of the noun. "Mi" can be used before all of the nouns in these cases.

These practice drills are vital for your progress. You must participate in all of them to advance your skills. You will be able to hear several of these sentences spoken by a Spanish-speaking person on Dr. Memory's™ web site. When you listen to them you will better understand the vocal downward intonation of affirmative statements.

As you start to make-up sentences, use the words on the brown door first and then use the words above, below and to the right of the that door in any order you may choose. Practice using all of the nouns to end your sentences to become more familiar with speaking Spanish in your first practice sentences. You may not say some of these made-up sentences in normal conversation, but the purpose of the drill is to get you started using Spanish sentences as well as becoming more secure with your Spanish vocabulary. It is also very important to become as comfortable as possible with the usage of "**el**" and "la" and "**un**" and "**una**" in Spanish.

It is imperative that you take the time to learn all the vocabulary words as you go. If you don't know them you will not be able to participate in Dr. Memory's™ unique learning drills. The drills become more interesting and more complex as you proceed through the course. These drills will enable you to become a Spanish-speaking person in a relatively short period of time, but you must know the vocabulary words. Dr. Memory™ has developed learning pictures to make learning vocabulary easier than ever. Make sure you have a little bit of discipline to review and retain the vocabulary words each time a new category is introduced. Have fun!

chin
ear
eye

		shoulder
		toe
		wrist

bee　eyebrow
bug　eyelash　animal
fly　face　bear
spider　forehead　bird
hair　cat

cow　head　chicken
dog　lip　deer
finger　neck　duck
beard　teeth　elephant
turkey　throat　fish
hand　tongue　fox
mouth　goat
bull　ankle　hen
ant　arm　horse
nose　back　lamb
biceps　lion
body　monkey

It is **the / a / my / the / a**

It is
my face.

blood　chest　pig
bone　elbow　rabbit
heart　fingernail　rooster
muscle　fist　sheep
skin　foot　snake
stomach　forearm　tiger
knee　turtle
leg　wolf

Negative Statements

A **switching of word order** takes place from English to Spanish when making negative statements with the verb "is." The same three example affirmative statements used earlier are now negative statements in the example sentences below.

<blockquote>
It is not the dog.   It is not my dog.   It is not the cow.
</blockquote>

The English word "not" is simply "no" in Spanish. The English word "no" is also "no" in Spanish. No picture is needed to learn this simple word. Just drop the letter "t" from the English word "not," and you have the Spanish equivalent of "no."

The placement of the negative word is the exact opposite in Spanish as it is in English. A **switch** takes place. In English the negative word "not" comes after the word "is," but in Spanish the negative word comes before "is," or "es." Notice the switching in the example sentences below. In each case the negative "no" comes before "es." This **switching of negatives** is something you will need to practice to become more comfortable with the word order. When making negative statements in Spanish, the intonation or speaking pattern is downward as it was with affirmative statements.

It is not the dog.	It is not my dog.	It is not the cow.
No es **el** perr**o**.	No es mi perro.	No es **la** vaca.

It is not a dog.		It is not a cow.
No es **un** perr**o**.		No es **una** vaca.

On the next page, you will see the same two doors and words that were used for affirmative statements. The words "it is" and "not" are to the left of the first door now. Nothing else has changed.

The purpose of this drill is to have you **make-up negative statements** in Spanish. After switching the negative to come before "es" use "the" or "my" before one of the English words you choose to make up a negative Spanish statement. Everything else is the same as far as masculine and feminine and the usage of the Spanish word "mi" for "my."

Once again, it is important to note that these practice drills are vital for your progress and success. You should participate in all of them to advance your skills. You will be able to hear several of these negative statements spoken by a Spanish-speaking person on Dr. Memory's™ web site. When you listen to them you will better understand that the vocal intonation is downward for negative statements as opposed to affirmative statements.

chin   shoulder
ear   toe
eye   wrist
eyebrow
bee   eyelash   animal
bug   face   bear
fly   forehead   bird
spider hair   cat
        head   chicken

It is   the   cow   lip   deer
        a   dog   neck   duck
        my   finger teeth   elephant
not   beard   throat fish
        the   turkey tongue fox
        a   hand   goat
                    mouth   ankle   hen
                    bull   arm   horse
                    ant   back   lamb
                    nose   biceps lion
                            body   monkey
It is not   blood   chest   pig
my nose.   bone   elbow   rabbit
                    heart   fingernail rooster
                    muscle fist   sheep
                    skin   foot   snake
                    stomach forearm tiger
                            knee   turtle
                            leg   wolf

Questions

When asking a question with the verb "is," or "es," you simply raise your vocal intonation at the end of the sentence. You do the same thing in English. The same three example English sentences using the verb "is" can be seen below. This time the sentences are now questions.

Is it the dog?   Is it a dog?   Is it my dog?   Is it the cow?   Is it a cow?

The words "it" and "is" were switched in English to change these statements to questions. "It is the dog" became "Is it the dog?" Since "es" is understood to be "it is" in Spanish there is no switching to take place. You can't switch the order of one word.

| Is it the dog? | Is it my dog? | Is it the cow? |
| ¿Es **el** perr**o**? | ¿Es mi perro? | ¿Es **la** vaca? |

| Is it a dog? | | Is it a cow? |
| ¿Es **un** perr**o**? | | ¿Es **una** vaca? |

One thing you will notice immediately is that there is an additional question mark in a Spanish question. This additional question mark not only comes before the Spanish question, it is also upside down. This is the proper punctuation for all Spanish questions. Other than the question marks there is no difference in these example sentences from the affirmative statements that were made earlier. To ask a question with the verb "es" all you have to do is change your vocal intonation from downward to upward at the end of the sentence. You simply raise the vocal intonation to ask a question.

To practice asking questions with these same example sentences simply turn back to page 104 and make up practice questions using the words by simply raising your vocal intonation at the end of the sentence. You will be able to hear several of these questions spoken by a Spanish-speaking person on Dr. Memory's™ web site. When you listen to them you will better understand that you simply raise your vocal intonation at the end of the sentence when asking a question.

Answering Questions

Before you learn how to answer questions you must learn how to say "yes" and "no" in Spanish. It has already been stated that "no" is the same in English and Spanish. They mean the same thing. The word "**yes**" in Spanish is simply "**sí.**" This is a very common word that most people hear in one way or another before even thinking of learning Spanish. It is so easy that no picture is needed. "Sí" meaning "yes" in Spanish has an accent mark. You will find out later that "si" without an accent mark means something else.

Affirmative Answers

When answering a question affirmatively, you simply say "yes," or "sí" at the beginning of the sentence and change to the downward vocal intonation of an affirmative statement.

Is it the dog?	Is it your dog?	Is it the cow?
Yes, it is the dog.	Yes, it is my dog.	Yes, it is the cow.
Sí, es **el** perro.	Sí, es mi perro.	Sí, es **la** vaca.

Is it a dog?		Is it a cow?
Yes, it is a dog.		Yes, it is a cow.
Sí, es **un** perro.		Sí, es **una** vaca?

Negative Answers

When answering a question negatively, you say "no" and change to the downward vocal intonation of a negative statement, but Spanish speakers usually state the word "no" twice. You will notice two negative words in the English answers to the questions below. "No" is used at the beginning of the sentence, and "not" is used after the word "is" in each example English sentence. As a result, there are two negative words in the Spanish answer as well. Since the word "no" means both "no" and "not" in Spanish, it is used two times in these Spanish negative answers to questions.

Is it the dog?	Is it your dog?	Is it the cow?
No, it is not the dog.	No, it is not my dog.	No, it is not the cow.
No, no es **el** perro.	No, no es mi perro.	No, no es **la** vaca.

Is it a dog?		Is it a cow?
No, it is not a dog.		No, it is not a cow.
No, no es **un** perro.		No, no es **una** vaca?

You can practice answering questions affirmatively and negatively by using the practice drill on the next page. Assume that you were asked a question about each of the nouns listed on the page. The imaginary questions would use either "the," "a" or "my" when asking about the noun. You should practice answering the imaginary questions with affirmative and negative replies. Once again, if you answer questions with all of the listed vocabulary your skill will improve dramatically.

chin
ear
eye
eyebrow
eyelash
face
forehead
hair
head
lip
neck
teeth
throat
tongue

shoulder
toe
wrist

animal
bear
bird
cat
chicken
deer
duck
elephant
fish
fox
goat
hen
horse
lamb
lion
monkey
pig
rabbit
rooster
sheep
snake
tiger
turtle
wolf

bee
bug
fly
spider

Yes, it is

No, it is not

the
a

my

the
a

cow
dog
finger
beard
turkey
hand
mouth
bull
ant
nose

Yes, it is my dog.

blood
bone
heart
muscle
skin
stomach

ankle
arm
back
biceps
body
chest
elbow
fingernail
fist
foot
forearm
knee
leg

CHAPTER 10

People

The next category of words you will learn is **people**. The people category in my comprehensive Spanish course has five sub-categories. Those are: general, by vocation, relatives, young people, and multiple people. You will learn 40 words from each of these categories in this survival Spanish book.

All of the learning pictures for the **people category** will be shown without any interruptions for review. You should still review this category as well as all of the words you have already learned after learning eight new words. You will not be as successful as you would like without these brief but important reviews. As stated before, the reward far surpasses the small investment of time required for these reviews.

Just as in the last segment, you should practice saying these words in Spanish out loud as you look at each English word during the review process. You should continue to review all of the words in every category each time you learn eight new words. Once you are sure you know the words well you need to continue preceding each word with either "**el**" or "**la**" depending on whether it is a **masculine** or **feminine** word while you practice saying the word in Spanish.

friend - amigo
ah - me - go

Ah, me go **now**!
Thanks, friend.

A friend in need is a friend indeed.

A friend taps his friend with a tongue depressor to show him the light is green. The man says, "Ah, me go **now**! Thanks, friend," as he prepares to cross the street. The sign reads, "A friend in need is a friend indeed."

boyfriend & girlfriend - novio & novia
no - vee - oh & no - vee - ah

Boyfriends and girlfriends with big noses and V-necks are so oh and ah.

Boyfriends and girlfriends are both nosy.

A boyfriend and girlfriend are talking. The boyfriend has a big nose and is wearing a V-neck shirt and overalls. The girlfriend also has a big nose and is wearing a V-neck sweater. She is Amish. The girl says, "Boyfriends and girlfriends with big noses and V-necks are so oh and ah."

man - hombre & woman - mujer
ohm - bray & moo - hair

This man at home is very brave.

This woman's moose needs longer hair.

Man meets woman.

Home For Sale

Bray

A man rides past his home on a braying donkey. The man is approaching a woman. The woman is riding a moose. The woman has very long hair. The sign reads, "Man meets woman."

barber - barbero
bahr - bear - oh

This barn barber is this bear's oldest buddy.

Bob the Barber

A barber outside a barn is cutting a bear's hair. The barber is wearing overalls. The sign reads, "Bob the barber." The bear says, "This barn barber is this bear's oldest buddy."

beautician - peluquera
pay - loo - kay - rah

Will you pay for this loop de doo hairdo, Kay, or will you hit your beautician with your curling rod?

Sweet Beautician Service

A Payday candy bar beautician holds a loop over a customer's head. The beautician's customer is named Kay. A large curling rod is held by the customer. The shop sign reads, "Sweet Beautician Service."

doctor - médico
may - dee - co

May I doctor you from over here, Miss Dee, the cobra?

Doctor Faraway

The doctor is wary of his patient. It is the month of May. He yells across the room at Dee, a female cobra. He is afraid to get too close to the snake, so she might not get the best of her doctor's medical care.

mechanic - mecánico
may - cah - knee - co

May the mechanic's concrete was needed along with my cobra to ruin this car.

Master Mechanic

A female mechanic named May, had a truck dump concrete under the hood of a car while her knees have a cobra on them. The owner of the car was fed up with the car and asked the mechanic to ruin it.

policeman - policía
poe - lee - sea - ah

No pogo stick leech policeman can catch this seahorse, ah, I'll get away.

A policeman is your best friend.

The policeman riding a pogo stick is a leech trying to catch a criminal. The criminal is a seahorse that just jumped on a tongue depressor, ah, to use it as a surfboard to make its get away. Another policeman is behind the sign that reads, "A policeman is your best friend."

waiter & waitress - camarero & camarera
cah - mah - rare - oh & cah - mah - rare - ah

A cahing crow waiter drags a mop while delivering a rare steak to a man wearing overalls. A cahing crow waitress drags a mop while delivering a rare steak to an Amish lady. The sign reads, "The world's best waiter and waitress."

aunt & uncle - tía & tío
tea - ah & tea - oh

Aunt T-square is using a tongue depressor (ah) as a cane, and uncle T-square is leaning on oats. A little T-square tells them they are both so square.

brother & sister - hermano & hermana
air - mah - no & air - mah - nah

A sister signaled her brother to jump off of a building onto an air bag. The brother is wearing moccasins and has a big nose. The sister is sitting on an air conditioner. She signaled her brother to jump with a mop. Her knees are knocking together from fear.

cousin - primo & prima
pre - moe & pre - mah

Cousins preserves are being judged. The boy cousin held up a jar of preserves to the judge and said, "Our cousin preserves are made in our mobile home." The girl cousin held up a jar of preserves toward the judge and said, "Our cousin preserves are made by my ma."

daughter & son - hija & hijo
ee - hah & ee - hoe

An eagle must learn to hoe, my son.

An eagle must work in a hot bed, my daughter.

Sons and Daughters of the Earth

Hot Bed

A mother eagle is showing her daughter how to work in a hot bed. The father eagle is teaching his son how to hoe in the family garden. The sign reads, "Sons and daughters of the earth."

father & mother - padre & madre
pah - dray & mah - dray

Mop the drapes open, mother.

Pop the drapes open, father.

A father, a pa-pa, is holding his baby son as he prepares to open the drapes. A mother holds her baby daughter in one hand and uses a mop with her other hand to open the other set of drapes.

grandfather & grandmother - abuelo & abuela
ah - boo - ay - low & ah - boo - ay - lah

bway

Grandfather and Grandmother

Ah bway low.   Ah bway lah.

A grandfather near an Amish man threw a boomerang to an Amish man. He missed , and a locust caught the boomerang. A grandmother near another Amish man threw a boomerang at that Amish man. She missed him, and a llama caught her boomerang.

husband & wife - esposo & esposa
ehs - poe - sew & ehs - poe - sah

An Eskimo husband and wife can't get away from polar bears. Sodas and sockets won't work.

Husband and wife Eskimos who are newlyweds are running away from a polar bear. The husband threw an ice cream soda at the bear, and the wife threw a socket set at it.

nephew & niece - sobrino & sobrina
sew - bree - no & sew - bree - nah

Nephews sew in breezes with nose problem.

Nieces have to sew in breezes with a knot head like you.

Nephew and niece sewing contest.

A nephew and a niece are both sewing in a breeze. The nephew has a big nose, and the niece has a knot on her head. The nephew says, "Nephews sew in breezes with nose problem." The niece says, "Nieces have to sew in breezes with a knot head like you."

parents - los padres
lohs - pah - drace

We are parents, so please close the drapes.

Pa will be happy to close the drapes.

Parents are paying attention to their babies. The mother says, "We are parents, so please close the drapes." The pa is holding his baby son as he prepares to close the drapes.

baby - bebé
bay - bay

My baseball missed the bale, and I'm crying like a baby.

Don't be such a baby.

A crying baby threw a baseball at a bale of hay and missed. The baby says, "My baseball missed the bale, and I'm crying like a baby. The sign reads, "Don't be such a baby."

boy & girl - muchacho & muchacha
moo - cha - cho & moo - cha - cha

Moo, Cha-choke, little boy!

Moo, Cha-cha, little girl!

Boy and Girl cha-cha

A boy and girl are holding hands as they watch young boy and girl cows dance. The boy mooing cow is doing the cha-cha while wearing a choke chain. The girl mooing cow is saying, "Cha-cha," as she dances the cha-cha.

children - hijos
ee - hohs

The eagle and heavenly hosts watch over children.

Children At Play

An eagle is perched on a cloud next to the heavenly host. The angels are overseeing the protection of some children below. The sign reads, "Children at play."

family - familia
fah - me - lee - ah

This fox loves meat, and I leap for my family, ah, let's eat it.

A Family Affair

Fox Family

A fox brought a piece of meat to his family and dropped it near the family den. A little fox leaped into the air and commented in anticipation of eating the meat. The sign reads, "A family affair."

group - grupo
grew - poh

I've never been in a group that grew to a post before.

Don't be a groupie.

Vines grew around a group of people and tied them to a post. The sign reads, "Don't be a groupie." A person in the group says, "I've never been in a group that grew to a post before."

lady & Mrs. - señora
say - nyoar - ah

A sailor and a nyoar always help a lady, ah, especially a Mrs.

Mrs. Lady docks here.

Ah

Ny

Mrs. Lady

A sailor and an onion are helping a lady, who is a Mrs., get into a boat. The onion, ny, is using an oar, and the sailor is using a tongue depressor, ah, to steady the boat. Notice that the name of the boat is "Mrs. Lady."

miss - señorita
say - nyoar - e - tah

A sailor and an onion (ny) with an oar both are red faced and look very embarrassed in the presence of the beautiful young Miss. An eagle in the background hides its face with its wing as its spins a toy top. It is also embarrassed. This Miss must have some captivating powers.

mister (Mr.) & sir - señor
say - nyoar

A sailor stands up next to an onion (ny) at an outdoor convention. The onion is waving an oar trying to get the attention of the convention chairman. The sailor yells, "**This sailor and the** nyoar **need attention,** Mister Chairman, sir."

people - gente
hen - tay

A hen is squawking while recording on a tape recorder. Some people seem to like it and dance, while other people don't like it and run away. The boy says, "I love to laugh at people when the hen tapes its squawks."

Family Tree

Dr. Memory™ has created a special Family Tree, so you can have a little more practice saying family words. Examine the Family Tree on the next page. You will notice that all of the masculine words are on the left of the tree, and all of the feminine words are on the right of the tree. The masculine side of the tree has a blue-sky background, and the feminine side of the tree has a pink-sky background. A blue letter "O" is on the ground on the left side of the tree, and a pink letter "A" is on the ground on the right side of the tree. The practice drill for this tree is simple.

When you see an English word in the boxes on the tree simply say the corresponding Spanish word for that word. You should have some fun with this Family Tree, and you will know the family words much better after the review. Remember to have a little bit of discipline and continue to review all of the words you have studied listed in the back of this book on a regular basis. Have fun!

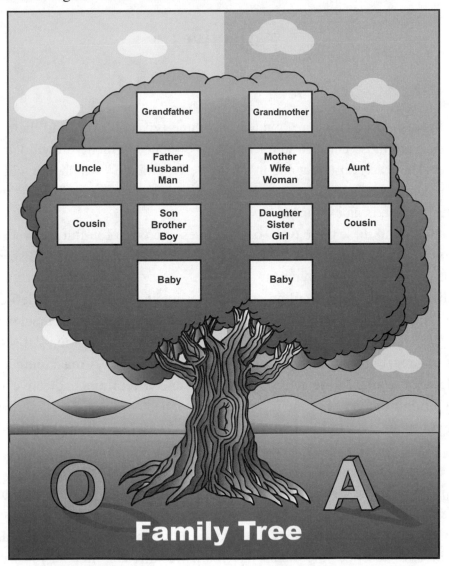

You have now studied and should know 120 words, 43 words relating to the body, 34 animal and insect words, 40 words in the people category and the words for "is," "my," "no" and "not." Make sure you continue to have **a little bit of discipline** with the review process. The reward far surpasses the small investment of time required for these reviews.

CHAPTER 11

Adjectives

In Spanish, adjectives are divided into three types according to their masculine ending. There are those that end in a letter "o." "Bueno," which you will learn soon, is an example. There are those that end in a letter "e." "Grande," which you will also learn soon, is an example. There are those which end with a consonant. "Joven," which you will also learn soon, is an example.

In addition to these three types of adjectives, there is a fourth type that is not classified according to their endings. These are adjectives of nationality. "Español" is an example of this type of adjective.

Adjectives may be **masculine** or feminine like the definite and indefinite article. "Hermos**o**" and "hermosa" both mean "beautiful" in Spanish, and, of course, the one ending in an "o" is **masculine**, and the one ending in an "a" is **feminine**. Adjectives must also agree in gender and number with the nouns they describe. A **masculine** adjective is used to describe a **masculine** noun or pronoun, and a **feminine** adjective is used to describe a **feminine** noun or pronoun. A **singular** adjective is used to describe a **singular** noun or pronoun, and a **plural** adjective is used to describe a **plural** noun or pronoun. When describing plural nouns adjectives must have plural endings.

The first two categories of adjectives you will learn are "description by size" and "how people look." The words in the "how people look" category can be used to describe nouns other than people as well. With these words you will be able to describe the body parts, animals, insects and people you have learned this far. You will also be able to use these adjectives to describe other nouns that you will learn later. In total you will learn 78 adjectives, or describing words. In these two categories there are 22 words. You will learn additional adjectives after you have learned more about verbs, because some adjectives are used with specific verbs. Study the pictures on the next five pages to make sure you know all 22 adjectives before continuing.

big & large - grande
grahn - day

Grr-Ron, my Great Dane is a big asset when I catch a large fish.

Grr

Ron

As Large as Life

"Grr" is directed at a fish from Ron, a big, large, Great Dane dog. Its owner says, "Grr-Ron, my Great Dane is a big asset when I catch a large fish." The sign reads, "As large as life."

high & tall - alto
ahl - toe

Look at that all-star toe tall drink of water fly high.

All Star Toe

An all-star high school basketball player that just happens to be a tall toe jumps up very high to practice dunking a basketball. Aren't most all basketball players tall? A fan says, "Look at that all-star toe tall drink of water fly high."

little & small - pequeño
pay - kay - nyoh

Kay

Payday bait allows Kay to cook a smallmouth for a Nyoh.

A little league baseball player is catching a small-mouth bass. He used a Payday candy bar as bait. Kay, his mother, is going to cook the smallmouth. His little friend is an onion, ny, wearing overalls.

long - largo
lahr - go

Lard makes a long-horned steer go a long way.

GO

The Long and the Slick of it

Lard

A long-horned steer slips in lard and slides a long way under a "go" traffic light. The sign reads, "The long and the slick of it."

short - corto
core - toe

A short apple core is standing in front of this totem pole.

Don't be caught short.

Short Cut

A short apple core wearing a short skirt looks up at a totem pole. The totem pole makes a short **remark**. One sign reads, "Don't be caught short." Another reads, "Short cut." This word is used for the length of things such as a "pencil" or "hair."

short - bajo
bah - hoe

Bah, do all short people use hoes?

Tall

Short

Yes, he is short.

A sheep asks a short man, "Bah, do all short people use hoes?" The ruler shows that the man is short. The sign reads, "Yes, he is short." This word is used for the stature of a person.

wide - ancho
ahn - cho

Open wide. On a good day I won't choke you.

ON   OFF

Stay wide awake.

A real wide on and off switch in the dentist's office has a choke chain hanging from it. The dentist says, "Open wide. On a good day I won't choke you." The sign reads, "Stay wide awake."

bald - calvo
cahl - voh

Caulk might help my bald head and my voting ability.

Vote Here

Bald is bare.

A bald man is squirting caulk from a caulk gun on his head while waiting to vote outside a voting station. He thinks it will help him grow hair. The sign reads, "Bald is bare."

beautiful - hermosa
air - moe - sah

A beautiful rose dropped from an airplane and fell near a motel. A soccer ball caught the beautiful rose before it hit the ground and said, "Airmo Airlines is beautiful for soccer balls." The motel is named, "The Beautiful Resting Place."

fat - gordo
gore - doe

The dog is very fat. He gorged himself with huge amounts of food for days. Doberman dogs are usually very trim. The sign reads, "Fat Farm." The Doberman says, "I live off of the gorged fat of Doberman land."

handsome & **good looking** - guapo
goo - ah - poe

A goose standing on a tongue depressor (ah) poses for a picture. The photographer says, "What a handsome goose." The sign reads, "Handsome photos are our specialty."

poor - pobre
poh - bray

A poor polar bear is wearing a brace. It is standing in front of a poorhouse. It says, "Poor me, this polar bear's brace hurts." A poor mouse says, "I'm poor as a church mouse."

A bow tie is tied around the knee of a pretty little girl tomahawk. She wants to know if she is pretty. The boy tomahawk answers, "You might be a bony tomahawk, but you sure are pretty." The sign reads, "Pretty as a picture."

The reward poster offers a $1,000,000 reward. A very rich cobra says, "That reward will make this cobra even richer." Another cobra says, "I could get to be a rich **cobra real** quick."

A flock of very skinny birds flies over a couple of thin cobras. One cobra says, "That flock sure is skinny." The other says, "**Yes, and we cobras sure are** thin."

A very strong fool, a court jester, is juggling three air conditioners while sitting on a table. he says, "A strong fool is an heir to bad table manners."

ugly - feo
fay - oh

You sure have an ugly face, Oh my.

As Ugly as Sin

young - joven
hoe - vehn

If that young hoe stays in front of that vent it won't be young long.

The Young and the Restless

A man looks at his wife while she is wearing a face pack. He is wearing overalls. He says, "You sure have an ugly face, Oh my." The sign reads, "As ugly as sin."

A young hoe is standing in front of a blowing vent with her hair blowing back. An old hoe comments. The sign reads, "The young and the restless."

Now that you have learned those 22 adjectives you will be able to practice using them in sentences. In the upcoming drill you will be describing what various nouns are like. You will have the choice of beginning your sentences with "my," "the," "a" or "an." If you choose an article it must match the gender of the noun it describes. "**El**" and "**un**" must be used with **masculine** nouns, and "**la**" and "**una**" must be used with **feminine** nouns. You will choose a noun from the next door. You will then use "es" in your sentence followed by an adjective to describe the noun. You should also use "y," which is "and," and add an additional adjective with some sentences. For instance, you might make-up this sentence, "Mi mano es grande." In English this is, "My hand is big." You might also make-up, "El mano es grande y flaco." In English this is, "The hand is big and skinny." You might also make-up, "Mi corazón es rico." In English this is, "My heart is rich." The verb "es," which you already know, will be used in all of these made up sentences.

You will follow that noun with "es" and an adjective or adjectives. You could even skip the door below the word "es" and just use the adjectives on the last door. You can pick and choose as you wish with any and all of Dr. Memory's™ drills. These drills were created to increase your skill and vocabulary knowledge, as well as help you with proper structure of Spanish sentences. Remember that there are two different words for "short." One describes only the stature of people.

Have fun as you create these sentences. Make up as many sentences as possible even though some sentences may not make sense. Your skills will improve as you participate in Dr. Memory's™ practice drills. Don't skip any drills and take your time as you go through them. A foreign language cannot be learned in a day, and you know that haste makes waste.

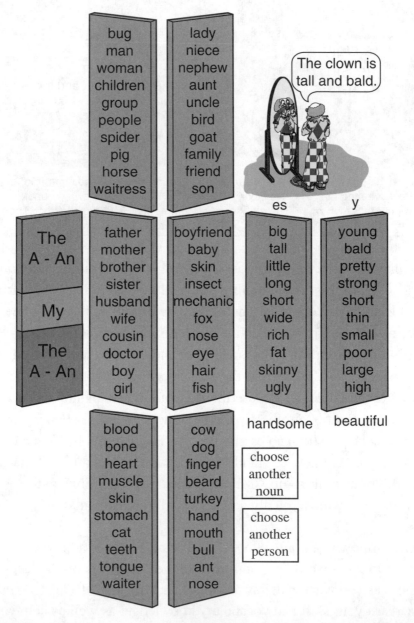

CHAPTER 12

Pronouns

From English grammar you will remember that a pronoun is a word that takes the place of a noun. It would be difficult to talk if we only had nouns to refer to persons, places, things or ideas. It would be awkward to speak without pronouns.

Even though this is a Spanish survival course you still don't want your speaking to be awkward by not using proper pronouns. The most commonly used pronouns are I, you, we, he, she and they. The first pronouns you will learn are "I," "you" and "we." They are called **subject pronouns**. Subject pronouns are pronouns that tell us who is doing something in a sentence such as, "I went," or "you go," or "we stopped." "I," "you" and "we" tell us who is doing something in those brief examples.

As usual Dr. Memory™ has special learning pictures for these words. The pronoun "I" is "**yo**" in Spanish. You will remember that blocks of **ice** stacked to look like a capital letter "I" were used to picture the letter "I" when you learned the sounds made by the Spanish alphabet. In the picture on the next page you see those blocks of **ice** playing with an **ice yo**-yo. This allows you to see that "**I**" means "**yo**" in Spanish. You also will see an arrow pointing from the **yo**-yo string to a box with a **light blue ice colored face** in it. The English word "**I**" and the Spanish word "**yo**" are above the box as a reminder of the Spanish meaning of this word. The light blue ice colored face also has an "**eye**" to remind you of the word "**I**." The mouth of the ice face is open as though it was speaking. Naturally, it is saying the Spanish word "**yo**." In practice drills to follow you also will say, "**yo**," when you see this ice face. Study this picture to make sure that you know that "**I**" means "**yo**" in Spanish before continuing.

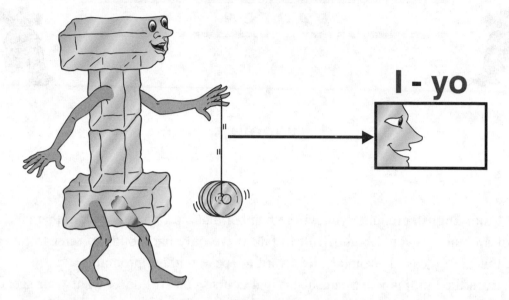

The pronoun "**you**" is "**tú**" or "**usted**" in Spanish. "**Tú**" is the familiar form of this word and "**usted**" is the formal form. Most likely you will be using the formal form of the word "you," since you will be a beginner in the Spanish language. It is considered ill mannered to use the familiar form of this word when speaking to strangers or people who are not very close friends. A "**ewe**," a female sheep, is used to picture the word "**you**," since "**ewe**" and "**you**" are pronounced exactly the same way. In the picture on the next page you see a **gray** "**ewe**" wearing a **tu**tu. You will notice an arrow pointing from the **tu**tu to the word "**tutu**." This allows you to see that "**you**" means "**tú**" in Spanish in the familiar usage. You also will see an arrow pointing from the ewe's face to a box with **her gray face** in it. Her eye is not in this image. The eye was in the ice face, because it represented the word "I." You will also notice another arrow pointing to a **gray human face** in a box. There is **no eye** on the human face as well. You will also notice that this face is pointed in the opposite direction of the ice face that represents the word "I" or "yo" in Spanish. The "I" or "yo" face has an eye and is light blue in color, and the "you" face has no eye and is gray like a "ewe." This will be important in the drills to follow.

Look back at the picture and you will notice that the ewe is looking down at and reaching toward her toy teddy bear. This is a very special teddy bear with moose-like antlers. The words "m**oos**e **ted**dy" are above the toy teddy. Notice that the letters "**oos ted**" are red in the words "m**oos**e **ted**dy" to make them stand out. The sounds "**oos ted**" are the exact syllable sounds heard in the Spanish word "**usted**," which is the formal form of the English word "**you**." This is the form you will learn to use as a beginner, but the picture also teaches you the other form of "tú." The English word "**you**" and the Spanish word "**usted**" are above the box that contains the gray human face as a reminder of the Spanish meaning of this word. The mouth of the gray face is open as though it was speaking. Naturally, it is saying, "**usted**." In practice drills to follow you also will say, "**usted**," when you see this gray face. You need to know the **plural** for usted as well. "Usted" simply becomes "**ustedes**" in the plural form. You will recall that plural rule number two stated that you add "es" to a word that ends with a consonant to form its plural. "**Ustedes**" would be used when addressing two or more people instead of a single person.

Since the faces in the boxes for "yo" and "usted" face in opposite directions from each other "yo" and "usted," or "I" and "you," could talk to each other. The three characteristics that distinguish these boxes from each other are different colors, different facing directions and the presence or absence of an eye. As a result, you will have no problem distinguishing them in practice drills.

The abbreviation for "usted" is "Ud." When you see "Ud." you will know that the word "usted" is being represented. "Ud. is always capitalized.

The pronoun "**we**" is "**nosotros**" in Spanish. The word "**we**" and the three syllable sounds in the Spanish word "**nosotros**" are pictured in Dr. Memory's™ picture seen below. You see the word "**weeds**" as well as "**weeds**" growing near the bottom of the picture. The first two letters in the word "**weeds**" will remind you of the English word "**we**." These "**weeds**" are **green**. The color "**green**" is the special color for the word "**we**" or "**nosotros**."

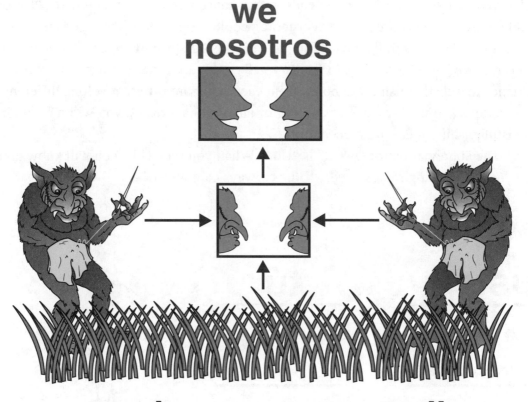

weeds - nose sew trolls

Notice the big **no**ses on the **sew**ing **trolls** that are standing in the "**weeds**." The red letters in the words "**nose sew trolls**" are the exact three syllable sounds heard in the word "**nosotros**." Now you can pronounce this word correctly, but you will hear it pronounced on Dr. Memory's™ web site.

Arrows are pointing from the trolls to the box between them. An arrow from the **green** "**weeds**" is also pointing to the box. The faces in the box are **green** like the "**weeds**." These faces represent the profiles of the trolls. Notice the big **no**ses and the **sew**n scars of the **trolls** on these faces. The references to the three syllables in "**nosotros**" are in these faces to help you understand the proper pronunciation of the word "**nosotros**." There are two faces in this box to represent at least two people in the word "**we**." These faces are also facing each other as though two people, or "**we**," were facing each other. They are **green** to represent the **green** color of "**weeds**."

Another arrow points up to two **green** human faces in a box above. The human faces are **green** to represent the word "**we**" or "**nosotros**." The **green** color comes from the "**weeds**." The mouths of the faces are open as though they are talking to each other. There are **no eyes** on these human faces. The only "eye" on these faces represents the word "I" or "yo."

Light ice blue is the color for "**yo**," **gray** is the color for "**usted**" and **green** is the color for "**nosotros**." Since the faces in the boxes for "**yo**" and "**usted**" face in opposite directions from each other in separate boxes, and the faces for **nosotros**" face each other in the same box there is no way you can confuse them in practice drills. "Nosotros" is used for all men or men and women, and "nosotras" is used for all women.

In the upcoming drill you will simply say "yo" when you see the light blue ice face with an "eye," "usted" when you see the gray face representing the "ewe," and "nosotros" when you see the green faces representing the "weeds." The faces will be mixed up to make it a little more fun. Go through the boxes saying the words at a normal rate the first time and then do it again seeing how fast you can say the words and complete the list. Have fun!

Pronoun Hand Jiving

You can also practice these three pronouns by using your hands in a special way. If you hold up your left hand as you see pictured on the left below it could represent the "yo" face speaking from the left, since the fingers will be pointing to the left. If you hold up your right hand as you see pictured on the right below it could represent the "usted" face speaking from the right, since the fingers are pointing to the right. If you hold up both hands facing each other as you see pictured in the middle below it could represent the "nosotros" faces speaking to each other from both directions. Practice holding up your hands as you see pictured below alternating them in various orders. Say the corresponding Spanish pronoun as you alternate your hands. See how fast you can perform this **pronoun hand jiving** drill. Have fun!

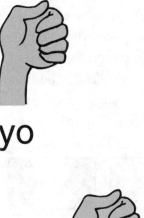

yo   usted

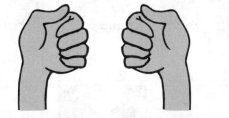

nosotros - nosotras

Subject Pronoun Ladders

Subject pronouns are pronouns that tell us who is doing something in a sentence. You just learned three subject pronouns. You will notice those three pronouns on the two ladders on the next page. One is an English ladder, and the other is a Spanish ladder. The top three spaces of the ladder on the left contain the words "I," "you" and "we." The top three spaces of the ladder on the right contain the corresponding Spanish words "yo," "usted" and "nosotros." The other spaces in these ladders will be filled in later when you learn more subject pronouns. Become familiar with these ladders. They will help you when you begin to study verb endings.

Dr. Memory™ lists "I," "you" and "we" first, because this grouping includes those who could talk to each other in a group of two or more. The grouping of "he," "she" and "they" which you will learn later are others who can't talk in our group. These are words that refer to people away from us. Some Spanish texts list these words in singular and plural groupings, but Dr. Memory™ believes groupings of "us" and "them," if you will, work better.

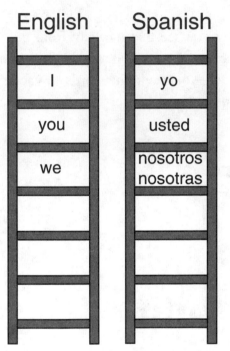

More Subject Pronouns

"**He**" in Spanish is "**él**." You already learned "**el**" when you learned the Spanish word for the definite article "the." "El" is used in both instances. The only difference is that "él" that means "he" has an accent. Dr. Memory™ uses an all blue outline of the original "él" picture to picture "he." In the picture on the next page you see **one blue outline** representing the word "**he**" with the Spanish word "**él**" next to it.

él

"**She**" in Spanish is "**ella**," which is pronounced "**ay-yah**." The red letters in the words "**a yacht**" are the exact Spanish sounds for the two-syllable word "**ella**." The letter "e" is pronounced like a long "a" in English, the double letter "l's" make the consonant letter "y" sound and the letter "a" makes the "ah" sound. Say "**ay-yah**" out loud several times to be more familiar with the sounds in the pronoun "**ella**."

In the picture below you see that the lady from the original "la" picture is now holding "**a yacht**" above her head to remind you that "she" in Spanish is "ella," which is pronounced like the red letters you see in the words "a **yacht**." In this picture she has the word "she" on her apron instead of the letter "a" as before.

Dr. Memory™ uses a pink outline of the original "la" picture to picture "she." To the right of the picture above you see **one pink outline** representing the word "**she**" with the Spanish word "**ella**" next to it.

"**They**" is the final subject pronoun to be learned at this time. When referring to two or more females when using the word "they," "ella" simply is made plural by adding a letter "s." So then "**ellas**" is the Spanish word used for "**they**" when referring to a **group of females**. Dr. Memory™ represents this with a picture of **two pink outlines** as seen below. The word "**ellas**" is below the two outlines.

When referring to two or more males when using the word "they" "**ellos**" is used, because the letter "**o**" is the masculine ending. As a result, "**ellos**" is the Spanish word used for "**they**" when referring to a **group of males**. Dr. Memory™ represents this with a picture of **two blue outlines** as seen below. The word "**ellos**" is below the two outlines.

The word "**ellos**" is also used when referring to a mixed group of males and females. A mixed group of males and females is represented with **one blue and one pink outline** as you also see below. The word "**ellos**" is also below these outlines.

ellas ellos ellos

More Subject Pronoun Ladders

You just learned three more subject pronouns. You will notice those three pronouns have been added to the two ladders on the next page. The bottom three spaces of the Spanish ladder contain the corresponding Spanish words "él," "ella" and "ellas & ellos." As was stated earlier, become familiar with these ladders, since they will help you when you begin to study verb endings and verb conjugation. The order of the placement of the words on the ladder is important for future study.

English	Spanish
I	yo
you	usted
we	nosotros nosotras
he	él
she	ella
they	ellas ellos

In the upcoming drill you will simply say "**él**" when you see the **all blue outline** of the original "**el**" picture. You will say "**ella**" when you see the **all pink outline** of the original "**ella**" picture. You will say "**ellas**" when you see **two all pink outlines** of the original "**ella**" picture in the box. You will say "**ellos**" when you see **two all blue outlines** of the original "**él**" picture in the box. You will also say "**ellos**" when you see **one all blue outline and one all pink outline** which represents a mixed group of males and females. The outlines will be mixed up to make it a little more fun. Go through the boxes saying the words at a normal rate the first time and then do it again seeing how fast you can say the words and complete the list. Have fun!

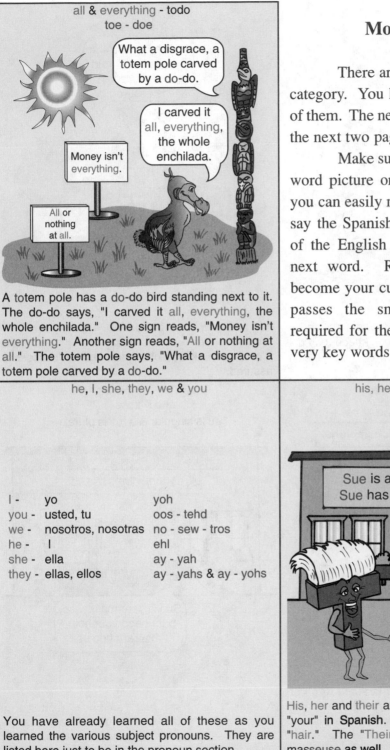

all & everything - todo
toe - doe

What a disgrace, a totem pole carved by a do-do.

I carved it all, everything, the whole enchilada.

Money isn't everything.

All or nothing at all.

A totem pole has a do-do bird standing next to it. The do-do says, "I carved it all, everything, the whole enchilada." One sign reads, "Money isn't everything." Another sign reads, "All or nothing at all." The totem pole says, "What a disgrace, a totem pole carved by a do-do."

More Pronouns

There are 18 words in the **pronoun** category. You have already learned many of them. The new pronouns are pictured on the next two pages.

Make sure to study each vocabulary word picture on the next two pages until you can easily recreate it in your mind and say the Spanish equivalent when thinking of the English word before going to the next word. Review the words as has become your custom. The reward far surpasses the small investment of time required for these reviews. Pronouns are very key words in any language

he, I, she, they, we & you

I -	yo	yoh
you -	usted, tu	oos - tehd
we -	nosotros, nosotras	no - sew - tros
he -	I	ehl
she -	ella	ay - yah
they -	ellas, ellos	ay - yahs & ay - yohs

You have already learned all of these as you learned the various subject pronouns. They are listed here just to be in the pronoun section.

his, her & their - su & sus
sue & soos

Sue is also their masseuse. Sue has his and her service.

Sue is his and her masseuse as well, but I bet their not all knotted up.

His, her and their are expressed the same way as "your" in Spanish. A "their" is a letter "T" with "hair." The "Their" says, "Sue is his and her masseuse as well. I bet their not all knotted up."

nobody & no one - nadie
nah - dee - ay

Knock-kneed demons are nobody to an angel.

Nobody but no one fears you.

A knock-kneed demon is pointing its finger at an angel. The angel says, "Knock-kneed demons are nobody to an angel." The sign reads, "Nobody but no one fears you."

our - nuestro
new - ehs - tro

I'm a new Eskimo troll hunter, and our success is assured.

Our day will come.

A gnu is being protected by two Eskimos. They are trying to drive a troll away. One of them says, "I'm a new Eskimo troll hunter, and our success is assured."

some & any - alguno
ahl - goo - noh

Few, if any, become champions.

Any all-star with goose bumps can wait no longer.

Some say yes, some say no.

An all-star basketball player with goose bumps also has a very big nose. He gets some goose bumps before every game and is afraid to go on the court. A twin teammate says, "We can't wait any longer." One sign on the wall reads, "Few, if any, become champions." The other sign reads, "Some say yes, some say no." Algunos is plural.

your - su & sus
sue & soos
su is singular & soos is plural

Sue - Your Masseuse

Sue is your masseuse, but I need your help. I'm all knotted up.

A letter "Y" is on the "oar," so it is a "Y-oar," or a "Your." The "Your" is walking up to a massage parlor. Sue, your masseuse, is the operator of the business. The "Your" expresses his need.

CHAPTER 13

Verbs

The next category of words you will learn is **verbs or action words**. This category has several sub-categories within it in the comprehensive course, but in survival Spanish they will grouped together simply as verbs or action words.

Before beginning to learn verbs, a car analogy with the vocabulary you are learning seems appropriate. The **body parts** words you learned could be the parts of a car. The **animals** could be the pets that might ride in the car. The **insects** could be the pests that buzz around the car. The people could be the occupants of the car, and the **adjectives** could be the words that describe the car. At this point about the only thing you could say about the car is that it **is** a car, because **"is"** or **"es"** is the only verb you have learned. The car has no power or **gas** to go anyplace. Dr. Memory™ thinks of verbs as the gas power that enables the car to travel and be useful. As long as it simply **is** a car it is of no use as transportation. The verbs you are about to learn, as well as others you will learn later, are the heart of the Spanish language. They are the **gas** power that causes it to operate. When you learn verbs and their functions you will be able to use your car to go shopping, drive to a restaurant, visit relatives and **empower** yourself to do anything else. It's time to begin to gas up. Your car has a big gas tank, and it's time to start filling it up with **verb power**.

If you look up a verb in a Spanish dictionary, the form you will find is called the **infinitive**. In English, the infinitive has the word "to" in front of it, such as "to walk," "to run," "to travel" or "to give." The infinitives in Spanish are expressed with only one word instead of two words as in English. You learned earlier that the words "it is" in English are expressed in the single Spanish word "es." Spanish infinitives are somewhat similar in that one word takes the place of two English words, but there is a difference. In Spanish, think of the word "to" as being represented by an "ar," "er" or "ir" ending added to the main part of the word, or verb.

Study the words on the next seven pages. Make sure to study each vocabulary word picture until you can easily recreate it in your mind and say the Spanish equivalent when thinking of the English word before going to the next word. Verbs are just as easy to learn as nouns, or any other part of speech, with Dr. Memory's™ pictures, since they are also made tangible.

Do a review of all of the verbs each time you learn eight new ones. You should still review all of the other categories you have learned to this point on a regular basis as well. You will not be as successful as you want to be without these brief but important reviews. Click on these words on Dr. Memory's™ web site to hear them pronounced by a Spanish-speaking person as you learn them. There are 33 verbs in this grouping. The last two words you will learn are "talk" and "want." They are taught out of alphabetical order with the next grouping for a reason that will become apparent to you later.

The sets of endings, which are added to the stem, or to the main part of the verb, to denote person, number and tense are called conjugation. You will learn about conjugation a bit later. With some verbs the main part of the verb, called the **stem**, does not change, but the endings of the verb do change when the verb is conjugated. These verbs are called **regular verbs**, because they follow the pattern of **no change to the stem**, or main part of the word. Irregular verbs can have dramatic changes, even in the main part of the word as you will find out later.

Dr. Memory™ has color coded verbs to denote whether they are regular or irregular verbs. Verbs listed in green type in the review list are regular verbs. Green on a traffic light means, "go," and with regular verbs you will be able to go faster, because they follow a pattern in conjugation. Verbs listed in red type in the review list are irregular verbs. Red on a traffic light means, "stop," and with irregular verbs you may have to stop and figure them out, because they do not follow a pattern in conjugation. You will learn about this soon. Dr. Memory™ just wanted you to be aware of the green and red colors as you study these verbs.

You will find a fun drill on our web site that will help you learn which verbs are regular and which are irregular.

to ache & to hurt - doler
doe - lair

This doe is hurt, so I will ache as I limp into that lair.

Lair

Will this hurt?

A doe deer is holding its leg up, because it is hurt. It is going to go into the animal lair to try to get away from predators. It says, "This doe is hurt, so I will ache as I limp into that lair." The sign reads, "Will this hurt?"

to buy - comprar
comb - prahr

A comb does not pry art very well when you want to buy it.

Art

Buy artwork here.

A person is using a comb to pry a piece of art off of a wall so he can buy it. The sign reads, "Buy artwork here."

to call - llamar
yah - mahr

Mr. Yacht is calling to Mars.

You can call a very long distance from this phone.

The Call of the Wild

A yacht is on the phone calling a person on the planet Mars. One sign reads, "You can call a very long distance from this phone." The other sign reads, "The call of the wild."

can or to be able to - poder
poh - dare

This polar bear is able to take the dare. I can do it.

Daredevil Gulch

You are able to if you think you can.

A polar bear took a dare to try to jump daredevil Gulch. He says, "This polar bear is able to take the dare. I can do it." The sign reads, "You are able to if you think you can."

to carry & to wear - llevar
yeah - vahr

A cheerleader just bought some varnish at a Wear and Carry store. She cheers, "Yeah, I love to carry varnish when I wear my outfit." The sign reads, "Don't carry on like that."

to change & to exchange - cambiar
cahm - bee - ahr

A comma held by the bee is a piece of art. The bee came to exchange it at the punctuation art exchange window. It says, "A comma can't bee the art I want to keep. I must change it."

to close & to shut - cerrar
say - rahr

A sailor yells, "Rah," at a suit of armor. The armor says, "Mr. Sailor, you better close your rah-rah mouth, or this armor will shut it for you." The sign reads, "Put up or shut up."

to do & to make - hacer
hah - sair

A hot dog making machine is being operated by a woman named Sarah. A man asked her, "What do you do?" She answered, "I make hot dogs, and I am Sarah." The saying on the machine reads, "Do you know how to make a friend?"

to drink - beber
bay- bair

Let's drink from the baby buggy if the bear will let us.

It's time we began to drink differently.

Have a drink.

A beggar says to a friend at a drinking fountain, "Let's drink from the baby buggy if the bear will let us." He answers, "It's time we began to drink differently." The sign reads, "Have a drink."

to eat - comer
co - mair

Cobras love to eat with good looking mares.

Eat here.

A cobra and a mare horse are preparing to eat. The sign simply says, "Eat here." The cobra says, "Cobras love to eat with good looking mares."

to end & to finish - terminar
tehr - me- nahr

This turtle with measles will finish this race to the end, Mr Narwhal.

You'll end up a winner.

Always finish what you start.

A turtle with measles is trying to finish a race as it approaches a narwhal. It says, "This turtle with measles will finish this race to the end, Mr Narwhal." A narwhal is an arctic whale with a slender, twisted tusk.

to find - encontrar
ehn - cone - trahr

Can you find the time to fix it?

This engineer wants that pine cone to find somewhere else to drive that Tropical Armored car.

Tropical Armored

Can you find your way?

A train engineer reprimands a pine cone when he finds a break in the tracks in the tropics. The pine cone's Tropical Armored car caused the break. The pine cone asks, "Can you find the time to fix it?" The sign reads, "Can you find your way?"

to give - dar
dahr

Give me a break.

Give me a dart.

You need a little give and take.

A boy says, "Give me a dart," to a man playing darts. The man says, "Give me a break." The sign reads, "You need a little give and take."

to go - ir
ear

Don't Go

This ear wants to go!

An ear is stopped at a traffic light waiting to go. It says, "This ear wants to go!"

to have - tener
tay - nair

Tapers have to use Nair in the summer to have short hair.

The Haves and the Have Nots

Nair Lotion hair remover

A taper wants to have short hair, so it is going to use Nair hair remover. It says, "Tapers have to use Nair in the summer to have short hair." The sign reads, "The haves and the have nots."

to hear - oír
oh - ear

I might be old, but I can still hear in this ear.

Now hear this.

An old man wearing overalls has a large hearing aid in his ear. He points to his hearing aid and says, "I might be old, but I can still hear in this ear." The sign reads, "Now hear this."

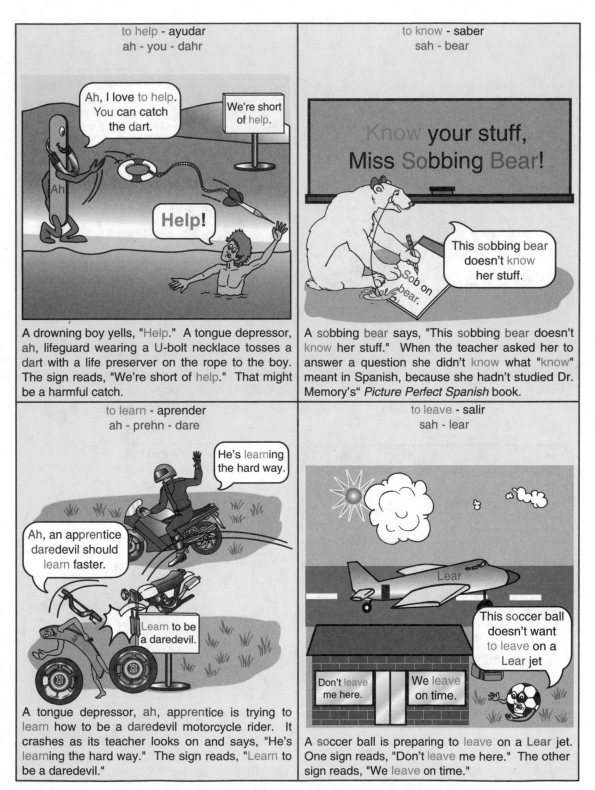

to help - ayudar
ah - you - dahr

Ah, I love to help. You can catch the dart.

We're short of help.

Help!

A drowning boy yells, "Help." A tongue depressor, ah, lifeguard wearing a U-bolt necklace tosses a dart with a life preserver on the rope to the boy. The sign reads, "We're short of help." That might be a harmful catch.

to know - saber
sah - bear

Know your stuff, Miss Sobbing Bear!

This sobbing bear doesn't know her stuff.

Sob on bear.

A sobbing bear says, "This sobbing bear doesn't know her stuff." When the teacher asked her to answer a question she didn't know what "know" meant in Spanish, because she hadn't studied Dr. Memory's " Picture Perfect Spanish book.

to learn - aprender
ah - prehn - dare

He's learning the hard way.

Ah, an apprentice daredevil should learn faster.

Learn to be a daredevil.

A tongue depressor, ah, apprentice is trying to learn how to be a daredevil motorcycle rider. It crashes as its teacher looks on and says, "He's learning the hard way." The sign reads, "Learn to be a daredevil."

to leave - salir
sah - lear

Lear

This soccer ball doesn't want to leave on a Lear jet

Don't leave me here.

We leave on time.

A soccer ball is preparing to leave on a Lear jet. One sign reads, "Don't leave me here." The other sign reads, "We leave on time."

to like - gustar
goose - tahr

I like goose tar.
I like goose tar.

Would you
like
to try this?

A goose is taking a bath in tar. It is saying, "I like goose tar. I like goose tar." It must be trying to convince itself. The sign reads, "Would you like to try this?"

to live - vivir
vee - vear

My V-neck caused me to veer, but I lived to tell about it.

Drive safely and live.

Live a happy life.

A man wearing a V-neck sweater veered on a road and had an accident. He said, "My V-neck caused me to veer, but I lived to tell about it." One road sign reads, "Drive safely and live." The other reads, "Live a happy life."

to need - necesitar
nay - say - sea - tahr

You can neigh, but this sailor needs to get to the sea, not tar.

Sea

My need is great.

My needs are few.

A neighing horse is ridden by a sailor. He needs to get back to the sea as he says, but his horse got stuck in tar. One sign reads, "My need is great." Another reads, "My needs are few."

to open - abrir
ah - brear

Ah, now that this is open, Brr should no longer be a problem, Mr. Ear.

Brr, every time this is open, I get cold.!

Open Here

An Open and Shut Case

An Amish man opened a package to get some earmuffs for a cold ear. "Brr," came from the cold ear. The Amish man says, "Ah, now that this is open, Brr should no longer be a problem, Mr. Ear." The sign reads, "An open and shut case."

A tongue depressor (ah) asks to talk to a sales clerk about an ink blotter it is holding. It asks, "Ah, may I speak to you about this blotter?" One sign reads, "Speak the truth." The other sign reads, "Talk is cheap."

A woman named Kay wants a rare steak. The waiter brought her a well done steak by mistake. She says, "Kay said she wanted a rare steak." The sign reads, "You don't always get what you want."

Verb Stems

Before using these 33 verbs in sentences you must know more about verb forms. You have already read that the sets of endings that are added to the stem, or to the main part of the verb, to denote person, number and tense are called conjugations. You have already learned that with some verbs the main part of the infinitive, called the **stem**, does not change, but the endings of the verb do change when the verb is conjugated. These verbs are called **regular verbs**, because they follow the pattern of **no change to the stem**, or main part of the word. Irregular verbs can have dramatic changes, even in the main part of the word as you will find out later.

The picture on the next page will help you better understand what is meant by the stem or main part of the verb not changing. In the top part of the picture you see the English word "walk" above the stem of the flower. In this case "walk" is the stem, or main part of the word. Three different endings that can be added to the word "walk" are on the flower petals. By using those endings "walk" can become "walked," "walking" or "walks." The three endings change the time of when the word "walk" happens. The main part, or stem, of the word did not change, but the meaning of the word did according to which ending was added to the stem.

In the bottom part of the picture you see the Spanish word "visit" above the stem of the flower. It is the stem, or main part, of a Spanish word. Does this look like a familiar word to you? Of course it does. The main part of the word "visit" is the same in English and Spanish. When "ar" is added to "visit" in Spanish it means "to visit" in English. The English word "to" is expressed in the "ar" ending of the Spanish word. Since many English and Spanish words have the same origin, it is possible to form Spanish infinitives directly from the English infinitives. You simply replace the preposition "to" with the suffix "ar" on the end of the Spanish stem word. In this case "visit" is the stem, or main part of the word. Three different endings that can be added to the Spanish word "visit" are on the flower petals. By using those endings "visit" can become "visito," "visita" or "visitamos." These three endings change the subject pronoun of the sentence. You don't yet know what these endings mean, but you will. There are also other endings that can be added to "visit" as you will soon find out. This is just an example to show you that the stem of regular verbs does not change when being conjugated. Once again, the main part, or stem, of the word did not change, but the meaning of the word did according to which ending was added to the stem and which person does the action.

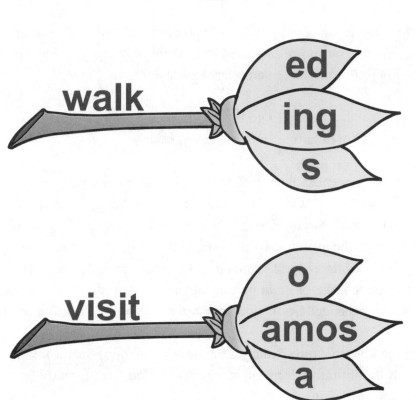

As was stated before, regular verbs do not change their stems when being conjugated while irregular verbs do change the stem spelling when being conjugated. Some of them even change their entire spelling in their conjugations. The verb "ir," for instance, becomes "voy" in the "I" or "yo" usage, which means that "I" is the subject pronoun with the "voy" usage. All of the many and varied forms of conjugation will not be taught in this course. It is not necessary for survival Spanish.

When using Spanish verbs you need to primarily know three things. They are: the meaning of the verb; who's doing the action; and the conjugated form of the verb to use. With Dr. Memory's™ learning pictures learning the meaning of the verbs is no problem. You have already learned 31 verbs. Who's doing the action isn't difficult either. What is most difficult for Spanish language students is the conjugation of the verbs. You are going to learn how to use Spanish verbs in two ways in Dr. Memory's™ survival Spanish program. You will be taught how to use the infinitive form in compound verb phrases. By learning just a few verbs outside of their infinitive forms you will be able to express yourself very well when using these verbs along with the infinitive forms of other verbs.

As an example, look at the sample sentences below. The words have been spaced so that the English and Spanish equivalents are directly above and below one another. The

Spanish word for "to" is simply "a," which is pronounced "ah." The Spanish word for "church" is "iglesia." You haven't studied its learning picture yet, but you will in the future. It is used here to form these sample sentences.

I   want   to go to the church.

Yo quiero   ir   a   la iglesia.

These sample sentences have two verbs forming a compound verb phrase. The verbs are "want" and "go." "Go" is in the infinitive or "to go" form. In the sample Spanish sentence the verb "want" is not used in its infinitive or "to want" form. You learned that "querer" is the infinitive form of the verb "want." It is used in its proper conjugated form with "I" as the subject pronoun in the above sample sentence. "Querer" is an irregular verb, so the stem, or main part of the verb, changed with the subject pronoun "yo" usage. The stem changed from "quer" to "quier." "Quiero" is pronounced like "key arrow" in English.

You will be able to express many sentences by learning just a few irregular verb forms to use with the infinitive form of other verbs. You have already learned 30 verb infinitives, and you will learn more later.

For example, if you knew "quiero," by changing the ending to the basic sample sentence above you could express many thoughts. "I want to go to the church" could easily become "I want to go to the bank," or "I want to go to the pharmacy." You could end the sentence with any word that told where you, or "I," want to go.

The irregular verb forms you will learn in addition to "to want" in order to communicate in a survival mode are: "to go," "to be able to or can," "to have," "to like" and "to know." You will also be taught to use "to need" with other verb infinitives. Knowing how to use these verbs in their various conjugated forms will allow you to communicate quite adequately.

You could also use the proper form of "to want" to express "I want to drink," or "I want to eat," or "I want to leave." You could insert any of the infinitives you have learned to follow "I want" or "quiero" to express yourself. With Dr. Memory's™ basic building block process you are getting closer to being able to express yourself with proper Spanish. You will not be using the elementary "Me Tarzan you Jane" type expressions. Your expressions will be grammatically correct, but before that can happen you must first learn some more words. For instance, if you wanted to say, "I want to go to the ____," you would have to know the word to fill in the blank.

Buildings and Places

When you learn the following words you can begin to make up full sentences to express many thoughts. The words you will learn now are from the buildings and places category.

Do a review of all of these words each time you learn eight new ones. You should still review all of the other categories you have learned to this point on a regular basis as well. You will not be as successful as you want to be without these brief but important reviews. Click on these words on Dr. Memory's™ web site to hear them pronounced by a Spanish-speaking person as you learn them. There are 27 words in this grouping. In addition you will also learn the word "where" in this grouping, so you can practice saying "where is something."

airport - aeropuerto
ah - air - oh - poo - air - toe

Ah, that airplane's overalls is a pwair this toad could wear at the airport.

pwair

An Amish man watches an airplane with a pair of overalls stuck on it circle an airport. A poodle is flying the airplane. A toad is also watching the plane.

apartment - apartamiento
ah - pahr - tah - me - ehn - toe

Apartment   For Rent

An Amish man got a par on a hole on top of an apartment building. A meteor fell, and he ran. The train engineer caddy's big toe is sticking out of one of his shoes. An "Apartment for rent" sign is on the apartment building.

bank - banco
bahn - co

BANK

A bonnet on a cobra is money in the bank.

Break the bank.

A bonnet is worn by a female cobra that is going into a bank. The sign reads, "Break the bank." The cobra says, "A bonnet on a cobra is money in the bank." This word also means "bench," and is taught elsewhere.

cafe - café
cah - fay

Outdoor Cafe

You cafe cockroaches can't face up to this gas.

Several cockroaches are in front of a cafe. Two of them are taunting the exterminator wearing a face mask. The cafe has been closed because of the cockroaches. The exterminator says, "You cafe cockroaches can't face up to this gas."

church - iglesia
e - glay - sea - ah

The eagle's eyes are glazed over. He sees in a different way now that he belongs to the church, ah.

Sea

The Church by the Sea

An eagle is pecking on the door of a church. The letters "gl" are on the ape that is praising God. The church is next to a sea, and an Amish man is walking out of the sea.

department store - almacén
ahl - mah - sehn

All-Star Department Store

1¢

All-Star

All-Star mops score with cents at the department store.

An all-star mop tosses a cent toward a basketball goal that is in front of a department store. It says, "All-Star mops score with cents at the department store."

drugstore & pharmacy - farmacia
fahr - mah - sea - ah

Drugstore - Pharmacy

Farmer's moccasins and seeds are, ah, free in the drugstore.

SEEDS

Farmers' Pharmacy

A farmer wearing moccasins walked out of a drugstore/pharmacy past sacks full of seeds after getting a free tongue depressor (ah).

hospital - hospital
ohs - pea - tahl

A roast is good medicine for a peacock with tall tales in a mental hospital.

Roast

Mental Hospital

A roast is being cooked in front of a hospital by a peacock that is very tall. This is a crazy thing to do, but maybe not, since the sign reads, "Mental hospital." The peacock comments.

hotel - hotel
oh - tehl

A man wearing overalls is looking through a telescope into a hotel. The sign reads, "The Peekaboo Hotel." He says, "Oh, what I could tell about this hotel."

house & home - casa
cah - sah

A cahing crow makes its home in a sock. The sign reads, "Home Sweet Home." A house of cards is the home on the left, and a houseboat is the house parked in the water to the right.

market - mercado
mare - cah - doe

A mare horse looks at a cahing crow wanting to feed it a donut it purchased at a market. The name of the market is, "Market Place." The sign on the market stand reads, "Corner the market."

post office - correo
core - ay - oh

An apple core and an ape wearing overalls are about to enter a post office. The apple core comments on their love for the post office.

restaurant - restaurante
rehs - tah - ooh - rahn - tay

I'm restless, and I bring a tomahawk into a restaurant.

Ooh, Ron, you upset your table.

A restless person in a restaurant swings a tomahawk to get some service. The waiter says, "Ooh," as the tomahawk approaches. The restless man is named Ron. Notice that he is also upsetting the table. The word "Restaurant" is on the window.

store - tienda
tea - ehn - dah

The Store of all Stores

This store is teariffic, Mr. Engineer. Let's dominate.

A tea bag, a train engineer and a domino discuss whether they should enter The Store of all Stores to shop. The domino says, "This store is teariffic, Mr. Engineer. Let's dominate."

street - calle
cah - yeah

They are on easy street.

Yeah!

Cah

Derby Street

A cahing crow and a boy who yells, "Yeah," are riding soap box derby cars down a closed off street named Derby Street. Someone in the crowd yells, "They are on easy street."

supermarket - supermercado
sue - pair - mair - cah - doe

Supermarket

Sue rides a pair of mares to the supermarket while I cah and ride a doe.

A girl named Sue is standing on, and riding, a pair of mare horses like a circus performer in front of a supermarket. A cahing crow riding a doe deer in the same way is following her.

center & downtown - centro
sehn - troh

A centipede with a trophy is the center of attention when downtown.

A centipede is holding up a trophy in the center of a circle in front of a community center in downtown Centerville. The sign reads, "The center of downtown."

city - ciudad
sea - ooh - dahd

This city will see me shoot Dodge full of holes.

An old western type city is by a sea. A cowboy is about to shoot his gun at the sign at the entrance to the city. As you can see it is Dodge City. The second "d" in "Dodge" is actually silent, but we will assume it is sounded for our purposes.

corner - esquina
ehs - key - nah

This Eskimo has the key to knotted traffic at corners.

An Eskimo holds a key while standing on a corner of a street. The Eskimo is knock-kneed. He says, "This Eskimo has the key to knotted traffic at corners." The sign reads, "Don't cut corners."

district & neighborhood - barrio
bah - ree - oh

This bottle is real. Ask my old buddies in the neighborhood.

A bottle watches a reel of film on a roller skate roll over a pair of overalls. The bottle says, "This bottle is real. Ask my old buddies in the neighborhood." The sign reads, "District three."

farm - granja
grahn - hah

Grr, Ron doesn't like farm work, but you don't have to ha-ha me.

Ha-ha

Farm

Ron

I'm am old farm hand.

movie **or** movies - cine
sea - nay

Movieland

Seahorses and neighing horses love movies.

Neigh

"Grr," comes out of the mouth of a boy named Ron who is working on a farm. He doesn't like the hard work. His friend laughs at him and says, "Ha-ha." The sign reads, "I'm an old farm hand."

A seahorse and a neighing horse are waiting to see a movie at Movieland. The seahorse comments on their love for movies.

The purpose of the upcoming drill is to have you **make up sentences** like you did before with "it is," which is "es" in Spanish. These practice sentences must be spoken in Spanish. That is why you can't participate in this drill without knowing the Spanish words in the buildings and places category. When you use the word "the" in a sentence you make- up, you will have to use the appropriate form of the definite article "the" in Spanish. If it is used before a **masculine** noun the usage must be "**el**," and if it is used before a **feminine** noun the usage must be "la."

For example, in the sample sentence "I want to go to the church," which is, "Yo quiero ir a **la** iglesia" in Spanish, you would have to use "**la**," since "iglesia" is a **feminine** noun. If you made up the sentence "I want to go to the bank," you need to learn something new. When the words "**to the**," which are "a **el**" in Spanish, are used before a **masculine** noun they must form the contraction "**al**." As a result, "I want to go to the bank," would be, "Yo quiero ir **al** banc**o**" in Spanish. You would have to use "**al**," since "banc**o**" is a **masculine** noun. Make sure to remember that anytime you **use "to the"** before a **masculine** noun it becomes "**al**." You will have an opportunity to practice it in the upcoming drill. So remember that "a + el" becomes "**al**." An asterisk mark follows the word "to*" in the practice drill to remind you to use "**al**" with masculine nouns.

You will notice that there is no apostrophe in this contraction as there is for "I'm" in English. Spanish contractions do not use apostrophes. This change is not optional. It must always be used when "a" directly precedes "el." Before "la," "las" and "los" there is no contraction.

"De" in Spanish means "of or from." Likewise, when the words "**of the**," which are "**de el**" in Spanish, are used before a **masculine** noun they must form the contraction "**del**." As a result, if you were using the phrase, "of the bank," it would be, "**del** banc**o**," in Spanish. You would have to use "**del**," since "banc**o**" is a **masculine** noun. Make sure to remember that anytime you **use "of the"** before a **masculine** noun it becomes "**del**" and not "de el." This change is not optional either. It must always be used when "de" directly precedes "el." Before "la," "las" and "los" there is no contraction.

These practice drills are vital for your progress. You must participate in all of them to advance your skills. You will be able to hear several of these sentences spoken by a Spanish-speaking person on Dr. Memory's™ web site. When you listen to them you will better understand the vocal intonation of all of the words.

The first sentence you will practice will begin with "I want to go to the," and all you will have to fill in will be the place to go. Of course, if you choose the definite article you will have to use "**el**" or "**la**" depending on the gender of the noun used to complete the sentence. If you choose to use the indefinite article you will have to use "**un**" or "**una**." Most of these words are masculine. You should also practice making the nouns plural and using plural definite and indefinite articles with the plural nouns. In that case you would use "**los**" or "**las**" or "**unos**" or "**unas**."

The second sentence you will practice will begin with "Where is the," and all you will have to fill in will be the place to go. As you start to make-up sentences, use the words on the brown door first and then use the words to the right of the that door in any order you may choose. Practice using all of the nouns to end your sentences to become more familiar with speaking Spanish in these practice sentences. Remember that "**quiero**" is pronounced like "**key arrow**" in English. Remember that "**where**" is pronounced "**dohn day**." You will also need to use a new form of the verb "is" in these sentences. "**Está**" is the form of "is" that is used **when locating things**. The word "**where**" is the key here, **because it asks for the location of something**. You have learned that "where" means "¿dónde? in Spanish. Have fun!

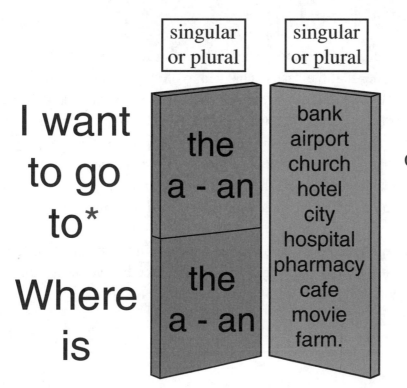

singular or plural	singular or plural

I want to go to*

the a - an

Where is

the a - an

bank
airport
church
hotel
city
hospital
pharmacy
cafe
movie
farm.

apartment
neighborhood
department store
home or house
post office
restaurant
supermarket
corner
downtown
market
street

Creating Other Verb Phrases

There are six other verbs with "yo" as the subject pronoun to learn that will be used with Spanish infinitives to create other compound verb phrases. The infinitive form of the verb can be used with these six verbs to express many more thoughts. The six verbs in the "yo" form with the Spanish equivalents and phonetic pronunciations are listed below.

English	Spanish	Phonetic Pronunciation
I'm going to	Yo voy a	yoh – voh – ee - ah
I can	Yo puedo	yoh – pway - doe
I have to	Yo tengo que	yoh – tehn – go - kay
I like	Me gusta	may – goose - tah
I need	Yo necesito	yoh – nay – say – sea – toe
I know how to	Yo sé	yoh – say

"Need" is the only regular verb of this group. The infinitive form of "to need" is "necesitar." You will learn later that the "ar" is changed to an "o" in conjugation when "I" is the subject pronoun. The only difference between "necesito" and "necesitar" is that the "ar" was changed to an "o." The stem, or main part of the verb, didn't change.

Some Spanish verbs must be used with prepositions like "a" or "de." You just have to learn the verbs and their accompanying prepositions as they come along.

You will also notice that "que" follows the "yo" form of "I have to." This expresses a necessity or that you "have to" to do something as opposed to simply "having" or "possessing" something.

The infinitive forms of the other six verbs, other than "to want," and the "yo" form of the verbs we are going to use in compound verb phrases are listed below. These are the most important verbs you will use in survival Spanish in addition to "to want."

English	Spanish Infinitive	Spanish Yo Form
to go to	ir	yo voy a
to be able - can	poder	yo puedo
to have to	tener	yo tengo que
to like	gustar	me gusta
to need	necesitar	yo necesito
to know	saber	yo sé

As you can see the "yo" forms of these irregular verbs vary a little or a lot. They are totally different from regular verbs, since the main parts, or stems, of regular verbs don't change. This survival Spanish course is not going to get into the many and varied forms of irregular verbs. This isn't necessary for you to communicate in a survival mode. These are the only irregular verbs, in addition to "ser," that you will need to learn. The verb "ser" means "to be" in English. You will learn it later.

It is important for you to learn a few irregular verbs in the "yo" form to be used with Spanish infinitives to express your thoughts in Spanish. The six that were just listed, along with "to want," are the most important for you to learn. They will be listed again so you can study them to not only be familiar with them but to know them. You have already familiarized yourself with "**I want**" or "**quiero**" when you took part in the last sentence drill. It is listed below as well. Go over these verb forms until you know them well before continuing. You can click on these words on Dr. Memory's™ web site to hear a Spanish-speaking person pronounce them.

English	Spanish	Phonetic Pronunciation
I want	Yo quiero	yoh – key - arrow
I'm going to	Yo voy a	yoh – voh – ee - ah
I can	Yo puedo	yoh – pway - doe
I have to	Yo tengo que	yoh – tehn – go - kay
I like	Me gusta	may – goose - tah
I need	Yo necesito	yoh – nay – say – sea – toe
I know how to	Yo sé	yoh – say

Notice that the words "how to" have now been added after "I know," because when "I know" is used with an infinitive it means "I know how to." If you simply said, "I know the number," for example, you are not saying, "I know how to the number." You are simply expressing that you know the number. So, when "I know" is used with an infinitive it actually means "I know how to" do something.

When you are sure you know these verb forms you can practice using them with Spanish infinitives. In the upcoming drill you will just speak compound verb phrases. After learning more words you will be able to speak complete sentences that begin with the verb phrases you will soon practice. You will be practicing using the last six "yo" verb forms listed above with the 30 Spanish infinitives you have already learned to form compound verb phrases. You will not be able to use all of the infinitives with each "yo" form, because they won't make sense, but use as many as you can in this very important practice drill.

The "yo" forms will be listed on the left door from the clown's make-up wardrobe in English, and the English infinitives will be listed on the right door. Select a "yo" form on the left door and say it with an infinitive on the right door. For instance, if you used the first verbs listed on both doors you would say, "Yo voy a vivir." This, of course, is "I'm going to live" in English. When you learn more words you will be able to finish the sentence with what ever you wanted to express. You could say, "I'm going to live in Mexico," or anyplace else. If you used the last verbs listed on the doors you would say, "Yo sé aprender." This, of course, is "I know how to learn" in English. You use fewer words in Spanish in this instance to express more English words. You will discover later that you will need to use more words in Spanish to express fewer words from English in some cases. After you have practiced with the infinitives on the door expand your practice by using the infinitives listed next to the door.

Spanish speakers usually omit the "yo" and all other subject pronouns when speaking. The form of the verb indicates the first person in the upcoming drill. As you do the following drill try leaving off the "yo" after you become comfortable making new sentences.

As has already been stated several times, these practice drills are vital for your progress and success. You must participate in all of them to advance your skills. You will be able to hear several of these sentences spoken by a Spanish-speaking person on Dr. Memory's™ web site. By listening to a Spanish-speaking person you will better understand Spanish vocal tendencies.

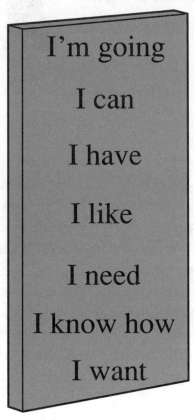

I'm going

I can

I have

I like

I need

I know how

I want

to live
to find
to drink
to leave
to talk
to eat
to call
to buy
to go
to learn

to like
to hear
to end
to close
to change
to carry
to wear
to give
to help
to need
to want
to make
to have
to be able

CHAPTER 14

Verb Classification and Conjugation

You have already learned that the sets of endings, which are added to the stem, or to the main part of the verb, to denote person, number and tense are called conjugations. Verbs are classified as verbs of the first, second or third conjugation according to the ending of the infinitive. First conjugation verbs end in "**ar**," second conjugation verbs end in "**er**" and third conjugation verbs end in "**ir**." The letters "**ar**" in Spanish sound like the beginning letters in the word "**art**," so Dr. Memory™ calls these the "**art**" conjugation verbs. The letters "**er**" in Spanish sound exactly like the English word "**air**," so Dr. Memory™ calls these the "**air**" conjugation verbs. The letters "**ir**" in Spanish sound exactly like the English word "**ear**," so Dr. Memory™ calls these the "**ear**" conjugation verbs. The infinitive endings of "ar," "er" or "ir" are dropped and other endings are added to the stem when the verb is used in various conjugated forms.

The first infinitives that will be discussed are verbs that end with "**ar**." It has already been mentioned that Dr. Memory™ calls them "**art** verbs." The word "**art**," which begins with the same two letters of the ending of "**ar**" verbs, will be used later in some of Dr. Memory's™ learning pictures.

The personal endings of the **first conjugation**, or "**art**" conjugation verbs, will be taught first. In English there is very little change to the stem for personal endings. For most subjects there is no additional ending added to the stem to denote the person doing the action of the verb. Let's look at the verb "visit" in English and notice the endings. You see them at the top of the next page.

visit

I	visit
you	visit
we	visit
he	visits
she	visits
they	visit

As you can see, only two of the subject pronouns, "he" and "she," have an ending added to the stem. In both cases the ending is a letter "s." In Spanish, it is much more complex, but Dr. Memory™ will make it easy to understand with his unique, learning pictures. In Spanish each subject pronoun: "yo," "usted," "nosotros," "él," "ella," "ellas" and "ellos" has a personal ending. The personal endings for Spanish are listed below. The ending for "yo" is "o." The ending for "usted" is "a." The ending for "nosotros" is "amos." The ending for "él" is "a." The ending for "ella" is "a." The ending for "ellas and ellos" is "an."

visitar

yo	visito
usted	visita
nosotros, nosotras	visitamos
él	visita
ella	visita
ellas, ellos	visitan

The "o" and "a" endings on verbs do not imply masculine or feminine gender as they do with nouns. "Yo" always ends in "o," and "usted" always ends in "a" with "ar" verbs regardless of the gender of the subject.

Since the personal ending clearly indicates the subject pronoun, subject pronouns are usually omitted in conversation although they may be used for emphasis or to make the meaning clear if one so desires. A Spanish-speaking person could say, "Yo visito la casa," which means "I visit the home." The present tense may be translated: I visit, I do visit, I am visiting, etc. So, "Yo visito la casa," can mean, "I am visiting the home."

However, most Spanish-speaking people do not use the subject pronoun in conversation. They would simply say, "Visito la casa." Since "o" is the ending for the subject pronoun "yo," Spanish speaking people know that the subject pronoun is "yo," because of the "o" ending on the stem "visit." You will get practice speaking all of these endings after you learn these subject pronoun endings with Dr. Memory's™ pictures.

In Dr. Memory's™ picture on the next page you see a female "**ar**tist." She is actually a model who is modeling her "**ar**tist" outfit. The "**ar**tist" and the "**ar**t" picture in the lower left identifies that the first, or "**ar**t," conjugation for infinitives ending in "ar" are being taught. A number "1" is also on the "**ar**tist" to show that this picture represents verbs of the **first** or "**ar**" **conjugation** class. The "**present**" with "**tents**" on it shows that the "**present tense**" is being discussed. This is not the past or future tense. These actions happen in the present or near future.

The present the artist presented to the "yo" was a pair of "O-brand" overalls with a letter "o" on them. She got them from the O-brand overall factory in the background. A **special conjugation adding machine** sucked a letter "O" off of a pair of overalls and added it to the "yo's" hand. There are enough letter "o's" in this picture for you to easily remember that a letter "o" is added to the stem of "**ar**" infinitives to form the personal subject pronoun ending of "o" for the "**yo**" subject pronoun. Also, notice that a letter "o" is on the top, or "**yo**" position, of the **ar**tist's dress below her belt. The "yo" says, "Yo visito la casa," to emphasize the "yo" ending of "o" on the stem word.

In Dr. Memory's™ picture on the next page you see the same female "**ar**tist." She will be in all of the first, or "**ar**," conjugation pictures. The present the **ar**tist presented to the "**ewe**" or "**usted**" was a toy "ape" with a letter "A" on it. She got it from the "Apes" gift shop at the zoo. The special **conjugation adding machine** sucked a letter "A" off of the sweater of the "ape" and added it to the "**ewe**'s" hoof. There are enough letter "a's" in this picture for you to easily remember that a letter "a" is added to the stem of "**ar**" infinitives to form the personal subject pronoun ending of "a" for the "**usted**" subject pronoun. Also, notice that a letter "a" is on the **ar**tist's dress below her belt in the "**usted**" position just below the "yo" position. The correct endings for the "**ar**" infinitives are beginning to line up in order on her dress. The "**ewe**" says, "Usted visita la casa," to emphasize the "**usted**" ending of "a" on the stem word.

In Dr. Memory's™ picture on the next page you see the same female "**ar**tist." The present the artist presented to the "troll" or "**nosotros**" was a toy "ape" with a letter "A" on it. It was dragged over from the "Apes" gift shop at the zoo. The special **conjugation adding machine** sucked a letter "A" off of the sweater of the "ape" and added it to the "troll's" **we**eds. An Amish man "mows" the **we**eds in this picture. An Amish man "mows" the **we**eds to picture the pronunciation of "amos." "Amos" sounds like the red letters in the words "Amish mows." This will help you to remember that the letters "amos'" are added to the stem of "**ar**" infinitives to form the personal subject pronoun ending of "amos" for the "**we**" or "**nosotros**" subject pronoun. Also notice that the letters "amos" are on the artist's dress below her belt in the "**nosotros**" position just below the "usted" position. There are now three correct endings for the "**ar**" infinitives lined up in order on her dress. This is the same order that appeared on the subject pronoun ladders before. In the picture the artist says, "Nosotros visit**amos** la casa," to emphasize the "**nosotros**" ending of "amos" that is added to the stem of the verb.

Take some time to review the "I," "you" and "we," or "yo," "usted" and "nosotros," endings on her dress to make sure you know them before continuing.

In Dr. Memory's™ picture on the next page you see the same female "**ar**tist." The present the artist presented to the "**he**-man" or "**él**" was also a toy "ape" with a letter "A" on it. She got it from the same "Ape" gift shop at the zoo. The special **conjugation adding machine** sucked a letter "A" off of the sweater of the "ape" and added it to the "**he**-man's" hand. There are enough letter "a's" in this picture for you to easily remember that a letter "a" is added to the stem of "**ar**" infinitives to form the personal subject pronoun ending of "a" for the "**él**" subject pronoun. Also notice that a letter "a" is on the artist's dress below her belt in the "**él**" position just below the "nosotros" position. One more correct ending for the "**ar**" infinitives is added to the line up on her dress. The "**he-man**" says, "El visita la casa," to emphasize the "**él**" ending of "a" on the stem word.

Make note that the "él" ending is the same as the "usted" ending.

In Dr. Memory's™ picture on the next page you see the same female "**ar**tist." The present the artist presented to the "**she**-woman" or "ella" was also a toy "ape" with a letter "A" on it. She got it from the same "Ape" gift shop at the zoo. The special **conjugation adding machine** sucked a letter "A" off of the sweater of the "ape" and added it to the "**she**-woman's" hand. The "**she**-woman" is holding "a yacht" up in the air to picture the pronunciation of "ella." "Ella" sounds like the red letters in the words "a yacht." There are enough letter "a's" in this picture for you to easily remember that a letter "a" is added to the stem of "**ar**" infinitives to form the personal subject pronoun ending of "a" for the "ella" subject pronoun. Also notice that a letter "a" is on the artist's dress below her belt in the "ella" position just below the "él" position. One more correct ending for the "**ar**" infinitives is added to the line up on her dress. The "**she**-woman" says, "Ella visita la casa," to emphasize the "ella" ending of "a" on the stem word.

Make note that the "ella" ending is the same as the "usted" and "él" endings.

In Dr. Memory's™ picture on the next page you see the same female "**ar**tist." She is representing the "**they**" subject pronoun in this picture.

You will recall that when referring to two or more females when using the word "**they**," "ella" simply is made plural by adding a letter "s." So then "**ellas**" is the Spanish word used for "**they**" when referring to a **group of females**. When referring to two or more males when using the word "**they**," "**ellos**" is used, because the letter "**o**" is the masculine ending. Consequently, "**ellos**" is the Spanish word used for "**they**" when referring to a **group of males**. You will also recall that the word "**ellos**" is also used when referring to a mixed group of males and females.

The present the artist presented to the "**he**-man and **she**-woman" or "**ellas**" was a toy "ape" with a letter "A" on it and a cigar store Indian with a letter "N" on it. She got them from the same "Ape" gift shop at the zoo. The special **conjugation adding machine** sucked a letter "A" off of the sweater of the "ape" and a letter "N" off of the cigar store Indian and added them to the "**he**-man and **she**-woman. This will remind you that the letters "an" are added to the stem of "**ar**" infinitives to form the personal subject pronoun ending of "an" for the "**ellas** and **ellos**" subject pronouns. Also, notice that the letters "an" are on the **ar**tist's dress below her belt in the "**ellas** and **ellos**" position just below the "ella" position. This is the final correct ending for the "**ar**" infinitives in the line up on her dress. The "**he**-man" says, "Ellos visitan la casa," to emphasize the "**ellas** and **ellos**" ending of "an" on the stem word.

Take some time to review the "I," "you," "we," "he," "she" and "they" or "yo," "usted," "nosotros," "nosotras," "él," "ella," "ellas" and "ellos" endings on her dress to make sure you know them before continuing.

The verb "to visit" is listed below again along with a special detective to make a point that will be extremely helpful with a special verb at a later time as well as helping you better understand these endings.

You can see that lines starting at the usted, él and ella positions converge at the same point. These are connected by lines, because they all have the same endings. Usted, él and ella always have the same endings in conjugations. Because of this there could sometimes be cause for confusion if usted, él or ella were not used to identify which subject pronoun was being discussed. It is obvious in most cases but in some instances they need to be **identified**. The Sherlock Holmes-like detective you see examining the point where the arrows join is looking for clues to **identify** the subject pronoun. We will call him **The Identifier**. He will be very useful in future applications. The lines he is examining also point out that usted, él or ella all have the same endings. He says, "I must identify who is being discussed."

The Identifier

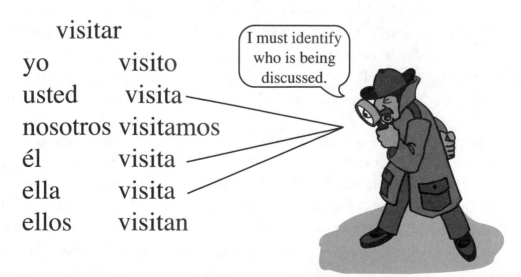

visitar

yo   visito
usted   visita
nosotros visitamos
él   visita
ella   visita
ellos   visitan

I must identify who is being discussed.

The "er," or "air," verbs and the "ir," or "ear," verbs are conjugated much the same way "ar" verbs are. On the next page you see a picture of three models. You recognize the "ar," or "art," model whom you have already studied. The model in the middle is modeling **air**line stewardess clothing to represent the "**er**," or "**air**," verbs. The model on the right is modeling **ear**rings to represent the "**ir**," or "**ear**," verbs. The conjugation endings for the present tense for subject pronouns are listed on each model. The endings can also be seen below.

You will remember that verbs are classified as verbs of the first, second or third conjugation according to the ending of the infinitive. First conjugation verbs end in "**ar**," second conjugation verbs end in "**er**" and third conjugation verbs end in "**ir**."

"ar" or "art" verbs	"er" or "air" verbs	"ir" or "ear" verbs
o	o	o
a	e	e
amos	emos	imos
a	e	e
a	e	e
an	en	en

Notice that the "yo" endings for all three classes of verbs is an "o." In addition, notice that all three letter "a" endings in the "**art**" class are simply changed to an "e" in the "**air**" and "**ear**" classes. You will also recall that the "you," "he" and "she," or "usted," "él" and "ella" endings are always the same. **The Identifier** showed you their pattern. That pattern makes them easier to remember. The letter "a" in "an" in the "they," or "ellas" and "ellos" position, of the "art" verbs also changes to a letter "e" and becomes an "en" in both the "air" and "ear" "they" positions. A helpful memory aid is that all letter "a's" from the "art" conjugation become letter "e's" except in the "we" or "nosotros" position.

Another helpful memory aid is that the "you," "he" and "she" positions all have the same endings in all three conjugations. They all end in "a" in the "art" conjugation, and they all end in "e" in the "air" and "ear" conjugations.

The last three letters of "mos" never change in the "we" or "nosotros" position. Only the beginning letter changes. A pattern makes this position easier to remember as well. This position always begins with the first letter of the infinitive ending. Thus, "**ar**" verbs have the "**amos**" ending, "**er**" verbs have the "**emos**" ending and "**ir**" verbs have the "**imos**" ending.

Review the models, the listing of endings and the memory aids a few times until these endings become knowledge. You will need to know them before you participate in an upcoming drill after you learn more verb infinitives.

CHAPTER 15

More Verbs

It is time to learn more **verbs or action words**. Study the words on the next six pages. Make sure to study each vocabulary word picture until you can easily recreate it in your mind and say the Spanish equivalent when thinking of the English word before going to the next word. You already know that verbs are just as easy to learn as nouns, or any other part of speech, with Dr. Memory's™ pictures, since they are also made tangible.

Do a review of all of the verbs each time you learn eight new ones. You should still review all of the other categories you have learned to this point on a regular basis as well. You will not be as successful as you want to be without these brief but important reviews. Having a little bit of discipline will pay off with exciting dividends. Click on these words on Dr. Memory's™ web site to hear them pronounced by a Spanish-speaking person as you learn them. There are 24 verbs in this grouping. They continue to be taught in alphabetical order.

to pay - pagar
pah - gahr

A garfish is paying for a bag of popcorn under a "Pay Here" sign. The garfish loves popcorn. The other sign reads, "Crime doesn't pay."

to place & to put - poner
po - nair

A polar bear is going to put a can of Nair hair remover into a garbage can, so it can't be used to remove his hair. The product works too well, and he needs his hair for the cold winter. The sign reads, "Place polar bear Nair here!"

to receive - recibir
ray - sea - beer

A manta ray and a sea horse are ready to receive a load of beer from the delivery truck. The manta says, "Manta rays and sea horses love to receive beer." The banner reads, "Receiving."

to repair - arreglar
ah - ray - glahr

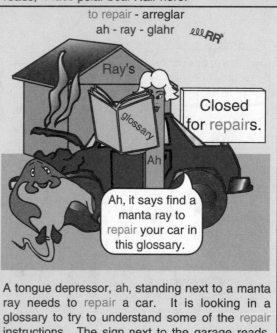

A tongue depressor, ah, standing next to a manta ray needs to repair a car. It is looking in a glossary to try to understand some of the repair instructions. The sign next to the garage reads, "Closed for repairs." The two sounds in the word "glossary" had to be used, because no word with the "glahr" sound could be found.

to ride - montar
moan - tar

I always moan when I have to ride through tar.

Do you have a ticket to ride?

The motorcycle rider loves to ride his bike, but he moans when he has to ride through tar. He says, "I always moan when I heve to ride through tar."

to run - correr
core - air

An apple core can run fast enough to catch an Airedale.

Airedale

He's on the run.

Run until you run out of money.

An apple core had been running after an Airedale on roller skates that was running away from it. It had run fast enough to grab its tail. One sign reads, "He's on the run." The other sign reads, "Run until you run out of money."

to say & to tell - decir
day - sear

Say there, this daisy would seriously like to help you.

Let me tell you, Mr. Daisy's petal is being seared.

I've had my say.

The daisy says to the pretty rose, "Say there, this daisy would seriously like to help you." The rose answers, "Let me tell you, Mr. Daisy's petal is being seared." The sign reads, "I've had my say."

to see - ver
vair

I see my varicose veins too easily.

See for yourself.

Let me see.

A lady looks down to see her varicose veins and says, "I see my varicose veins too easily." One sign reads, "See for yourself." Another reads, "Let me see."

sell - vender
vehn - dare

Mr. Vent, will you sell this barn real cheap to a daredevil?

Will Sell Cheap

I'll sell, and you can jump.

Don't sell out!

A vent is trying to sell a barn to a daredevil, so he can jump over it. He asks, "Mr. Vent, will you sell this barn real cheap to a daredevil?" The sign reads, "Don't sell out."

to send - enviar
ehn - vee - ahr

She must send you.

Engineers don't veer when sending with argyle socks.

Send early.

A train engineer wearing a V-neck sweater and argyle socks is handing a package to a mailman. He is sending it to his sweetheart. The mailman says, "She must send you," as he reaches for the package. The sign reads, "Send early."

to sleep - dormir
door - mear

z z Z

Doors with Mirrors For Sale

Sleep like a log.

The man is sleeping against a door with a mirror in it. The sign reads, "Sleep like a log."

to take - tomar
toe - mahr

Market

Will you take my tote bag to the market for me?

I'd take it anywhere for you.

That takes the cake.

Tote

The little girl asks a boy, "Will you take my tote bag to the market for me?" The boy answers, "I'd take it anywhere for you." The sign reads, "That takes the cake."

A V-neck vest is worn by the Amish man who is traveling down a road on harvesting machinery. He says, "Mr. Veeah can't travel fast on this harvesting machinery." The sign reads, "Don't travel too fast."

An instructor sees that a comb being used by an apprentice hair dresser was broken on a dairy product. He yanked on her hair and commented. The apprentice says, "I'm an apprentice. Should I understand yet?"

Oil oozes out of the bottom of a can of sardines as a lady uses a key opener to open the sardines. One sign reads, "Use your brain." The other sign reads, "I could use a drink."

A V-neck sweater is worn by a seahorse that came to visit a sick seahorse that is stuck in tar. The sick seahorse says, "Mr. V-sea, thank you for coming to visit this sick seahorse in tar."

to walk - caminar
cah - me - nahr

Cah, meteors don't stop my walk, Mr. Narwhal.

This is the corner of Walk and Walk streets.

Walk a mile with me.

Walk St.

A cahing crow walks up to a meteor as it walks toward a crosswalk to greet a narwhal. A narwhal is an arctic whale with a long twisted tusk. The sign reads, "Walk a mile with me."

to wash - lavar
lah - vahr

This llama is going to wash that man right out of my hair with varnish, no less.

Wash something here.

Varnish

A llama is using varnish to wash its hair. She says, "This llama is going to wash that man right out of my hair with varnish, no less." The sign reads, "Wash something here." This is not for washing yourself but something like a dish or car. That is why the sign reads as it does.

to work - trabajar
trah - bah - hahr

That trombone, boxcar and harmonica music is great while at work.

Men at work.

Three men are supposed to be at work. One is playing a trombone. The next man is actually working to free the box car. The other man is playing a harmonica. The sign reads, "Men at work." It should say, "Man at work."

to write - escribir
ehs - cree - beer

Eskimo Creek is a great place to write with beer along.

Did I write that?

Creek

An Eskimo floats down a creek on a writing desk while writing on a writing pad. Bottles of beer are floating down the creek with him. The Eskimo discusses a great place to write. The sign reads, "Did I write that?"

there is **&** there are - hay
eye

There is **an** eye in my hand.

There are **two** beautiful eyes in front of me.

The eyes have it!

A "there" is a letter "T" with "hair." The "T-hair" on the left says, "There is an eye in my hand." The "T-hair" on the right says, "There are two beautiful eyes in front of me." This is a very useful word, since it means either "there is" or "there are."

Subject Pronoun and Regular Verb Practice

In the upcoming drill you will simply say "yo" when you see the light blue ice face with an "eye," "usted" when you see the gray face representing the "ewe," and "nosotros" when you see the green faces representing the "weeds." You will also say "él" when you see the **all blue outline** of the original "él" picture. You will say "ella" when you see the **all pink outline** of the original "ella" picture. You will say "ellas" when you see **two all pink outlines** of the original "ella" picture in the box. You will say "ellos" when you see **two all blue outlines** of the original "él" picture in the box. You will also say "**ellos**" when you see **one all blue outline and one all pink outline** which represents a mixed group of males and females. The outlines will be mixed up to make it a little more fun.

These are the same boxes you used in previous drills, but there is an addition in this drill. Dr. Memory™ has placed regular infinitive verbs in English next to the boxes. The purpose of this drill is to speak the subject pronoun represented in a box followed with the proper conjugated verb from of an infinitive verb next to the box. As usual you will see English verbs that you need to translate to Spanish as you practice with this drill. You will need to know if the verb is an "ar," "er" or "ir" verb to select the correct conjugated form to speak. Review the three models one more time before the upcoming drill.

As an example of what you will be doing look at the top box on the page 187x. You see the "yo" image in the box, which means you will have to use the "yo" conjugated form of the regular infinitive verbs next to the box. The first verb is "to visit," so you would say, "Yo visito." As was stated earlier the purpose of this drill is to have you get used to using the correct conjugated form of regular verbs with all of the subject pronouns. You will be able to add additional words to make complete sentences with these words when you learn more vocabulary. When that time comes you will be able to easily complete full sentences with what you will learn in the upcoming drill.

If "to visit," for example, was used with all of the subject pronouns they would be as listed below, since "visit**ar**" is an "**ar**" verb.

English Infinitive	Conjugated Spanish Verb Form
I visit	Yo visit**o**
You visit	Usted visit**a**
We visit	Nosotros visit**amos** – Nosotras visit**amos**
He visits	El visit**a**
She visite	Ella visit**a**
They visit	Ellas visit**an** – Ellos visit**an**

If "to drink," for example, was used with all of the subject pronouns they would be as listed below, since "beb**er**" is an "**er**" verb.

English Infinitive	Conjugated Spanish Verb Form
I drink	Yo beb**o**
You drink	Usted beb**e**
We drink	Nosotros beb**emos** – Nosotras beb**emos**
He drinks	El beb**e**
She drinks	Ella beb**e**
They drink	Ellas beb**en** – Ellos beb**en**

If "to live," for example, was used with all of the subject pronouns they would be as listed below, since "viv**ir**" is an "**ir**" verb.

English Infinitive	Conjugated Spanish Verb Form
I live	Yo viv**o**
You live	Usted viv**e**
We live	Nosotros viv**imos** – Nosotras viv**imos**
He lives	El viv**e**
She lives	Ella viv**e**
They live	Ellas viv**en** – Ellos viv**en**

The Spanish present tense has a broader range of meaning than the English present tense. It is important to know these meanings before participating in the next drill. As in English, the Spanish present tense may be used for action occurring in the present or near future. Before looking at the example below you must know that "today" is "hoy" in Spanish. You will be given a learning picture for "today" in its proper category later. It is used here to help you better understand the different uses of the Spanish present tense.

"I visit today" in English is "Yo visito hoy" in Spanish. The present tense may as well refer to an action in the near future. As a result, "Visito mañana,"could mean, "I will visit tomorrow."

In addition to this obvious use, the Spanish present tense may also be used to refer to what is known as the English emphatic present tense. Look at the example below for more understanding.

"I do visit today" in English is also "Yo visito hoy" in Spanish.

In addition to this these uses, the Spanish present tense may also be used to refer to what is known as the English present progressive tense. Before looking at the example below you must know that "now" is "ahora" in Spanish.

"I am visiting now" in English is "Yo visito ahora" in Spanish.

So then, the Spanish present tense can be translated in four ways: I visit, I do visit, I am visiting or I will visit. This is the case with any verb. The Spanish present tense can present an action happening in the present or near future.

The four sample sentences below are simple actions in the present tense that express four present tense actions. Since you have not learned some of the words used in the sample sentences yet you won't fully understand the Spanish. You will learn the words in later categories.

I travel today.   You work soon.
Yo viajo hoy.   Ud. trabaja pronto.

I do travel today.   You do work soon.
Yo viajo hoy.   Ud. trabaja pronto.

I am traveling now.   You are working now.
Yo viajo ahora.   Ud. trabaja ahora.

We walk now.
Nosotros caminamos ahora.

We will walk tomorrow.
Nosotros caminamos mañana.

We are walking now.
Nosotros caminamos ahora.

In the upcoming drill you should go through all of the boxes saying the subject pronouns with the correct conjugated form of the verbs. Although most Spanish-speaking people do not use the subject pronoun in all instances, because most of them are understood, you should say all subject pronouns when participating in this most important drill. If you don't know all of the Spanish infinitive verbs that have been taught to this point you should review them to know them well before participating in this drill.

It cannot be said enough that these practice drills are vital for your progress and success. You must participate in all of them to advance your skills. All of these word combinations may not be used in normal conversation, but they are important for your ongoing progress. When you have gone through the entire drill you can then mix and match any box with any verb for even more practice. You will be able to hear several of these words spoken by a Spanish-speaking person on Dr. Memory's™ web site. By listening to a Spanish-speaking person you will better understand them.

After you have become more familiar with the subject pronouns and verbs next to the boxes you can return and make-up complete sentences using the words at the upper right of the page along with the people names. If you haven't had **a little bit of discipline** to review all of the words you have learned on a regular basis, you will have to review the people words for this drill. For instance, you could then say, "I am visiting my grandmother," in Spanish by saying, "Yo visito a mi abuela." In Spanish a **personal "a" must come before a person who is the direct object of a sentence**. Since "my grandmother" is the object person of the visit, the personal "a" must precede "mi abuela."

You can also complete sentences by using the definite article "the" before one of the listed words. For instance, you might make up this sentence, "I am visiting the doctor." In Spanish that sentence would be "Yo visito al médico." Since the doctor is the object person of the visit, the personal "a" must be used. It would then be "a el medico," but it must be "al." You have already learned that "a el" must be contracted to "al" for proper use. The more you practice the better. You cannot practice too much.

You can also use the word "with" in this practice drill. "With" means "con" in Spanish and is pronounced "cone." You might want to say, "I am learning with my friend." In Spanish that sentence would be, "Yo aprendo con mi amigo."

After you become more familiar with these subject pronouns and verb forms, make up as many sentences as possible. Of course, you will not be able to use some of the names of the people with some of the verbs, because they will not make sense. Have fun!

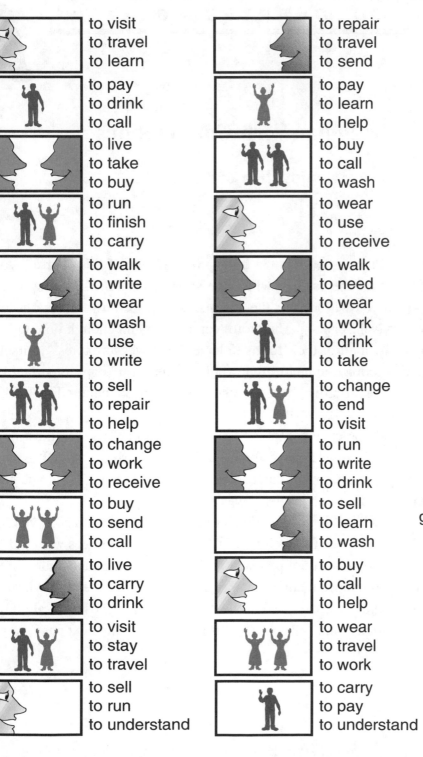

to visit to travel to learn	to repair to travel to send
to pay to drink to call	to pay to learn to help
to live to take to buy	to buy to call to wash
to run to finish to carry	to wear to use to receive
to walk to write to wear	to walk to need to wear
to wash to use to write	to work to drink to take
to sell to repair to help	to change to end to visit
to change to work to receive	to run to write to drink
to buy to send to call	to sell to learn to wash
to live to carry to drink	to buy to call to help
to visit to stay to travel	to wear to travel to work
to sell to run to understand	to carry to pay to understand

the
my
the

with my

friend
boyfriend
girlfriend
man
woman
barber
beautician
doctor
mechanic
policeman
waiter
waitress
aunt
brother
cousin
daughter
father
grandfather
grandmother
husband
mother
nephew
niece
parents
sister
son
uncle
wife

CHAPTER 16

Irregular Verb Conjugations

Conjugation of "To Go"

What you are about to learn is the **high-powered gas** of this course. You have already read that verbs are the gas that will make your car useful. In this section seven important verbs which you will learn is the **gas** that is so **high-powered** that it might be called **jet fuel** for survival Spanish. Therefore, you must spend enough time to learn the upcoming conjugations in all of their forms to have the power to express yourself comfortably and properly from a grammatical viewpoint. These verbs are important because they can be used with the infinitive forms of other verbs to make hundreds of verb phrases to express yourself.

You have already practiced speaking the "yo" form of the seven most important verbs with the infinitive form of other verbs when forming verb phrases. It is now time to learn the other conjugated forms of these seven most important verbs, so you can practice using them in verb phrases and full sentences later as well.

The first listing will be the conjugation for the irregular verb "to go," which is "ir." This verb is very irregular, since the spelling of the verb totally changes when it is conjugated. The subject pronouns will not be listed in the phonetic pronunciations, since you already know how to pronounce them. Only the pronunciation of the verb will be listed. Only "nosotros" and "ellos" will be listed in the "we" and "they" positions although they could also include :nosotras" and "ellas." The listing begins on the next page, so you can see the entire conjugation on one page.

English	Spanish	Phonetic Pronunciation
I'm going	yo voy	voh – ee
You're going	usted va	vah
We're going	nosotros vamos	vah – mohs
He's going	él va	vah
She's going	ella va	vah
They're going	ellos van	vahn

When you examine the conjugation you will notice that the "you," "he" and "she" forms are all the same as always. **The Identifier Detective** pointed this out to you earlier. You will also notice that "we" and "they" follow the basic pattern you learned for regular verbs. "We" has an "amos" ending, and "they" has an "an" ending. The "mos" and "n" endings follow the basic pattern. Although you have already practiced the "yo" form of "voy a" with other infinitives it will still be included in the upcoming drill. You have not practiced using it with full sentences yet.

When you are sure you know these verb forms you can practice using them with Spanish infinitives in the upcoming drill. In this drill you will just speak compound verb phrases as you did before with the "yo" forms. After learning more words you will be able to speak complete sentences that begin with the verb phrases you will soon practice. You will not be able to use all of the infinitives with each form, because they won't make sense, but use as many as you can in this very important practice drill.

The various forms are represented by boxes on the left side of the page. You are already familiar with these boxes. "Ellos" for all men or a mixture of men and women for the "they" form will be represented by one blue and one pink figure in this and other upcoming drills. Select a verb form on the left and say it with an infinitive on the first door. For instance, if you used the first form listed on the left with the first infinitive on the door you would say, "Usted va a correr." This, of course, is "We're going to run," in English. You should practice speaking verb phrases of all of the forms first. After you have practiced with the infinitives on the door expand your practice by using the infinitives listed above and below the door.

After you have practiced with verb phrases you can practice complete sentences by using the other words listed on the page. For instance, you could say, "Usted va a correr a la farmacia." In English this is "You are going to run to the pharmacy." The "building and places" category has been listed for this practice drill. Use as many of these words as possible while you practice. If you are not sure of all of the "building and places" words go back and review them briefly until you know them well. If you have been following Dr, Memory's™ regular review process by having **a little bit of discipline** you will already know them well. You have a few suggestions between the doors of words to be used between the infinitive and the "buildings and places" words.

You will have to use "**el**" or "**la**" depending on whether the building or place is **masculine** or **feminine**. You will also notice that you have the choice of using "a" or "an" before the building or place. When you use this indefinite article you will have to use "**un**" or "**una**" depending on whether the building or place is **masculine** or **feminine**. You should also practice making the nouns **plural** while using **plural** definite and indefinite articles with the **plural** nouns. In that case you would use "**los**" or "**las**" or "**unos**" or "**unas**." You need practice using the **plural** form of the definite and indefinite articles.

You might make up, "Ellos van a vender las casas." In English this is "They're going to sell the houses." Practice using all forms of the verb "to go" with as many verbs and buildings and places as possible. You can never practice too much.

As has already been stated several times, these practice drills are vital for your progress and success. You must participate in all of them to advance your skills. Practice makes perfect. You will be able to hear several of these sentences spoken by a Spanish-speaking person on Dr. Memory's™ web site. By listening to a Spanish-speaking person you will better understand Spanish vocal tendencies. Remember that "in" is "en" in Spanish in the upcoming drill, and "to" is "a."

A red asterisk mark precedes the words "*to the" in the practice drill to remind you to use "**al**" with masculine nouns.

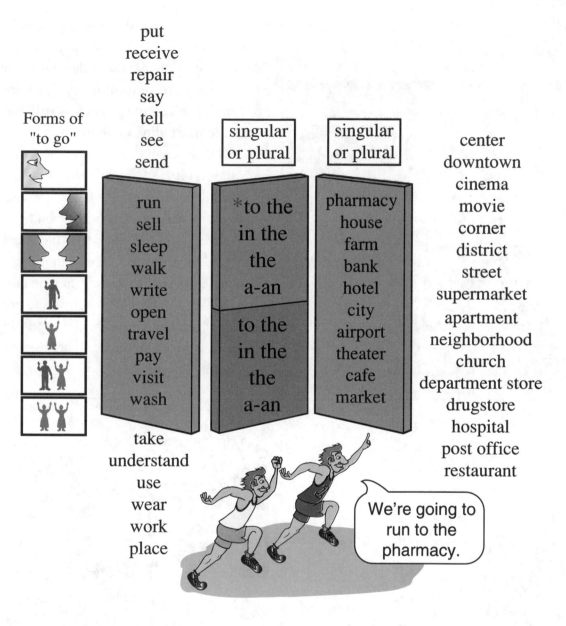

put
receive
repair
say
tell
see
send

Forms of "to go"

run
sell
sleep
walk
write
open
travel
pay
visit
wash

take
understand
use
wear
work
place

singular or plural

*to the
in the
the
a-an

to the
in the
the
a-an

singular or plural

pharmacy
house
farm
bank
hotel
city
airport
theater
cafe
market

center
downtown
cinema
movie
corner
district
street
supermarket
apartment
neighborhood
church
department store
drugstore
hospital
post office
restaurant

We're going to run to the pharmacy.

Clothing

Before you learn the conjugation of another of the seven very important verbs Dr. Memory™ wants you to learn three more categories of vocabulary words, so you can use them in the next practice drill. The first category is **clothing**.

Study the words on the next four pages. Make sure to study each vocabulary word picture until you can easily recreate it in your mind and say the Spanish equivalent when

necktie & tie - corbata
core - bah - tah

I want a tie to match my core in the bottle, Mr. Tomahawk.

The World's Best Necktie Store

An apple core is inside the bottle that is shopping for a tie. A tomahawk sales person wearing a tie is helping the bottle select a necktie. The sign reads, "The world's best necktie store."

thinking of the English word before going to the next word. The words in the review list will be **blue** or **pink** depending on whether they are **masculine** or **feminine**. For future use you must know whether the words are **masculine** or **feminine**.

Do a review of all of the words each time you learn eight new ones. You should still review all of the other categories you have learned to this point on a regular basis as well. You will not be as successful as you want to be without these brief but important reviews. Click on these words on Dr. Memory's™ web site to hear them pronounced by a Spanish speaking person as you learn them. There are 17 words in this category.

shirt - camisa
cah - me - sah

Cah, this meteor should give me enough power to tug the shirt away from the soccer ball.

Me

I'm going to lose my shirt.

Keep your shirt on.

A cahing crow standing on a meteor reaches for a shirt. A soccer ball reaches for the shirt from the other side. They want to have a shirt tug of war. The sign reads, "Keep your shirt on."

pants - pantalones
pahn - tah - low - neighs

Pants Shop

Top

Pontoon

Mayonnaise

Locust

Mayo-naise

Pants are floating around a pontoon with a toy top on top of it. A locust standing on a jar of mayonnaise is holding up another pair of pants next to a pants shop on the edge of the lake.

suit - traje
trah - hay

A trombone makes a great suit hanger for a stack of hay.

A Musical Suit

A suit is hanging on the end of a trombone that a stack of hay is holding. The sign reads, "A musical suit."

T-shirt & undershirt - camiseta
cah - me - say - tah

T-shirt Store

You stole my undershirt.

A cop with measles should leave a sailor, his tomahawk and his T-shirt alone.

A cop with measles pulled a T-shirt away from a sailor who stole it. The sailor has a tomahawk hooked to his side. The letter "T" is on the T-shirt. This all happens in front of a T-shirt store.

blouse - blusa
blue - sah

This blouse blew a blue sock quite nicely.

The Blouse that Blew

A blouse just blew up a sock like it was a balloon. Notice that it is a blue sock.

dress - vestido
vehs - tea - doe

Dressmaker to the Stars

A vest looks great over a dress on a teaspoon. Don't you know that!

A vest is held by a female teaspoon as it looks at a dress in front of a dress shop with a dome over it. The name of the dress shop is, "Dressmaker to the Stars."

skirt - falda
fahl - dah

This false face looks great with this polka dotted skirt.

Skirts Galore

Don't skirt the issue.

The girl with the false face is wearing a polka dotted skirt while looking at other skirts in a skirt store. The sign reads, "Don't skirt the issue."

clothes & clothing - ropa
row - pah

This robot's pontoon is used to store clothing.

Used Clothes

A robot stuck in a pontoon is holding up some clothes in front of a "Used Clothes" store. Used clothing is all over the place.

coat - saco
sah - co

This sock coat looks great on a cobra.

Coat Sale

A sock is being tried on by a cobra as a coat in the coat department of a department store.

glove - guante
goo - ahn - tay

This goose is on top of this glove despite the tape. gwahn

ON
OFF

It fits like a glove.

A glove is pecked by a goose that is in front of an on and off electrical switch. A roll of tape is stuck to the goose. The sign reads, "It fits like a glove."

hat - sombrero
sohm - brair - oh

That sewn "M" won't keep my hat warm. Brr, this air is cold, Mr. Oak.

Hats for sale.

A large sombrero hat is worn by a shivering hat salesman. A sewn letter "M" is on the ground next to him. He says, "Brr, this air is cold." The oak tree hat salesman has all kinds of hats. Cold air is blowing on the man from the North. The tree says, "Hats for sale."

jacket - chaqueta
cha - kay - tah

Cha-cha Kay does the jacket dance!

I can top that.

A cha-cha dance is being performed by a lady named Kay and a toy top. They are dancing around a jacket on the floor.

shoe - zapato
sah - pah - toe

Socks polish shoes well on toadstools.

If the shoe fits, wear it.

A man is using a sock to polish his shoes. One shoe is propped on a toadstool while he polishes it. The sign reads, "If the shoe fits, wear it."

sock - calcetín
cahl - say - teen

Put a sock in it, teenager.

This call is safe, Miss teenage sock.

A telephone call is being made by a sock with a safety pin pinned to it. The teenage girl sock is making the phone call to her boyfriend. Apparently her father left the "Put a sock in it, teenager" sign to try to curtail the length of her calls. The boy sock says, "This call is safe, Miss teenage sock."

Colors

The next category of words you will learn before using the next important verb is **colors**. Colors are adjectives since they help us describe something.

Study the words on the next three pages. Make sure to study each vocabulary word picture until you can easily recreate it in your mind and say the Spanish equivalent when thinking of the English word before going to the next word.

Do a review of all of the words each time you learn eight new ones. You should still review all of the other categories you have learned to this point on a regular basis as well. You will not be as successful as you want to be without these brief but important reviews. Click on these words on Dr. Memory's™ web site to hear them pronounced by a Spanish speaking person as you learn them. There are 10 words in this category.

black - negro
nay - grow

A black widow spider has nasal spray sprayed at it in front of Mr. Black's Black Grocery Store. Black pepper is displayed next to the store. Notice that Mr. Black is dressed in all black clothing, and he has a black eye.

blonde - rubio
roo - bee - oh

A blonde, rude bee in overalls is throwing a blonde wig at a bald man. The sign reads, "Blondes have more fun." The bee says, "I'm a rude, blonde bee in overalls." The sign reads, "Blondes have more fun."

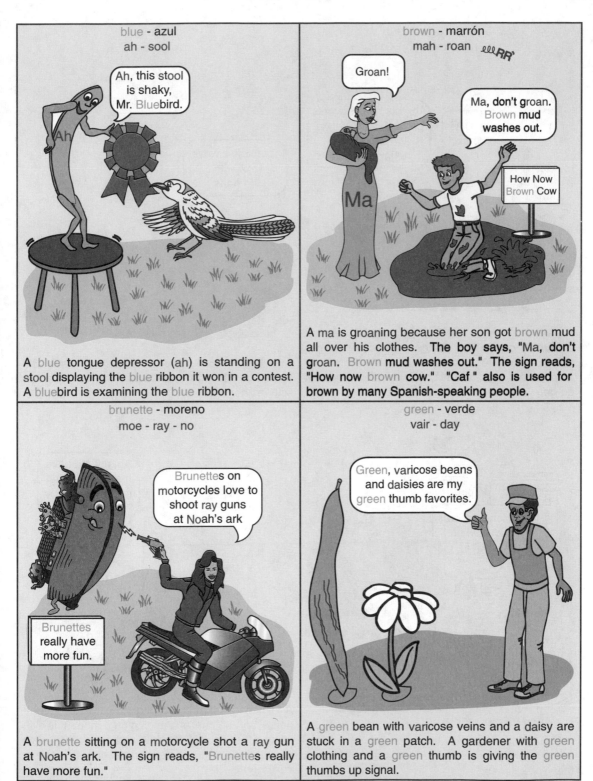

blue - azul
ah - sool

Ah, this stool is shaky, Mr. Bluebird.

A blue tongue depressor (ah) is standing on a stool displaying the blue ribbon it won in a contest. A bluebird is examining the blue ribbon.

brown - marrón
mah - roan

Groan!

Ma, don't groan. Brown mud washes out.

How Now Brown Cow

A ma is groaning because her son got brown mud all over his clothes. The boy says, "Ma, don't groan. Brown mud washes out." The sign reads, "How now brown cow." "Caf " also is used for brown by many Spanish-speaking people.

brunette - moreno
moe - ray - no

Brunettes on motorcycles love to shoot ray guns at Noah's ark

Brunettes really have more fun.

A brunette sitting on a motorcycle shot a ray gun at Noah's ark. The sign reads, "Brunettes really have more fun."

green - verde
vair - day

Green, varicose beans and daisies are my green thumb favorites.

A green bean with varicose veins and a daisy are stuck in a green patch. A gardener with green clothing and a green thumb is giving the green thumbs up signal.

orange - anaranjado
ah - nah - rahn - ha - doe

A playful orange squirted orange colored water on an Amish man. The orange water came from a nozzle. The Amish man's name is Ron. He laughs and says, "Ha-Ha," while stroking his pet do-do. The orange comments.

red - rojo
row - hoe

A redbird is rowing a red boat on the red sea with red hoes. It says, "Redbirds don't normally row with red hoes."

white - blanco
blahn - co

A blonde haired cobra with very large white fangs is examining a pair of white birch trees in front of the White House.

yellow - amarillo
ah - mah - ree - yo

A yellow jacket is flying toward a tongue depressor, ah, that is standing on a mop. It is also using a fishing reel string to make a yellow yo-yo go up and down. The sign reads, "Beware of yellow fever."

Food

The third and last category you will learn before studying the conjugation of another of the seven very important verbs is **food**.

Study the words on the next eleven pages. Make sure to study each vocabulary word picture until you can easily recreate it in your mind and say the Spanish equivalent when thinking of the English word before going to the next word. The words in the review list will be **blue** or **pink** depending on whether they are **masculine** or **feminine**. For future use of the words you must know whether they are **masculine** or **feminine**.

Do a review of all of the words each time you learn eight new ones. You should still review all of the other categories you have learned to this point on a regular basis as well. You will not be as successful as you want to be without these brief but important reviews. Click on these words on Dr. Memory's™ web site to hear them pronounced by a Spanish-speaking person as you learn them. There are 44 words in this category. This is an extensive category, so don't get in a hurry as you study the pictures. Take your time and make sure you know all of the pictures before continuing.

beans - frijoles
free - hoe - lace

Notice the free beans sign. A hoe was used by a shoe to knock the beans over. I guess that makes it easier to get the beans, since its lace is untied. The shoe says, "These free beans were hoed by me and caused my lace to untie."

bread - pan
pahn

A piece of bread just fell off of a pontoon into a pond. Other pieces of bread as well as loaves of bread are floating on the pond. It came from the bread truck. There are two words with the "pon" sound to help you in this picture.

burrito - burrito
boo - ree - toe

A ghost with the word "Boo" on it is reading the menu at a burrito shop. It is taking too much time, so a tomato kicks it. The ghost says, "Boo-hoo, I want a burrito with real tomatoes."

cheese - queso
kay - sew

A sewing machine named Kay is sewing up holes in Swiss cheese. A mouse says, "Kay, you sew cheese very well." It wants the sewing machine to leave, so it can eat the cheese.

food & meal - comida
co - me - dah

Food Store
Cheap Meals

Cobras with measles must pay a dollar for food and a **good** meal.

I hope I don't get food poisoning from this cheap meal.

A cobra with measles paid a dollar to buy a meal at a food store. The cobra says, "I hope I don't get food poisoning from this cheap meal."

French fries - papas fritas
pah - pahs - free - tahs

Free Tomahawks

Papa's French Fries

Papa's free tomahawks are needed for these huge French fries.

Papa's French Fries is a famous fast food restaurant. Papa gives away free tomahawks with every order, so the customers can cut the very large French fries.

hamburger - hamburguesa
ahm - booer - gay - sah

I'm a booer.

What a hamburger. An omelet booer at a game of soccer.

A ghost is cooking an omelet on a grill. Another ghost is booing because it wants a hamburger, so it is a "booer." A game of soccer is being played by hamburgers in the background. Another hamburger says, "What a hamburger. An omelet booer at a game of soccer."

taco - taco
tah - co

Tony's Tacos

A man ordered a taco at a taco shop. There is no need for any additional information, because this word is pronounced the same in both languages.

carrot - **zanahoria**
sah - nah - oar - ee - ah

These socks don't hide my knocked-knees. An oar and an eagle can't help this carrot, ah.

A carrot wearing wild looking socks is knock-kneed, because an oar was used by an eagle, along with its own tongue depressor (ah) to hold its knees in.

lettuce - **lechuga**
lay - chew - gah

I lay and chew lettuce in goggles every day.

A hen that just layed eggs is chewing on a head of lettuce in a lettuce patch while wearing goggles.

onion - **cebolla**
say - bow - yah

Sailors only wear bow ties when eating onions on yachts.

The Onion Skin

A sailor wearing a bow tie is eating onions while sitting on a yacht. The yacht is full of onions. The name of the yacht is "The Onion Skin."

potato - **papa**
pah - pah

Potatoes   Potatoes   Potatoes

Pa-pa potato!

A little potato holds out its arms and says, "Pa-pa, potato," to its father, the big potato.

salad - ensalada
ehn - sah - lah - dah

Endive salad is a soccer ball's favorite.

Llamas get dotted with joy as well.

Salad Oil

Salad Days

A very large endive lettuce salad is being eaten by a soccer ball and a llama. Polka dots are on the large salad bowl and the llama. Salad oil is on the table, and the sign reads, "Salad days."

tomato - tomate
toe - mah - tay

The tomato toe of this mop should not be on the table.

A tomato is stuck on the toe of a mop. The mop placed his leg on a table to have another mop try to pull the tomato off. The mop says, "The tomato toe of this mop should not be on the table." A tomato plant is growing in the window.

vegetable - vegetal
vay - hay - tahl

Vases and hay that are tall attract vegetable customers.

A vase full of vegetables and a stack of hay that are very tall are in front of a vegetable stand. The vegetable salesman says, "Vases and hay that are tall attract vegetable customers."

meat - carne
car - neigh

Meat Shop

Meat Carved Daily

I'm a meat carving, neighing horse.

Don't complain, Meathead.

A side of meat is being carved by a neighing horse in front of the meat shop where it works. The sign reads, "Don't complain, Meathead." The horse says, "I'm a meat carving neighing horse." This word also means "flesh."

fish - pescado
pehs - cah - doe

Pesticide, cah, sprayed through a donut makes great tasting fish.

A fish has pesticide sprayed on it by a cahing crow. This crow has a funny way of eating fish. The pesticide is sprayed through a donut. There is another word for "fish" when it is a live fish, and not a fish to be eaten. That word is taught in the animals category.

ham - jamón
hah - moan

This ham hops and moans because of its toe.

What a ham!

A large ham is hopping around and moaning, because it stubbed its toe. Another ham says, "What a ham."

pork - cerdo
sair - doe

If you had eaten more pork, Sarah says you might not be extinct, you do-do.

Pork is the new white meat.

Sarah

A girl named Sarah is feeding pork to a do-do bird. She says, "If you had eaten more pork, Sarah says you might not be extinct, you do-do." The sign reads, "Pork is the new white meat."

seafood - mariscos
mah - rees - cohs

Ma's Reese's should be on the coaster with the seafood.

A ma is holding a little baby that loves Reese's Peanut Butter Cups. She placed a bowl of seafood on a very large coaster on the dining table. She says, "Ma's Reese's should be on the coaster with the seafood."

turkey - pavo
pah - voh

This turkey reads this pocket book over and over to try to learn Spanish vocabulary.

A turkey is reading a pocket book about Spanish vocabulary. He is doing it the hard way. What a turkey. He needs to talk turkey with Dr. Memory". This picture is repeated, because this word means the same as a live animal or as meat.

coffee - café
cah - fay

I'm a cop who loves coffee and party favors.

A cop at a party is serving coffee. Coffee cans full of party favors are around the room. Other people at the party are also drinking coffee.

juice - jugo
who - go

Got juice?

SNAP

In the name of juice, who goes there?

A container of juice that is a bodyguard says, "In the name of juice, who goes there," after it hears a noise. A thief is hiding behind the giant juice advertising sign in the background.

milk - leche
lay - chay

I will lay in chains because I'm a milk thief.

Milk Store

Skim Milk

The Milk of Human Kindness

A prisoner lays his head in his hand, because he dropped a carton of milk. He has a chain around his legs. He was arrested for stealing milk from the milk store in the background. He is known as the milk bandit.

soda - soda
sew - dah

I sew dollars onto soda.

So, that's why they call soda sew - dah.

Fountain

A lady is sewing a dollar bill onto a bottle of soda at a soda fountain counter. The soda jerk says, "So, that's why they call soda sew - dah."

water - agua
ah - goo - ah

Bottled Spring Water

Ah, water for my iguana.

gwah

Spring Water

An Amish man has his pet iguana on a leash. He stopped and bought bottled spring water for his pet. He says, "Ah, water for my iguana." The water is very refreshing on the hot day.

chocolate - chocolate
cho - co - lah - tay

Chocolate Charlie's Chocolate House

Choke this cobra, Mr. Llama, but I'll get that chocolate on the table.

The choke chain on the cobra is held by a llama to keep it away from all of the chocolate on the table in front of the chocolate shop. The name of the chocolate shop is "Chocolate Charlie's Chocolate House."

dessert - postre
pos - tray

I'm a post with a tray full of dessert.

What's for dessert?

Various kinds of desserts are on a post in a tray. The sign reads, "What's for dessert?"

ice cream - helado
ay - lah - doe

An ape, a llama and a do-do all scream for ice cream.

An ape has hoarded some ice cream as a llama and a do-do prepare to eat their ice cream. **The llama says, "An ape, a llama and a do-do all scream for ice cream."**

apple - manzana
mahn - sah - nah

An apple tree a day keeps the monster and its saucer away.

Knock knock!

A monster that came from the flying saucer in the background is watching an apple use a door knocker. It devoured a whole apple tree from an apple orchard in one gulp.

banana - banana
bah - nah - nah

The banana bottle knot knock is great.

Plantation

A bottle used a banana to knock a knot hole out of a fence. It split the banana, and the banana landed in a banana split bowl. The bottle says, "The banana bottle knot knock is great."

fruit - fruta
froo - tah

I'm a frugal tomahawk, and your fruit is too expensive.

Fruit Stand

A frugal tomahawk is bartering with a fruit stand owner about the price of his fruit. He says, "I'm a frugal tomahawk, and your fruit is too expensive." A fruit bat to the side is going to eat a fruit cake.

lemon - limón
lee - moan

Leeches moan when sucking sour lemons.

Lemon juice sucks.

A leech is moaning loudly as it sucks on a lemon. The sign reads, "Lemon juice sucks."

orange - naranja
nah - rahn - ha

Ha-ha!

This nozzle works great, Ron. Oranges love this, ha-ha!

Ron

A playful orange squirted water out of a nozzle onto a boy named Ron. Ron seems to enjoy it, because he laughs and says, "Ha-ha," along with the orange. Orange trees are in the background.

butter - mantequilla
mahn - tay - key - yah

Monocles and tape are the key to good yachting. What could be butter than this?

Butter

The Buttercup

A package of butter wearing a monocle blew a roll of tape at a key standing on a yacht. The name of the yacht is "The Buttercup."

pepper - pimienta
pea - me - ehn - tah

A peacock and a meteor in an end zone are hotter than pepper to this tomahawk.

P

END ZONE

A peacock with a pepper shaker in its mouth watched a meteor that fell toward a football end zone. A tomahawk was painting the stripes in the end zone when the meteor fell. The goalposts are made of big pepper shakers. The tomahawk comments on the events.

salt - sal
sahl

Solitaire is this salt's favorite game.

S

The Salt of the Earth

A salt shaker with salt flying out of it is playing solitaire on a globe of the earth. The sign reads, "The salt of the earth."

sugar - azúcar
ah - sue - cahr

Ah, Sue knows that carnation sweetened sugar is the best.

Sugar

Ah Sue

I need some sugar, Daddy.

An Amish woman named Sue is wearing a carnation while pouring sugar from a box of sugar into a sugar bowl. The sign reads, "I need some sugar, Daddy."

breakfast - desayuno
day - sah - you - no

This daisy with one sock is serving "U" breakfast.

No, breakfast is not the most important meal.

A good looking breakfast is on the table. The daisy that prepared it for a letter "U" said, "This daisy with one sock is serving "U" breakfast." The letter said, "No, breakfast is not the most important meal."

lunch - almuerzo
ahl - moo - air - sew

mwair

All-star Moo Air soda delivery for lunch.

Moo!

All Star

The Lunch Bunch

Lunch

An open box lunch is on the picnic table. An all-star cow basketball player is mooing as it looks into the lunch box. An airplane just dropped a soda pop for the cow to drink with its lunch. The soda says, "All-star Moo Air soda delivery for lunch." Moo Air is a brand new airline company.

dinner & supper - cena
say - nah

Is dinner served, Mr. Sailor, nah, but it will be soon.

That sailor likes to take naughty girls to supper.

A candlelight dinner is about to be enjoyed by a sailor and a naughty girl at supper time. The waiter has disappointing news. The girl says, "That sailor likes to take naughty girls to supper."

Conjugation of "To Have"

The second of the seven important verbs to conjugate is the irregular verb "to have," which is "ten**er**." This is also an "**er**" or "**air**" verb and the endings will follow the "**er**" conjugation pattern. Again, the subject pronouns will not be listed in the phonetic pronunciations, since you already know how to pronounce them.

English	Spanish	Phonetic Pronunciation
I have to	yo tengo que	tehn – go – kay
You have to	usted tiene que	tea – ehn – ay - kay
We have to	nosotros tenemos que	tay – nay – mohs - kay
He has to	él tiene que	tea – ehn – ay - kay
She has to	ella tiene que	tea – ehn – ay - kay
They have to	ellos tienen que	tea – ehn – ehn - kay

When you examine the conjugation you will notice that the "you," "he" and "she" forms are all the same as always. **The Identifier Detective** pointed this out to you earlier. You will also notice that "we" and "they" follow the basic pattern you learned for regular verbs. "We" has an "emos" ending, and "they" has an "en" ending. The "mos" and "n" endings follow the basic pattern. Although you have already practiced the "yo" form of "yo tengo que" with other infinitives, it will still be included in the upcoming drill. You have not practiced using it with full sentences yet.

When you are sure you know these verb forms you can practice using them with Spanish infinitives in the upcoming drill. In this drill you will first speak compound verb phrases as you did with the forms of "to go." You will then be able to speak complete sentences that begin with the verb phrases and end with the words from the "clothing," "color" and "food" categories. You will not be able to use all of the infinitives with each form, because they will not make sense, but use as many as you can in this very important practice drill.

The various forms will be represented by boxes on the left side of the page as before. Again, you will select a verb form on the left and say it with an infinitive on the first door. For instance, if you used the first form listed on the left with the first infinitive on the door you would say, "Nosotros tenemos que comer." This, of course, is "We have to eat," in English. You should practice speaking verb phrases of all of the forms first. After you have practiced with the infinitives on the door expand your practice by using the infinitives listed above and below the door.

After you have practiced with verb phrases, you can practice complete sentences by using the other words listed on the page. For instance, you could say, "Nosotros tenemos que comer el queso." In English this is "We have to eat the cheese." You could then expand the sentence to say, "Nosotros tenemos que comer el queso en el restaurante." In English this is "We have to eat the cheese at the restaurant." An explanation of the "en" used in this sentence is imperative. You have learned that "at" means "a," but, in this sentence "en" has been used. "A" is used when you are "at" or "only up to something." For instance, you could be "at" the door. You would use "a" in this case. However, in the sentence, "Ella compra un sombrero en la farmacia," "en" is used. In English this means, "She buys a hat at the pharmacy." In this case she is not just at the door of the pharmacy, but she actually is in the pharmacy buying the hat. Another sample sentence with this usage is, "Yo bebo el café en el restaurante." This means, "I drink the coffee at the restaurant." The coffee isn't being drunk at the door, but actually "in" the restaurant. You might as well use the "buildings and places" category to expand your sentences since you have learned those words.

By now you know the make-up drill procedure. Use as many of these words as possible during your practice. If you are not sure of all of the "building and places" words go back and review them briefly until you know them well. You will continue to have to use "el" or "la" depending on whether the food or clothing is **masculine** or **feminine**. It would also be good practice for you to use "los" or "las" and make the words **plural**. You could use some more practice using the plural form of the definite article.

You will also notice that you have the choice of using "a" or "an" before the food or clothing. When you use this indefinite article you will have to use "un" or "una" depending on whether the food or clothing is **masculine** or **feminine**. It would also be good practice for you to use "unos" or "unas" and make the words **plural**. You might say, "Ellos tienen que vender las manzanas." In English this is "They have to sell the apples." Practice using all forms of the verb "to have" with as many words as possible. You can never practice too much.

A different set of verbs than were used in the "to go" drill are being used in this drill. If you haven't been disciplined enough to review your words on a regular basis as Dr. Memory™ routinely suggests, you might have to go back and review the verbs used in this drill.

As has already been stated several times, these practice drills are vital for your progress and success. You must participate in all of them to advance your skills. Practice makes perfect. You will be able to hear several of these sentences spoken by a Spanish-speaking person on Dr. Memory's™ web site. By listening to a Spanish-speaking person you will better understand Spanish vocal tendencies. Remember that "in" and "at" are "en" in Spanish, and "to" is "a".

A red asterisk mark precedes the words "*to the" in the practice drill to remind you to use "al" with masculine nouns. The practice drill is on the next page.

More Practice

Use as many of these words as possible while you practice. If you are not sure of any of the words listed on the next page go back and review them briefly until you know them well. You will continue to have to use "**el**" or "**la**" depending on whether the food or clothing is **masculine** or **feminine**. It would also be good practice for you to continue to use "**los**" or "**las**" and make the words **plural**.

Again you have the choice of using "a" or "an" before food or clothing. When you use this indefinite article you will have to use "**un**" or "**una**" depending on whether the building or place is **masculine** or **feminine**. You might make up, "El tiene que comer la manzana verde." In English this is "He has to eat the green apple." Practice using all forms of the verb "to have" with as many words as possible in this list and use a color with each food or clothing item to describe it by color. You can never practice too much.

You could also say, "Ella tiene que llevar una falda roja." In English this is "She has to wear a red skirt." Go color crazy with this drill. You may make up some weird sentences, but it is always good to speak Spanish as much as possible in the learning stages.

You will be able to hear several of these sentences spoken by a Spanish-speaking person on Dr. Memory's™ web site. By listening to a Spanish-speaking person you will better understand Spanish vocal tendencies.

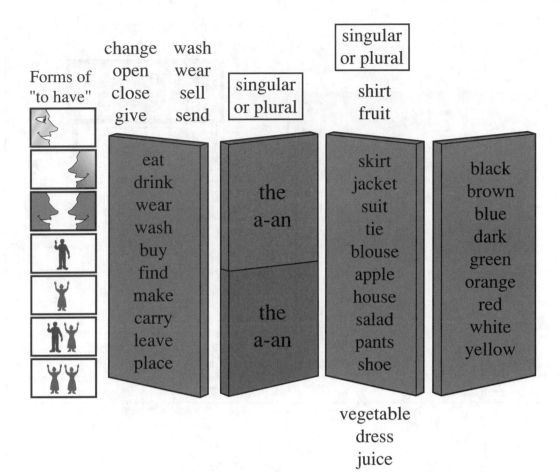

Vehicles

Before you learn the conjugation of another of the seven important verbs Dr. Memory™ wants you to learn three more categories of vocabulary words, so you can use them in the next sentence make-up practice drill. The first category is **vehicles**.

Study the words on the next two pages. Make sure to study each vocabulary word picture until you can easily recreate it in your mind and say the Spanish equivalent when thinking of the English word before going to the next word. The words in the review list will be **blue** or **pink** depending on whether they are **masculine** or **feminine**. For future use, you must know whether thethe words are **masculine** or **feminine**.

There are only seven words in this category. Review the words several times before going on to the next category. Click on these words on Dr. Memory's™ web site to hear them pronounced by a Spanish-speaking person as you learn them.

bicycle - bicicleta
bee - sea - clay - tah

Mr. Bee, the sea bicycle has been clayed by a tomahawk.

Sea

A bee examines a bicycle that washed ashore from the sea. A hunk of clay was thrown at the bicycle by a tomahawk.

bus - autobús
ah - ooh - toe - boos

The bus stops here.

Ah, ooh, the toe needs a boost to get on the bus.

Good boost.

An Amish man says, "Ooh," as he gives a toe a boost into a bus at a bus stop. The sign reads, "The bus stops here." Many Spanish-speaking people just say "boos" and do not use the first three syllables. It is like saying "car" instead of "automobile."

car - carro
cahr - oh

That car passes this oak faster than other cars.

Oak

CAR

A car with the word "car" on it is chasing a roller skate. It is nearing an oak tree. The oak says, "That car passes this oak faster than other cars." The word "car" is on the car, to emphasize that this particular car is used for the word "car," because there are other cars in other pictures.

motorcycle - motocicleta
mo - toe - sea - clay - tah

Motorcycle Convention

Sea

No Mohawk toes on sea motorcycles are allowed on this clay beach, Tom.

A Mohawk haircut is worn by the big toe sitting on a motorcycle near a sea. Clay pots are thrown at the motorcycle by a tomahawk. Some Spanish speakers simply say "moto" for motorcycle.

taxi- **taxi**
tahk - sea

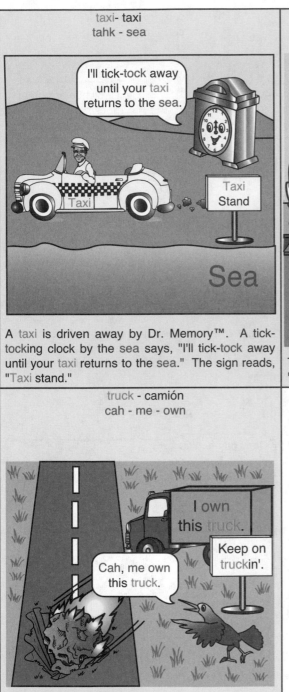

A **taxi** is driven away by Dr. Memory™. A tick-tocking clock by the **sea** says, "I'll tick-tock away until your **taxi** returns to the sea." The sign reads, "**Taxi** stand."

train - **tren**
trehn

The **train** derailed and dug a trench. The word "Train" is on the side of the **train**.

truck - **camión**
cah - me - own

A **truck** owned by a cahing crow is on the side of a road. It got out to see where the meteor landed. The sign on the truck reads, "I own this **truck**." The sign reads, "Keep on **truckin'**."

Travel

The next category of words you will learn is **travel**. Study the words on the next three pages. Make sure to study each vocabulary word picture until you can easily recreate it in your mind and say the Spanish equivalent when thinking of the English word before going to the next word. The words in the review list will be **blue** or **pink** depending on whether they are **masculine** or **feminine**. For future use of the words you must know whether they are **masculine** or **feminine**.

There are 10 words in this category. Review the words several times before going on to the next category.

backpack - mochila
moe - chee - lah

The motor in this cheese's backpack is heavy. I need to lock this thing away.

Backpack Trail

A motor is in a backpack carried by a piece of cheese. A lock fell out of the backpack. The sign reads, "Backpack Trail." The cheese says, "The motor in this cheese's backpack is heavy. I need to lock this thing away."

camera - cámara
cah - mah - rah

Cobwebs are great mockingbird camera rock subjects.

Camera Rock

A cobweb is being photographed by a mockingbird perched on a rock. Its camera is new and fully automatic. The mockingbird is camera crazy.

country - país
pah - ees

We love our country.

Popcorn and geese are loyal to our country.

A bag of popcorn and two geese are holding their hands, wings, over their hearts to honor their country as the flag of the United States flutters. One of the geese holding up a map of the United States says, "We love our country."

film - película
pay - lee - coo - lah

Don't pay for this film, Mr. Leech, or you're as cuckoo as that llama.

Coo

s Film Stor

PayDay

Just Out Laser Film

A Payday candy bar ripped the film out of a leech's camera as a cooing dove and a llama look on. They are all in front of a film store. The sign reads, "Just out laser film." This also means a "movie" or "film" you would go see.

flight - vuelo
voo - ay - low

My voodoo vway has hexed this flight.

vway

This wing is low.

Flight 13

A voodoo doll and an ape are on the wings of an airplane while in flight. It causes one wing to tip down lower than the other wing. A sign on the plane reads, "Flight 13." The flight number may be a sign of bad luck.

liter - litro
lee - troh

Leaves and trolls have liter or no trouble.

Do not liter.

Liter

A leaf is dropping leaves into a liter **container in front of** a troll. The leaf says, "Leaves and trolls have liter or no trouble." The sign reads, "Do not liter." This is the Spanish volume measurement.

map - mapa
mah - pah

I'll mop up this map faster than you can say, "Pop, pop."

Map

Maps Unlimited

A mop is used by a box of popcorn to clean off a map in a map room. The sign reads, "Maps unlimited."

passport - pasaporte
pah - sah - poor - tay

This possum's passport smells like a sock. He has poor taste.

Passports checked here.

A possum with a sock on its tail is very poor. Its passport was taped on to it so it wouldn't lose it. The sign reads, "Passports checked here." The agent says, "This possum's passport smells like a sock. He has poor taste."

suitcase - maleta
mah - lay - tah

This mop will help me lay my suitcase near my tomahawk.

Suitcase City

A suitcase is being carried on a mop handle by a laying hen with a tomahawk stuck in its belt. She is entering Suitcase City.

trip - viaje
vee - ah - hay

Mr. Veeah left this hay on his last trip.

When you take a trip, don't trip.

A V-neck sweater is next to a stack of hay. The tongue depressor, ah, is feeding hay to a horse. It is going to take a trip on the horse. It says, "Mr. Veeah left this hay on his last trip." The sign reads, "When you take a trip, don't trip."

Elements

The third and last category you will learn before studying the conjugation of another of the seven important verbs is **elements and environment**.

Study the words on the next four pages. Make sure to study each vocabulary word picture until you can easily recreate it in your mind and say the Spanish equivalent when thinking of the English word before going to the next word. The words in the review list will be **blue** or **pink** depending on whether they are **masculine** or **feminine**. For future use, you must know whether the words are **masculine** or **feminine**.

Do a review of all of the words each time you learn eight new ones. You should still review all of the other categories you have learned to this point on a regular basis as well. You will not be as successful as you want to be without these brief but important reviews. Click on these words on Dr. Memory's™ web site to hear them pronounced by a Spanish-speaking person as you learn them. There are 17 words in this category. Take your time and make sure you know all of the pictures before continuing.

beach - playa
plah - yah

A yacht plopped down on a beach. The yacht sank into the beach, because it is so heavy. The sign reads, "Don't be a beach bum." A voice from the yacht says, "This plopped yacht sank in the beach."

cloudy - nublado
new - blah - doe

A gnu looks up at a cloudy sky and sees a blob and a donut shaped cloud. The weather sign reads, "Today's weather is cloudy."

earth, ground & land - tierra
tea - air - ah

A teacup rocket Air Express landed on the ground next to a globe of the earth. As the rocket landed some of the ground and the land at the landing site flew up and hit an Amish man. The sign reads, "Earth to ground. Land here."

fire - fuego
foo - ay - go

A fool, a court jester, is juggling stuffed toy apes that are on fire while preparing to ride a goat through a wall of fire. The sign reads, "Don't play with fire."

lake - lago
lah - go

I love to do the llama go-go at the lake.

Lakefront Lots For Sale

Lake Trout For Sale

Lake

A llama watches a go-cart splash into a lake as it does the llama go-go dance. One sign reads. "Lakefront lots for sale." Another reads, "Lake trout for sale."

moon - luna
loo - nah

Lulu got knots from the green cheese on the moon.

Don't get moonstruck.

A girl named Lulu has knots on her head from green cheese that fell from the moon and hit her. She says, "Lulu got knots from the green cheese on the moon." The sign reads, "Don't get moonstruck."

mountain - montaña
moan - tah - nyah

I'm a moaning, mountain tomahawk, and he's a non-climbing nyah.

Ny

Mountain Men

A moan comes out of a tomahawk that is climbing a mountain. An onion (ny) with a tongue depressors, ah, headdress isn't climbing. The sign near the mountain reads, "Mountain men."

rain - lluvia
you - vee - ah

Hey, univee, ah, it's raining.

Ah

Come out of the rain.

A unicycle is being ridden in the rain by a boy wearing a V-neck sweater. Some of the rain is bouncing off of an Amish man who is watching the boy. The sign reads, "Come out of the rain."

river - río
ree - oh

A reward poster if floating down a river on a pair of overalls. A boy on the bank of the river says, "I'd sell my brother down the river for that reward on overalls." The sign on the river bank reads, "River of regret."

sea - mar
mahr

Bags of marshmallows are floating in a sea. A **mar**shmallow jumped out of one of the bags and said, "I'm a marshmallow at sea."

sky - cielo
sea - ay - low

A skywriter made clouds in the sky that look like a sea horse, an ape and a locomotive. His comment proves that he is a little loco himself. The plane is pulling a sign that reads, "Skywriter."

snow - nieve
knee - ay - vay

An ape drops snow on its knees. The ape is asked to fill the vase with snow by the snowman. The sign reads, "Watch out for snow jobs." The snowman says, "I need some, Mr. Ape. Please fill my vase with snow."

Conjugation of "To Be Able" or "Can"

The third listing will be the conjugation for the irregular verb "to be able to" or "can," which is "pod**er**." Since this is an "**er**" or "**air**" verb the endings follow the "**er**" conjugation pattern. Again, the subject pronouns will not be listed in the phonetic pronunciations, since you already know how to pronounce them.

English	Spanish	Phonetic Pronunciation
I can	yo puedo	pway – doh
You can	usted puede	pway – day
We can	nosotros podemos	poh – day - mohs
He can	él puede	pway – day
She can	ella puede	pway – day
They can	ellos pueden	pway – dehn

When you examine the conjugation you will notice that the "you," "he" and "she" forms are all the same as always. **The Identifier Detective** pointed this out to you earlier. You will also notice that "we" and "they" follow the basic pattern you learned for regular verbs. "We" has an "emos" ending, and "they" has an "en" ending. The "mos" and "n" endings follow the basic pattern. Although you have already practiced the "yo" form of "yo puedo" with other infinitives it will still be included in the upcoming drill. You have not practiced using it with full sentences yet.

When you are sure you know these verb forms you can practice using them with Spanish infinitives in the upcoming drill. In this drill you should first speak compound verb phrases as you did before with the other verb forms. You will then be able to speak complete sentences that begin with the verb phrases and end with the words from the "vehicles," "travel" and "elements and environment" categories. You will not be able to use all of the infinitives with each form, because they won't make sense, but use as many as you can in this very important practice drill.

The various forms will be represented by boxes on the left side of the page as before. Once again, you will select a verb form on the left and say it with an infinitive on the first door. For instance, you could say, "Nosotros podemos llevar." This is, "We can carry," in English. You should practice speaking verb phrases of all of the forms first. After you have practiced with the infinitives on the door expand your practice by using the infinitives listed above and below the door.

After you have practiced with verb phrases you can practice complete sentences by using the other words listed on the page. For instance, you could say, "Nosotros podemos llevar la maleta al tren." This is, "We can carry the suitcase to the train," in English. You can also skip the next to last door when making up some sentences and perhaps say, "Ella puede caminar en la playa." This means, "She can walk on the beach," in English. Since you are making up the sentences, you can do anything you would like, and the more you do the better.

Use as many of these words as possible during your practice. If you are not sure of all of the words go back and review them briefly until you know them well. You will continue to have to use "**el**" or "**la**" and "**un**" or "**una**" depending on whether the noun is **masculine** or **feminine**. It would also be good practice for you to use "**los**" or "**las**" and make the words **plural**. You could use some more practice using the plural form of the definite article. Practice using all forms of the verb "can" with as many words as possible. You can never practice too much.

As has already been stated several times, these practice drills are vital for your progress and success. You must participate in all of them to advance your skills. Practice makes perfect. You will be able to hear several of these sentences spoken by a Spanish-speaking person on Dr. Memory's™ web site. By listening to a Spanish-speaking person you will better understand Spanish vocal tendencies. Remember that "in" and "at" are "en" in Spanish, and "to" is "a".

A red asterisk mark precedes the words "*to the" in the practice drill to remind you to use "**al**" with masculine nouns. The drill is on the next page.

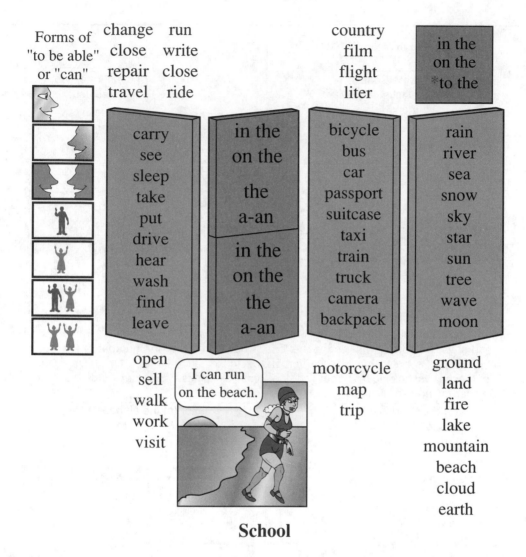

Forms of "to be able" or "can"

change run
close write
repair close
travel ride

country
film
flight
liter

in the
on the
*to the

carry
see
sleep
take
put
drive
hear
wash
find
leave

in the
on the
the
a-an

in the
on the
the
a-an

bicycle
bus
car
passport
suitcase
taxi
train
truck
camera
backpack

rain
river
sea
snow
sky
star
sun
tree
wave
moon

open
sell
walk
work
visit

I can run on the beach.

motorcycle
map
trip

ground
land
fire
lake
mountain
beach
cloud
earth

School

The next category of words you will learn are words that might be used in **school**. Of course, they might be used in other conversation as well. There are 11 new words in this category, and six of them are verbs relating to school. These verbs will be able to be used with other applications, but they fit this category best. These six verbs offer more possibilities for using them as infinitives along with the seven important verbs you are learning.

Make sure to study each vocabulary word picture until you can easily recreate it in your mind and say the Spanish equivalent when thinking of the English word before going to the next word. The reward far surpasses the small investment of time required for these reviews.

answer - contestar
cone - tehs - tahr

With Miss Cone's test you must target your answers.

I know the answer.

A student in class has his hand up to answer a question and says, "I know the answer." The ice cream cone teacher is giving her class a verbal test. The teacher is holding a target, so the students can target their answers."

count - contar
cone - tahr

I count one, two, three, four cones in tar.

Count your blessings.

Don't count me out.

A boy is counting the number of ice cream cones he found stuck in tar. One sign reads, "Count your blessings." Another reads, "Don't count me out."

draw - dibujar
dee - boo - hahr

Dee is crying boo-hoo, because she can't draw a harp as well as I can.

Boo-hoo

Don't draw back.

The little boy says, "Dee is crying boo-hoo, because she can't draw a harp as well as I can." The sign reads, "Don't draw back."

letter (of the alphabet) - letra
lay - trah

The letters of the day are "L" and "T."

Lei   Tropical

I just used the letters of the day in "Lei" and "Tropical."

A girl wearing a lei is standing in tropical plants while writing letters on the board. She says, "I just used the letters of the day in 'Lei' and 'Tropical.'"

paper - papel
pah - pehl

Popcorn and paper easily fit in a pelican's mouth.

Pelican

Pop

Paper Drive

A paper box full of popcorn and several pieces of paper were in the pelican's mouth. The pelican is dumping them into a huge stack of paper. The sign reads, "Paper drive."

pen - pluma
ploo - mah

Practice good penmanship. Pen a story about Pluto.

A Pluto in moccasins has to think of a good pen name.

The planet Pluto wears moccasins while writing with a very large pen. It says, "A Pluto in moccasins has to think of a good pen name."

pencil - lápiz
lah - piece

I'm a llama piece of pizza pencil pusher.

A llama is spinning a piece of pizza on the end of its pencil. Another large pencil is in the pencil sharpener. The llama says. "I'm a llama piece of pizza pencil pusher."

to read - leer
lay - air

I love to lay on air as I read.

Read a book a week.

A laying hen is on an air conditioner while reading Dr. Memory's™ Picture Perfect Spanish book. She says, "I love to lay on air as I read." The sign reads, "Read a book a week." Other reading material is between the hen's legs.

school - escuela
ehs - coo - ay - lah

kway

This Eskimo in no kway wants to go to school with an ape and llama.

I love school.

SCHOOL

An Eskimo and a cooing dove are coming to school from the left. An ape and a llama are coming to school from the right.

to study - estudiar
ehs - two - dee - ahr

Study Hard

The Eskimo, two Dee, "R" two, did study and passed the test.

The same female student Eskimo still has a number two and the name Dee on her. The archery teacher is about to shoot an arrow into a "Study Hard" banner. Her name is a little play on Star Wars.

teacher - profesor
pro - fehs - oar

The teacher's program will tell you all about the Festival of Oranges.

Pro-gram

The Festival of Oranges

Teacher knows best.

A teacher is holding a program about the Festival of Oranges. The teacher is teaching about the festival. The sign reads, "Teacher knows best." A female teacher is a "profesora."

word - palabra
pah - lah - brah

The word of the day is "word."

Pasta lobbing into a bra helps me remember the word "word."

I need a word with you.

A boy in school says, "Pasta lobbing into a bra helps me remember the word 'word.'" The sign reads, "I need a word with you."

Jewelry

The next category of words you will learn is **jewelry**. There are only four words in this category. A "watch" could be considered jewelry, but it means the same thing as "clock" and is taught in the "home" category.

Make sure to study each vocabulary word picture until you can easily recreate it in your mind and say the Spanish equivalent when thinking of the English word before going to the next word. The reward far surpasses the small investment of time required for these reviews.

bracelet - brazalete
brah - sah - lay - tay

This brahma bull will sock it to that layer with my bracelet if the table isn't full of eggs.

A large bracelet is held by a brahma bull only wearing one sock. A hen is laying eggs on the table. The bull shows its bracelet to the hen and says, "This brahma bull will sock it to that layer with my bracelet if the table isn't full of eggs."

earring - arete
ah - ray - tay

Ah, these manta ray earrings take my breath away.

A female tongue depressor (ah) is wearing a pair of manta ray earrings. She is trying on earrings laid out on the table. She says, "Ah, these manta ray earrings take my breath away."

Days of Week

The next category of words you will learn is the **days of the week**. Naturally there are only seven words in this category.

Make sure to study each vocabulary word picture until you can easily recreate it in your mind and say the Spanish equivalent when thinking of the English word before going to the next word. The reward far surpasses the small investment of time required for these reviews.

Sunday - domingo
doe - mean - go

A Doberman dog that looks really mean is chasing a go-cart. The man is going to church, because it is Sunday. A Sunday newspaper headlines news about the dog. The days of the week are not capitalized in Spanish.

Monday - lunes
loo - nace

A loony bird is going to work on a Monday with an ace of cards. A letter "N" is in the lunch box the mad ace dropped. The bird says, "What a loony thing to do on a Monday, Mr. Nace." The sign reads, "Monday morning quarterback."

Tuesday - martes
mahr - tace

A card game just ended at a Ruby Tuesday's Restaurant. One of the players just marked a letter "T" on one of his aces.

Wednesday - miércoles
me - air - co - lace

The cobra has measles. An air compressor is being sprayed on the cobra. It thinks it can blow its measles away. A shoelace is on the side of the compressor. The sign reads, "A windy Wednesday." Please excuse the bad grammar in the cobra's comment.

Thursday - jueves
who - ay - vase

A thirsty hoot owl says, "Hoot," as it throws a stuffed toy ape into a vase. "Thirsty" will help remind you of Thursday. The sign reads, "Thirsty Thursday."

Friday - viernes
vee - air - nace

A V-neck sweater uses an air compressor and forces a letter "N" into an ace of cards. The sweater says, "Mr. "V" loves to spray air on an ace on Friday." Notice the fish fry taking place in the background. It is a fry day to remind you of Friday.

Saturday - sábado
sah - bah - doe

A soccer ball hit a lamb, and it said, "Bah." The ball was kicked by a Doberman dog. The Doberman says, "A Saturday soccer kick makes lambs go "bah" in the Doberman league." The sign reads, "Soccer Saturday."

Months

The next category of words you will learn is the **months** of the year. There are 13 words in this category, because the word "month" is also included.

Make sure to study each vocabulary word picture until you can easily recreate it in your mind and say the Spanish equivalent when thinking of the English word before going to the next word. The reward far surpasses the small investment of time required for these reviews.

January - enero
ay - nair - o

"This ape used Nair to prepare my old body for January and the new year."

An ape used Nair to take hair off of its body. The Nair is on overalls. The ape is getting ready to ring in the new year at a January the first New Year's party. Notice the month of January on the calendar.

February - febrero
fay - brair - o

"Fay is a bee that is rare in old February."

Fay is the name of a bee that is cooking a rare steak on a grill while standing on a box of oats. A valentine with the month of February on it is in the background. She is cooking steaks for her boyfriend who says, "Fay is a bee that is rare in old February."

March - marzo
mahr - sew

"We love to march in March with marshmallows sewn to us."

A couple of marching soldiers have bags of marshmallows sewn to their uniforms. They are marching in front of calendar month of March.

April - abril
ah - breel

"Ah, April showers and a bee reel are good for fishing."

An Amish man and a bee are fishing with rods and reels. The bee says, "Ah, April showers and a bee reel are good for fishing."

May - mayo
mah - yo

A ma with a yo-yo loves May flowers.

A ma is playing with a yo-yo with one hand while holding her baby in her other arm. She is standing in May flowers in front of a calendar month of May. She says, "A ma with a yo-yo loves May flowers."

June - junio
who - knee - o

I give a hoot on my knees for this old June bride.

A female hoot owl is on her knees. A pair of overalls cushions them. A seamstress is making an adjustment to the top part of her wedding gown. The owl is going to be a June bride. A calendar month of June is in the background.

July - julio
who - lee - o

Who can this leech in overalls trust on the Fourth of July?

An owl screams, "Who," at a leech that is wearing overalls at a Fourth of July fireworks display. A calendar month of July is in the background The leech asks, "Who can this leech in overalls trust on the Fourth of July?"

August - agosto
ah - ghos - toe

Ah, that's no August ghost totem pole.

An Amish man saw a ghost and climbed on top of a totem pole using a ladder that spells out the month of August. The sun is blazing in the hot August sky. A calendar month of August is starting to burn on the ground, because it is so hot.

September - septiembre
sehp - tea - ehm - bray

British Embassy

We septuplets see tea time at the British Embassy every September, don't we, Braydy.

Septuplets are going to school during the first week of September. A man is having tea in front of the British Embassy they are passing. The donkey brays as they pass.

October - octubre
oak - two - bray

An oak tree with two braying donkeys can give us no treats in October.

An oak tree has two braying donkeys tied to it. A Halloween jack-o-lantern is in front of the tree. Trick or treaters are walking in the background. It is obviously October.

November - noviembre
no - vee - ehm - bray

No V-neck or emery board is necessary for November thanks, Mr. Braydy.

Noah's ark has only a donkey in front of it. The rest of the animals have already gone away. The donkey is handing a V-neck sweater and an emery board to Noah. It is braying as it looks at a November Thanksgiving dinner. Noah makes a gracious comment to the donkey.

December - diciembre
dee - sea - ehm - bray

Dee kicked me into the cold December sea on the emery board. Bray, it is cold.

Sea

A lady named Dee kicked a donkey into the sea. It reached for a floating emery board. The donkey is braying. Santa Clause, representing the month of December, watches. The donkey is afraid he won't get out of the sea in time to get his December gifts from Santa.

month - mes
mace

A can of mace is spraying on a calendar month.
One sign reads, "Not in a month of Sundays."
Another sign reads, "Monthly reports are due." If
people in your area say "mehs," simply see the
month being messy after being sprayed.

Printed Material

The next category of words you will learn is **printed material**. There are only 4
words in this category, and one of them has already been taught.

Make sure to study each vocabulary word picture until you can easily recreate it
in your mind and say the Spanish equivalent when thinking of the English word before
going to the next word. The reward far surpasses the small investment of time required
for these reviews.

Conjugation of "To Need"

The fourth listing will be the conjugation for the regular verb "to need" which is "necesit**ar**." Since this is an "**ar**" or "**art**" verb the endings follow the "**ar**" conjugation pattern. This is the only **regular verb** in Dr. Memory's™ important seven verbs, so the stem does not change during conjugation. You will recall that these verbs are important, because they can be used with the infinitive form of other verbs to form hundreds of verb phrases. The subject pronouns will not be listed in the phonetic pronunciations, since you already know how to pronounce them.

English	Spanish	Phonetic Pronunciation
I need	yo necesito	nay – say – sea - toe
You need	usted necesita	nay – say – sea - tah
We need	nosotros necesitamos	nay – say – sea – tah - mohs
He needs	él necesita	nay – say – sea - tah
She needs	ella necesita	nay – say – sea - tah
They need	ellos necesitan	nay – say – sea - tahn

When you examine this conjugation you will notice that the "you," "he" and "she" forms are all the same as always. **The Identifier Detective** pointed this out to you earlier. You will also notice that "we" and "they" follow the basic pattern you learned for regular "ar" or "art" verbs. "We" has an "amos" ending, and "they" has an "an" ending. The "amos" and "an" endings follow the basic pattern for "art" verbs. Although you have already practiced the "yo" form of "yo necesito" with other infinitives it will still be included in the upcoming drill. You have not practiced using the verb with full sentences yet. Since this is a regular verb all of the forms begin with "necesit." Likewise, the first three syllables are all "nay – say – sea." That is why regular verbs are easier than irregular verbs.

When you are sure you know these verb forms you can practice using them with Spanish infinitives in the upcoming drill. In this drill you should first speak compound verb phrases as you did before with the other verb forms. You will then be able to speak complete sentences that begin with the verb phrases and end with the words from the "school," "jewelry," "days" and "months" categories. You won't be able to use all of the infinitives with each form, because they won't make sense, but use as many as you can in this very important practice drill.

The various verb forms will be represented by boxes on the left side of the page just like before. You will select a verb form on the left and say it with an infinitive on the first door. For instance, you could say, "Ella necesita lavar." This is, "She needs to wash," in English. You should practice speaking verb phrases of all of the forms first. After you have practiced with the infinitives on the door expand your practice by using the infinitives listed above and below the door.

After you have practiced with verb phrases you can practice complete sentences by using the other words listed on the page. For instance, you could say, "Ella necesita lavar el anillo en lunes." This is, "She needs to wash the ring on Monday," in English. "On" with days of the week is "el" or "los." A red asterisk will be in the drill to remind you of this. You might also say, "Yo necesito usar el lápiz el sábado." This is, "I need to use the pencil on Saturday," in English.

You also have an opportunity to use the words "with the" in this practice drill. With is "con" in Spanish, which is pronounced "cone." For instance, you could say, "El necesita estudiar cone el profesor en viernes." This is, "He needs to study with the teacher on Friday," in English. A helpful tip is to remember that the days of the week are all masculine.

You could also practice shorter sentences such as, "Yo necesito visitar la escuela." This means, "I need to visit the school," in English. Another possibility is "Abren la escuela en septiembre." This is, "They open the school in September." Use as many of these words as possible during your practice. If you are not sure of all of the words go back and review them briefly until you know them well. You will continue to have to use "**el**" or "**la**" and "**un**" and "**una**" depending on whether the noun is **masculine** or **feminine**. It would also be good practice for you to use "**los**" or "**las**" and make the words **plural**. You could use some more practice using the plural form of the definite article. Practice using all forms of the verb "can" with as many words as possible. You can never practice too much.

Another principle must be discussed before you begin this practice drill. You must use "a" before a person when the person is a direct object in the sentence. For instance, you would not say, "Necesito llamar la policía," instead you must say, "Necesito llamar a la policía." In the case of a masculine noun "a el" would be contracted to be "**al**" as you have already learned.

As has already been stated several times, these practice drills are vital for your progress and success. You must participate in all of them to advance your skills. Practice makes perfect. You will be able to hear several of these sentences spoken by a Spanish-speaking person on Dr. Memory's™ web site. By listening to a Spanish-speaking person you will better understand Spanish vocal tendencies. Remember that "in" and "at" are "en" in Spanish, and "to" is "a".

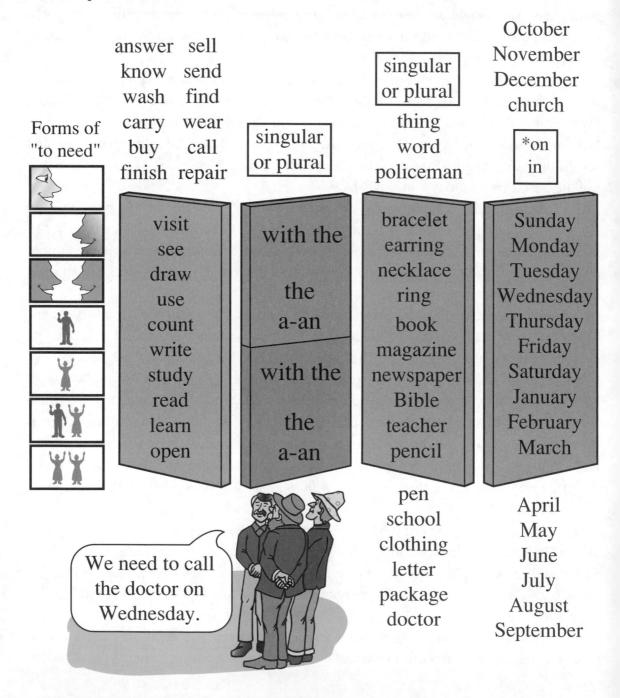

Home

The next category of words you will learn is words relating to the **home**. This category includes rooms in a home, appliances found in a home and other items that might be found around a home. As with all categories, these words will be taught in alphabetical order. Rooms will be taught first. A swimming pool is included in this grouping. Although it isn't a room it is found around the home and had to be put someplace. Appliances and items around the home will follow. There are 25 words in this category.

Make sure to study each vocabulary word picture until you can easily recreate it in your mind and say the Spanish equivalent when thinking of the English word before going to the next word.

You have been told several times to make sure to review all of the words regularly. Having **a little bit of discipline** in this fashion will pay big rewards. The reward far surpasses the small investment of time required for these reviews.

bathroom - **baño**
bah - nyoh

Bah, nyoh **onion should wash me in the** bathroom.

A baby lamb says, "Bah," while taking a bath in a bathroom. An onion (ny) wearing overalls is washing the little lamb.

bedroom - **dormitorio**
door - me - tore - ee - oh

Door me, that meteor tore me up. Oh, the bedroom will be a mess.

This bedroom is a disaster area.

Oh!

A door to a bedroom was struck by a meteor. The meteor tore a hole in the door and hit an eagle. The eagle yelled, "Oh." The sign reads, "This bedroom is a disaster area." This word also means "dormitory" and is taught elsewhere.

dining room - comedor
co - may - dohr

A cobra sees a maid after coming through a door into a dining room. A plaque on the wall reads, "Dining Room."

garage - garaje
gah - rah - hay

Goggles are worn by the robin that is pulling a stack of hay into the garage. The garage door fell and hit it on the head.

kitchen - cocina
co - sea - nah

A cobra accidentally sprays a seahorse with a nozzle while washing down a kitchen. The seahorse says, "We are the kitchen police."

living room - sala
sah - lah

A soccer ball is kicked into a living room by a lobster. The framed sign above the living room reads, " The living room is the place to live."

room - cuarto
coo - ahr - toe

A Room with a View

Ladies' Room

Men's Room

Room for Rent

Coo, I love a room full of art, especially totem art.

kwar

A cooing dove is enjoying a room full of art. It especially likes the painting of the totem pole. Some of the art on the wall is unusual signs. One reads, "Room for rent." Another reads, "A room with a view." Another reads, "Ladies' room," and one, "Men's room."

swimming pool - piscina
pea - sea - nah

Peace on earth and plenty of seahorse, swimming pool, egg nog this holiday.

Swimming Pool Filled with the Holiday Spirit

Egg Nog

Egg Nog

Egg Nog

Egg Nog

A pea threw a seahorse into a swimming pool with egg nog cartons all around it. The sign reads, "Swimming pool filled with the holiday spirit." The seahorse says, "Peace on earth and plenty of seahorse, swimming pool, egg nog this holiday."

bed - cama
cah - mah

Ah

Ah

Ah

Ah

Comma Ah Bed for Sale

A large comma punctuation mark is on a tongue depressor, ah, four-poster bed. Some people pronounce "comma" as "cah-mah," but some as "cah-muh," thus the tongue depressors to make sure you pronounce it with the "ah" sound.

bottle - botella
bow - tay - yah

A bow tie is normal for a taper on a bottled yacht.

Bottled Up

A bow tie is worn by the taper on the yacht. It is throwing bottles with messages in them into the sea, because the yacht is stranded. The name of the yacht is "Bottled Up." Notice the bottles lining the deck of the yacht.

chair - silla
sea - yah

Charlie's Chairs

Yacht

Sea

Won't you please take a chair.

A large chair in front of a chair store has a sea on it, and a yacht is floating on the sea. The sign reads, "Won't you please take a chair."

clock & watch - reloj
ray - low

Captain Clock's Clock Shop

Don't work around the clock.

Rays and locusts love to set clocks and watches.

A manta ray and a locust are resetting a clock in a clock shop. The sign reads, "Don't work around the clock."

cup - taza
tah - sah

Cup your hands and play a cup.

This cup makes a great tom-tom at soccer practice.

An upside down cup is being used as a tom-tom by a soccer ball. The sign reads, "Cup your hands and play a cup."

dish - plato
plah - toe

Dizzy's Dishes

Did you ever plop a tomato on a dish?

Plop

Can you dish it out?

A plopping sound was made by a tomato that was slapped by a dish. The sign reads, "Can you dish it out?" The dish asks, "Did you ever plop a tomato on a dish?"

flower - flor
flohr

A beautiful flower is growing in the middle of a tile floor. The sign reads, "The latest in flower floors." This word does not sound exactly like floor, but it does sound like floor if the "oo" sound is shorter and quicker.

fork - tenedor
tehn - ay - door

An octopus used a tentacle to throw a fork at an ape that is running away. Luckily the fork missed the ape and stuck in a door. The sign reads, "Watch out for flying forks."

glass - vaso
vah - sew

A vaudeville routine is being performed on a large upside down glass by a bar of soap. Notice the "Vaudeville Soapy" sign on stage. The bar of soap is juggling glasses during its act.

knife - cuchillo
coo - chee - yo

A cooing dove uses a knife to cut a piece of cheese on a large yo-yo. Another knife is on the ground. The dove thinks he is Rocky.

magazine - revista
ray - vees - tah

Maggie's Magazines

This ray had a Visa card and a tomahawk fall from its magazine.

Rays

VISA

A manta ray in front of a magazine stand shook a magazine. A Visa card and a tomahawk fell from the magazine. The first three letters in "visa" are combined and run together for the "vees" sound.

napkin - servilleta
sair - vee - yeah - tah

Does Sarah Vee have to yell, "Yeah," and wave her napkin, Mr. Tomahawk?

Sarah

Napkin Nonsense

V

A girl named Sarah Vee is seated at a table with a letter "V" on it. She is waving her napkin and screaming, "Yeah," very loudly at a tomahawk waiter. Her companion is trying to calm the situation. The sign reads, "Napkin nonsense."

party - fiesta
fee - ehs - tah

The feet of that Eskimo sure top off this party.

Party Time

The feet of an Eskimo are huge and talented. He uses them to spin a top at a party. The man says, "The feet of that Eskimo sure top off this party." The sign reads, "Party time."

radio - radio
rah - dee - oh

Rockin' demons love to listen to the Olympics on the radio.

RADIO

Radio's Demon Dandies

A rocker is the resting place for a demon listening to the Olympics on a radio. It says, "Rockin' demons love to listen to the Olympics on the radio. The sign reads, "Radio's demon dandies."

refrigerator - refrigerador
ray - free - hair - ah - door

"Rays love free refrigerator food, but hairy, ah doors kind of spoil it."

Free Food

Ah

A manta ray looks into a refrigerator. A "Free Food" sign is near the hairy tongue depressor, ah, **on the** door. The ray says, "Rays love free refrigerator food, but hairy, ah doors kind of spoil it."

spoon - cuchara
coo - cha - rah

"Coo, cha-cha, rah-rah, Mr. Spoon!"

"Rah-rah!"

I was spoon fed.

A cooing dove and a spoon are doing the cha-cha. The spoon waves a pompom, and the dove says, "Coo, cha-cha, rah-rah, Mr. Spoon," as they dance. The sign reads, "I was spoon fed."

stove - estufa
ehs - two - fah

"That Eskimo bought two stoves, and this fox has to carry one of them."

An Eskimo with a number two on him and a fox are each carrying a stove. The fox says, "That Eskimo bought two stoves, and this fox has to carry one of them."

table - mesa
may - sah

"This maid wants this flying saucer off of this table."

Maid

We turned the tables on you.

A maid reaches for a flying saucer that swooped down and landed on a table. The exhaust from the flying saucer turned two other tables over as it landed. The sign reads, "We turned the tables on you."

television - televisión
tay - lay - vee - sea - own

A tailor is measuring the laces in a V-neck sweater in front of his television. Water from a sea scene on the television flows out of the screen. The tailor says, "Sometimes I wish I didn't own a real life experience television."

thing - cosa
co - sah

A cobra snaps a sock at a "Thing." The "Thing" is a character created by Dr. Memory" to picture the word "Thing." The sign reads, "A thing of beauty."

Seasons

The next category of words you will learn is **seasons**. Obviously, this category only includes four words, since there are only four seasons.

Make sure to study each vocabulary word picture until you can easily recreate it in your mind and say the Spanish equivalent when thinking of the English word before going to the next word.

autumn - otoño
oh - toe - nyoh

Oh, my toes are nyoh comparison to autumn colors.

A man wearing overalls wiggles his toes in autumn leaves while watching a painter. An onion in overalls (nyoh) is painting a picture of autumn leaves. The man comments on his feeling for autumn.

spring - primavera
pre - mah - vair - ah

I love to eat pasta primavera in the spring.

Big Spring Sale

Spring is in the air.

The man says, "I love to eat pasta primavera in the spring." The ad on the television reads, "Big spring sale." The sign reads, "Spring is in the air." Pasta primavera is an Italian dish. Make sure to pronounce the letter "a's" with an "ah" sound instead of the "uh" sound as in primavera.

summer - verano
vair - ah - no

Various animals, ah, got off of Noah's Ark in the summer.

Varicose veins are worse in the summer.

Noah's Ark

Ah

Summer Festival

Varicose veins are on the tongue depressor (ah) leaning against Noah's ark. A voice from the ark says, "Various animals, ah, got off of Noah's Ark in the summer." The tongue depressor says, "Varicose veins are worse in the summer."

winter - invierno
een - vee - air - no

This teen in his "V" hates cold winter air. No, it's not fun.

Winter sports are fun.

Noah's Ark

A teenager wearing a V-neck sweater braces himself against a blast of air from Old Man Winter. The winter blast has frozen Noah's Ark to the ground. The sign reads, "Winter sports are fun."

Directions

The next category of words you will learn is **direction** words. There are six words in this category.

Make sure to study each vocabulary word picture until you can easily recreate it in your mind and say the Spanish equivalent when thinking of the English word before going to the next word. The reward far surpasses the small investment of time required for these reviews.

above, up & upstairs - arriba
ah - ree - bah

A tongue depressor (ah) is leaning against a reward poster up above the male bobcat. The bobcat says, "Ah, I'll read about Bob, the thief above." A female bobcat up above in the tree pokes her head out and yells, "Go all the way up." The sign reads, "Orders from above."

down, below & downstairs - abajo
ah - bah - hoe

A tongue depressor (ah) walks toward a flight of steps to go downstairs. A bottle and a hoe are already down. The tongue depressor says, "I'm on my way down. I'll be downstairs **soon**." The sign reads, "Down below."

left - izquierda
eas - key - air - dah

An Easter basket has a large chocolate key in it. An Airedale dog is protecting the basket. A Doctor is holding out his left hand. They are in left field on a baseball field. "Lefty" is on the mound. The sign reads, "Lefty is warming up."

right - derecha	straight - derecho
day - ray - cha	day - ray - cho

This daisy's ray gun causes right hand chops.

Ah, just right!

Keep to the right.

This daisy's manta ray **needs to be** choked straight away.

Oh, that won't straighten me out.

Straighter is better.

A daisy shot a ray gun at a man and caused him to karate chop with his right hand. The sign reads, "Keep to the right." The man says, "Ah," to remind you that right ends with a letter "a."

A daisy is mad at a manta ray, **so it** choked it straight away. The sign reads, "Straighter is better." The manta says, "Oh," to remind you that straight ends with a letter "o."

Conjugation of "To Want"

The fifth listing will be the conjugation for the regular verb "to want" which is "quer**er**." Since this is an "**er**" or "**air**" verb the endings follow the "**er**" conjugation pattern. The subject pronouns will not be listed in the phonetic pronunciations, since you already know how to pronounce them.

English	Spanish	Phonetic Pronunciation
I want	yo quiero	key - arrow
You want	usted quiere	key – air - ay
We want	nosotros queremos	kay – ray - mohs
He wants	él quiere	key – air - ay
She wants	ella quiere	key – air - ay
They want	ellos quienen	key – ehn - ehn

When you examine this conjugation you will notice that the "you," "he" and "she" forms are all the same as always. **The Identifier Detective** pointed this out to you earlier. You will also notice that "we" and "they" follow the basic pattern you learned for regular verbs. "We" has an "emos" ending, and "they" has an "en" ending. The "mos" and "n" endings follow the basic pattern. Although you have already practiced the "yo" form of "yo quiero" with other infinitives it will still be included in the upcoming drill. You haven't practiced using it with full sentences yet.

When you are sure you know these verb forms you can practice using them with Spanish infinitives in the upcoming drill. In this drill you should first speak compound verb phrases as you did before with the other verb forms. You will then be able to speak complete sentences that begin with the verb phrases and end with the words from the "home," "seasons" and "directions" categories. You may not be able to use all of the infinitives with each form, because they may not make sense, but use as many as you can in this very important practice drill.

The various forms will be represented by boxes on the left side of the page as before. You will select a verb form on the left and say it with an infinitive on the first door. For instance, you could say, "Yo quiero usar." This is, "I want to use," in English. You should practice speaking verb phrases of all of the forms first. After you have practiced with the infinitives on the door expand your practice by using the infinitives listed above and below the door.

After you have practiced with verb phrases you can practice complete sentences by using the other words listed on the page. For instance, you could say, "Yo quiero usar la cuchara en la cocina." This is, "I want to use the spoon in the kitchen," in English. You also might say, "Nosotros queremos ir a la piscina en el verano." This is, "We want to go to the swimming pool in the summer."

Use as many of these words as possible during your practice. If you are not sure of all of the words go back and review them briefly until you know them well. You will continue to have to use "**el**" or "**la**" and "**un**" and "**una**" depending on whether the noun is **masculine** or **feminine**. It would also be good practice for you to use "**los**" or "**las**" and make the words **plural**. You could use some more practice using the plural form of the definite article. Practice using all forms of the verb "can" with as many words as possible. You can never practice too much.

As has already been stated several times, these practice drills are vital for your progress and success. You must participate in all of them to advance your skills. Practice makes perfect. You will be able to hear several of these sentences spoken by a Spanish-speaking person on Dr. Memory's™ web site. By listening to a Spanish-speaking person you will better understand Spanish vocal tendencies. Remember that "in" and "on" are "en" in Spanish, and "to" is "a". You must also know that "from" is "de," which is pronounced "day."

An asterisk mark precedes the words "*to the" in the practice drill to remind you to use "**al**" with masculine nouns.

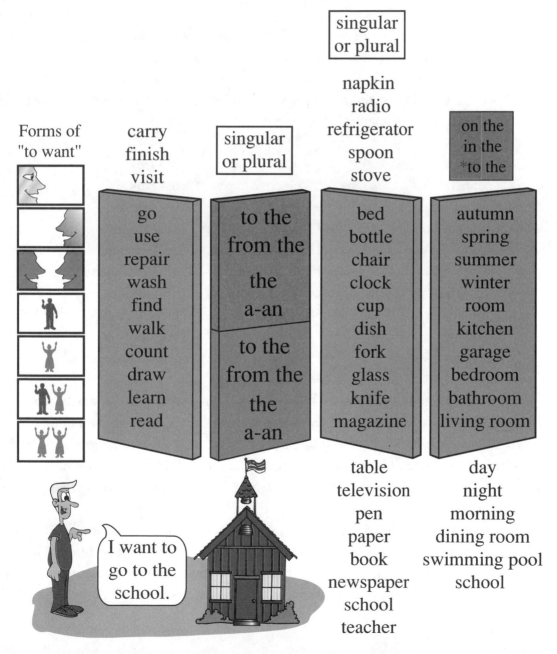

Forms of "to want"	carry finish visit	singular or plural	singular or plural napkin radio refrigerator spoon stove	on the in the *to the
	go use repair wash find walk count draw learn read	to the from the the a-an / to the from the the a-an	bed bottle chair clock cup dish fork glass knife magazine	autumn spring summer winter room kitchen garage bedroom bathroom living room
			table television pen paper book newspaper school teacher	day night morning dining room swimming pool school

I want to go to the school.

For your information you can make any of these sentences, and other sentences with these important verbs, negative by simply putting "no" before the verb. You can also turn any statement into a question by simply inflecting your voice at the end of the sentence.

Numbers

The next category of words you will learn is **numbers**. This category includes 30 number words. The basic numbers needed for Spanish survival are in this list. More complex numbers will be taught in Dr. Memory's™ comprehensive Spanish course.

Below is a listing of the numbers you will learn in this category. The Spanish equivalent is listed next to each number.

1 - uno	2 - dos	3 – tres
4 - cuatro	5 - cinco	6 – seis
7 - siete	8 - ocho	9 – nueve
10 - diez	11 - once	12 – doce
13 - trece	14 - catorce	15 – quince
16 – dieciseis	17 – diecisiete	18 – dieciocho
19 – diecinueve	20 - veinte	30 – treinta
40 - cuarenta	50 - cincuenta	60 – sesenta
70 - setenta	80 - ochenta	90 – noventa
100 - cien	1,000 - mil	Dozen – docena

Make sure to study each vocabulary word picture until you can easily recreate it in your mind and say the Spanish equivalent when thinking of the English number before going to the next word. The reward far surpasses the small investment of time required for these reviews. Take plenty of time with these pictures. There are a lot of them, and they are very important for your needs. Know all of these numbers well before going on to the next category.

No pictures are needed for 16, 17, 18 and 19. The number 16 used to be diez y seis, which is 10 and 6. You will learn those numbers in the upcoming pictures. The numbers 17, 18 and 19 follow the same pattern The new spellings for 16, 17, 18 and 19 are listed above. These spellings mean the same thing as diez y seis, which is 10 and 6, for example.

one (1) - uno
ooh - no

I'm glad the number one runner has no ooze from his big nose.

One is the loneliest number.

A person with a number one (1) on his jersey won a race. He held up one finger as he crossed the finish line. It must have been a long race, because something is oozing out of his shoes. Notice his big nose. The sign reads, "One is the loneliest number."

two (2) - dos
dohs

It takes two doses to tango.

Two Doses

Two Doses

Two for the Show

Two doses of medicine with number two's on them are doing the tango, because it takes two to tango. The sign reads, "Two for the show." One bottle says, "It takes two doses to tango."

three (3) - tres
trace

Number threes love to trace.

A number three is tracing on three pieces of tracing paper on a three-legged table. It is seated on a three-legged stool. Notice that the number three is wearing 3-D glasses to help it see to trace better.

four (4) - cuatro
coo - ah - tro

kwah

Kumquats and trolls love four fireworks on Fourth Street.

Fourth St.

A kumquat and a troll holding up four fingers are going to watch four fireworks on the Fourth of July on Fourth Street. Notice the four-leaf clover near their feet.

five (5) - cinco
scene - co

These five scenes by a cobra are scenesational.

Five and Dime

Five mountain scenes were drawn by a cobra with its flicking tongue. A number five is on the cobra. The sign reads, "Five and Dime."

six (6) - seis
sace

That S-ace will get you a load of this six shooter.

A six shooter was pulled out of the holster of one of the six cowboys who were playing cards. He saw a letter "S" on the ace that one of the players had up his sleeve.

seven (7) - siete
sea - ay - tay

Seventh Heaven

The 7-up sea has an ape from a table in it.

Sea

A sea of 7-Up has a toy ape with a seven on it floating in it. Notice all of the empty 7-Up cans that filled the sea. As you can see the ape fell off of a table in the seventh heaven and fell into the 7-Up sea.

eight (8) - ocho
oh - cho

Oh, this eight ball is all choked up.

Eight is not enough.

Overalls are worn by an eight ball with a choke chain around its neck. Another eight ball is connected to the choke chain. The eight ball says, "Oh, this eight ball is all choked up."

nine (9) - nueve
new - ay - vay

I'm learning a nway to get a nine vase spare.

nway

Dressed to the Nines

A gnu with a number nine on it is trying to get a spare in bowling. An ape gets a close look and makes a comment. Notice that the bowling pins are nine vases instead of bowling pins.

ten (10) - diez
dee - ehs

The Ten Commandments

Dee, the Eskimo, knows all ten.

Dee is the name of the female Eskimo who is teaching the Ten Commandments to children in a Sunday School class. She is holding up ten fingers denoting the number of commandments. The words, "The Ten Commandments," are written on the wall.

eleven (11) - once
ohn - say

Eleven o'clock and all is well. This phone could save the world.

11 12
9   3
Eleven
6

Eleven

Eleven red phones are just outside the oval office. A sailor is reaching for one of them for the president. He will need to use one of them at the eleventh hour to stop a disaster. The word eleven is on the clock and the counter.

twelve (12) - doce
doe - say

Twelve donuts for a sailor make a nice breakfast.

A year has twelve months.

Twelve donuts are on the table in front of a sailor. The sailor says, "Twelve donuts for a sailor make a nice breakfast." The sign reads, "A year has twelve months."

thirteen - trece
tray - say

I'm thirteen years old.

The tray this sailor is holding has thirteen gallons of water on it.

Thirteen isn't unlucky.

A tray with thirteen gallons of water on it is held by a sailor. The sailor says, "The tray this sailor is holding has thirteen gallons of water on it." The water bottle says, "I'm thirteen years old."

fourteen - catorce
cah - tore - say

It's fourteen hundred hours.

I cahed and tore that sailor's towel fourteen times.

A cahing crow tore a sailor's towel at fourteen hundred hours in military time. The crow says, "I cahed and tore that sailor's towel fourteen times." A number fourteen is on the clock.

fifteen - quince
keen - say

This fifteen pound skein of yarn has been owned by this sailor since I was fifteen.

Skein Sailor Desk

A fifteen pound skein of yarn is on the desk in front of a sailor. The sailor says, "This fifteen pound skein of yarn has been owned by this sailor since I was fifteen."

twenty - veinte
vane- tay

I thought we twin tea bags had 20/20 vision.

Yeah, but that looks like a weather vane on the table to me.

Twin tea bags are discussing the weather vane It on the table, One twin tea bag says, "I thought we twin tea bags had 20/20 vision." The other one replies, "Yeah, but that looks like a weather vane on the table to me."

thirty - treinta
train- tah

Even though I've been retired thirty years, I still play with my train and my top.

Thirty Years and Still Counting

The train engineer has been retired thirty years. He says, "Even though I've been retired thirty years, I still play with my train and my top." The sign reads, "Thirty years and still counting."

forty - cuarenta
coo - ah - rehn - tah

kwah

We're ten, so that makes us forty together.

These quads rented top hats for our forty year celebration.

Quadrental Top Hats - Forty Cents

A set of quadruplets are celebrating their tenth birthday, so they have forty years among them. One quad says, "These quads rented top hats for our forty year celebration." The sign reads, "Quadrental top hats - forty cents."

fifty - cincuenta
scene - coo - ehn - tah

kwehn

That scene is about fifty-fifty on these quints top fifty list.

A mountain scene is being enjoyed by a set of quintuplets. A toy top with a number fifty on it is in the scene. One boy says, "That scene is about fifty-fifty on these quints top fifty list."

sixty - sesenta
say - sehn - tah

Tacos - Sixty Cents

This sailor paid sixty cents for this taco.

A sailor was sent to by sixty tacos by his commanding officer. He says, "This sailor paid sixty cents for this taco."

seventy - setenta
say - tehn - tah

This sailor crushed the tent with the tomahawk, but it took seventy swings.

A sailor took seventy swings to crush the tent with a tomahawk. The reason it was so difficult is that the tent has seventy layers of waterproofing.

eighty - ochenta
oh - chehn - tah

This old chain engineer can still be on top even though I'm eighty.

Spin Limit
80 Miles
Per Hour

Overalls are worn by an eighty year old. A chain is in front of him. He is a retired train engineer. He used the chain to spin a toy top. The sign reads, "Spin limit 80 miles per hour."

ninety - noventa
no - vehn - tah

No, the ninety mile per hour wind from that vent blew the topping from my cake.

May you have ninety more.

A chef just finished baking a birthday cake for a ninety year old, but disaster struck. The chef says, "No, the ninety mile per hour wind from that vent blew the topping from my cake."

hundred - cien
sea - ehn

Anyone can see that this engineer is one hundred years old.

How old are you?

A
Hundred
Percent

A sea horse asks an old train engineer, "How old are you?" The old man answers, "Anyone can see that this engineer is one hundred years old." The sign reads, "A hundred percent."

The man says, "They can't possibly serve a thousand meals a day." The sign on the restaurant reads, "Over 1,000 meals served per day."

A donut is held up by a sailor who is standing in front of a knot. He says, "Donuts, sailors do not want a dozen."

Time of Day

The next category of words you will learn is **time of day** words. These words are not an actual time such as three o'clock but words like "morning" and "afternoon." There are 11 words in this category.

Make sure to study each vocabulary word picture until you can easily recreate it in your mind and say the Spanish equivalent when thinking of the English word before going to the next word. The reward far surpasses the small investment of time required for these reviews.

afternoon & late - tarde
tahr - day

"We're having tarts late in the afternoon, Miss Daisy."

Tarts are being eaten at an afternoon tea party. Daisies are on the table cloth. One lady says, "We're having tarts late in the afternoon, Miss Daisy."

day - día
dee - ah

"Demons hate the day, ah, there is too much light."

Ah

Day in and Day Out

A demon holds up a tongue depressor (ah) to try to block the sun from hitting it. The demon says, "Demons hate the day, ah, there is too much light." The sign reads, "Day in and day out."

evening & night - noche
no - chay

"No, my evening gown!"

"I love a chase at night."

This evening will make a great night.

A girl in an evening gown says, "No, my evening gown," to a boy who is chasing her with a water pistol. As you can see it is night. The sign reads, "This evening will make a great night."

hour - hora
oar - ah

"What hour is it?"

Ah

"My oar and my ah say it is after hours!"

An oar and a tongue depressor (ah) are the hands on a clock. They are on the hour of three o'clock. An hourglass looking at the clock asks, "What hour is it?" The clock replies, "My oar and my ah say it is after hours!"

An Amish man looks at the yukky stuff below as he flies an airplane. He says, "Ah, I past that same yukky air yesterday." The name of the airlines is "Yesterday Airlines." The sign on the ground reads, "I did it yesterday."

Adverbs

The next category of words you will learn is **adverbs**. If you are going to be asked questions you will have to know adverbs for the answers. There are 23 words in this category. Make sure to study each vocabulary word picture until you can easily recreate it in your mind and say the Spanish equivalent when thinking of the English word before going to the next word. Make sure to follow the normal review process. You will not use some of these words in a drill until much later, but you should learn them all now anyway. The reward far surpasses the small investment of time required for these reviews.

afterwards & later - despu s
dehs - poo - ehs

pwace

It's later than I thought. A desert is a terrible pwace to be lost.

I'll see you afterwards.

An ace from a deck of cards is lost in a desert. It says, "It's later than I thought. A desert is a terrible pwace to be lost." It has a lisp and said "pwace" instead of "place."

almost - casi
cah - sea

The Collie almost made it, but it fell into the sea.

The

Sea

A Collie dog tried to jump on a ship that was pulling away from a dock. It almost made it but hit the back of the ship and is sliding down into the sea. The name of the ship is "The Almost." An onlooker says, "The Collie almost made it, but it fell into the sea."

always & forever - siempre
sea - ehm - pray

Do you see this emery board flying. Pray forever.

Always and forever

The seesaw has an emery board and a praying mantis on it. The emery board says, "Do you see this emery board flying. Pray forever." The song playing on the radio is "Always and forever."

during - durante
dew - rahn - tay

I will duel you, Ron. This tailor will measure up during the duel.

I'm Ron.

No Noise During Duels

A duel is about to take place. A man named Ron and a tailor have a dispute to settle. Ron shamed the tailor during a sewing contest. The tailor says, "I will duel you, Ron. This tailor will measure up during the duel."

generally - generalmente
hehn - air - ahl - mehn - tay

Hen air on an all-star generally blows the menu off of the table.

A hen directs the air from an air compressor on an all-star basketball player. A menu is on the table in the restaurant. The hen comments on the situation. General Lee is the waiter to help remind you of the word "generally."

here - aquí
ah - key

This ostrich wants you to come here, Mr. Key.

Here is the place.

An ostrich speaks to a key. It says, "This ostrich wants you to come here, Mr. Key," as it points to the "here" spot. The sign reads, "Here is the place."

how much - ¿cuánto?
coo - ahn - toe

A dove kwahns to buy the stone, Mr. Toe. For how much?

For how much?

A cooing dove wants to buy an onyx stone. The salesman is a toe. The dove asks, "A dove kwahns to buy the stone, Mr. Toe. For how much?" The toe repeats, "For how much," as though it is trying to arrive at a price.

less - menos
may - nohs

May, my nohs hurts less than it did yesterday.

Don't take less.

A majorette named May hit her boyfriend in the nose, no less, the last time he came to visit. She is about to do it again. He says, "May, my nohs hurts less than it did yesterday." He can't pronounce "nose" properly, because of the bandage on his nose. He says, "Nohs."

more - más
mahs

The lady is collecting moss. She says, "I always want more and more moss." One sign reads, "The more moss the merrier." Another sign reads, "And what's more."

never - nunca
noon - cah

At noon the cahing crow says, "It's noon, and I never cah before noon." One sign reads, "Never, never cah before noon." The other sign reads, "Never say never."

now - ahora
ah - oar - ah

An Amish man is in an aerobics class. An oar is held by an Amish woman in the class. The instructor asks, "Amish or Amish, are you ready now?" The sign reads, "Now I am committed to aerobics." Another reads, "Do it now."

quickly, rapidly & fast - rápido
rah - pea - doe

A fast cheerleader is cheering quickly. The peanut says, "For cheering, "Rah," rapidly, this peanut will give you a donut." The sign reads, "Don't live the fast life."

Conjugation of "To Know"

The sixth listing will be the conjugation for the regular verb "to know" which is "sab**er**." Since this is an "**er**" or "**air**" verb the endings follow the "**er**" conjugation pattern. The subject pronouns will not be listed in the phonetic pronunciations, since you already know how to pronounce them.

English	Spanish	Phonetic Pronunciation
I know	yo sé	say
You know	usted sabe	sah - bay
We know	nosotros sabemos	sah – bay - mohs
He knows	él sabe	sah - bay
She knows	ella sabe	sah - bay
They know	ellos saben	sah – behn

When you examine this conjugation you will notice that the "you," "he" and "she" forms are all the same as always. **The Identifier Detective** pointed this out to you earlier. You will also notice that "we" and "they" follow the basic pattern you learned for regular verbs. "We" has an "emos" ending, and "they" has an "en" ending. The "emos" and "en" endings follow the basic pattern. Although you have already practiced the "yo" form of "yo sé" with other infinitives it will still be included in the upcoming drill. You have not practiced using it with full sentences yet.

When you are sure you know these verb forms you can practice using them with Spanish infinitives in the upcoming drill. In this drill you should first speak compound verb phrases as you did before with the other verb forms. You will then be able to speak complete sentences that begin with the verb phrases and end with the words from the "numbers" and "time of day" categories. You won't be able to use all of the infinitives with each form, because they won't make sense, but use as many as you can in this very important practice drill.

The various forms will be represented by boxes on the left side of the page as before. You will select a verb form on the left and say it with an infinitive on the first door. For instance, you could say, "Ella sabe visitar." This is, "She knows how to visit," in English. You should practice speaking verb phrases of all of the forms first. After you have practiced with the infinitives on the door expand your practice by using the infinitives listed above and below the door.

After you have practiced with verb phrases you can practice complete sentences by using the other words listed on the page. Choose a verb form from the left of the page to go with a verb listed on the first door. Then choose a number from the next door to go with a noun on the next door. Then select a word or words from the blue and pink door and finish the sentence with a word from the door below. You can also finish the sentence with one of the words to the right of the door below. For instance, you could say, "Sabemos leer ocho libros en un día." In English this is, "We know how to read eight books in a day." You can also skip a door if you so desire, if the sentence will make sense. You could also say, "Yo sé escribir diez cartas en dos horas." In English this is, "I know how to write ten letters in two hours."

Use as many of these words as possible during your practice. If you are not sure of all of the words go back and review them briefly until you know them well. You will continue to have to use "**el**" or "**la**" and "**un**" and "**una**" depending on whether the noun is **masculine** or **feminine**. It would also be good practice for you to use "**los**" or "**las**" and make the words **plural**. You could use some more practice using the plural form of the definite article. Practice using all forms of the verb "can" with as many words as possible. You can never practice too much.

As has already been stated several times, these practice drills are vital for your progress and success. You must participate in all of them to advance your skills. Practice makes perfect. You will be able to hear several of these sentences spoken by a Spanish-speaking person on Dr. Memory's™ web site. By listening to a Spanish-speaking person you will better understand Spanish vocal tendencies. Remember that "in" and "at" are "en" in Spanish, and "to" is "a".

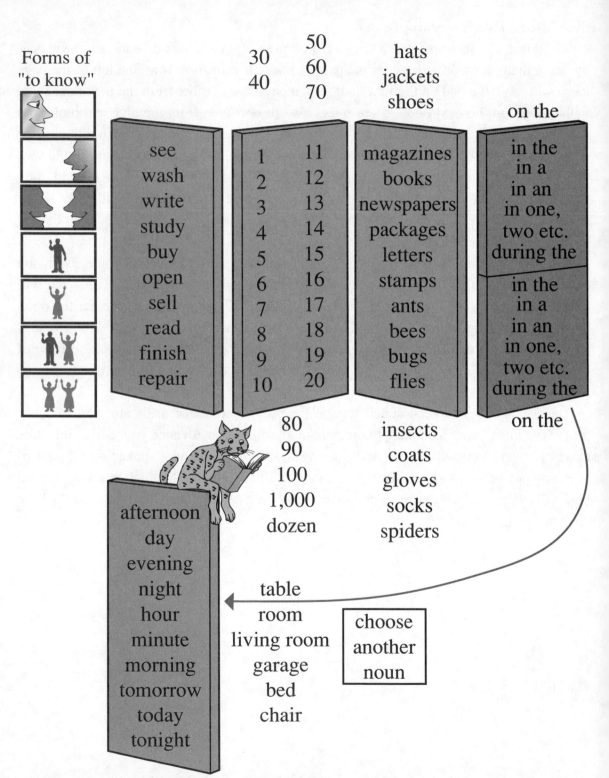

Forms of "to know"

see
wash
write
study
buy
open
sell
read
finish
repair

30	50
40	60
	70

1	11
2	12
3	13
4	14
5	15
6	16
7	17
8	18
9	19
10	20

80
90
100
1,000
dozen

hats
jackets
shoes

magazines
books
newspapers
packages
letters
stamps
ants
bees
bugs
flies

insects
coats
gloves
socks
spiders

on the
in the
in a
in an
in one,
two etc.
during the

in the
in a
in an
in one,
two etc.
during the

on the

afternoon
day
evening
night
hour
minute
morning
tomorrow
today
tonight

table
room
living room
garage
bed
chair

choose
another
noun

Restaurant

The next category of words you will learn is **restaurant** words. There are only four words in this category, but many food words and other words you have already learned will be used in a restaurant.

Make sure to study each vocabulary word picture until you can easily recreate it in your mind and say the Spanish equivalent when thinking of the English word before going to the next word. The reward far surpasses the small investment of time required for these reviews.

bill & check - **cuenta**
coo - ehn - tah

kwehn

"Kwehn will I pay this bill. Check out this tomahawk."

Bill

Check | Encyclopedia

Not Happy, no Bill or Check

A man wearing a coonskin cap uses an encyclopedia as a cutting block to cut a bill and a check in half with a tomahawk. The food at the restaurant must have been pretty bad. The sign reads, "Not happy, no bill or check."

booth - **banca**
bahn - cah

"Your bonnet will make me cah when you get in the booth."

Only Two to a Booth

A lady wearing a bonnet is entering a booth as a crow waiter cahs. The sign reads, "Only two to a booth." The crow comments.

A maid and a gnu are looking at a large menu. The gnu says, "I wish the maid knew why they don't call a menu a womenu."

A pro golfer hits a tip to a peacock, because it was such a good caddy. Notice that the peacock is standing on a doorknob. The peacock says, "Pro golfers need to tip peacocks more money, not!"

Shopping

The next category of words you will learn is **shopping** words. There are seven words in this category.

Make sure to study each vocabulary word picture until you can easily recreate it in your mind and say the Spanish equivalent when thinking of the English word before going to the next word. The reward far surpasses the small investment of time required for these reviews.

cash & money - dinero
dee - nair - oh

Demons shoot "N" air on overalls to get money, money, cash, cash, cash.

Out of Pocket Cash

A demon has a letter "N" on the air pump it is using to pump cash out of the pockets of a pair of overalls. The demon comments on his love for money and cash. The sign reads, "Out of pocket cash."

cent - centavo
sehn - tah - voh

Centipedes use tomahawks and Vogue mags to be cent centilating.

I don't have half a cent to my name.

A centipede uses a tomahawk to cut a cent in half. It placed the cent on a Vogue magazine so it wouldn't cut the table. The sign reads, "I don't have half a cent to my name."

coin - moneda
moe - nay - dah

Three Coins in a Fountain

This Mohawked neighing horse will catch that domino's coins.

A Mohawk haircut is on a neighing horse that is trying to catch three coins that were thrown toward a fountain by a large domino. The sign reads, "Three coins in a fountain."

to cost - costar
co - stahr

What is the cost of this coat? I'm a star, you know.

I'll sell it to you at cost.

Buy at any cost.

A coat is held by a Hollywood star. She asks, "What is the cost of this coat? I'm a star, you know." The sales clerk replies, "I'll sell it to you at cost." The sign reads, "Buy at any cost."

client & customer - cliente
clee - ehn - tay

dollar - dólar
doe - lahr

Since I'm your client, do cleats look good on an engineer, Mr. Tailor?

The customer is king.

I'm no do-do when it comes to large dollars.

This client measures up.

A dollar saved is a dollar earned.

Lard

A shoe with cleats is held by a train engineer who is being measured for a new uniform by a tailor. The tailor says, "The customer is king." The sign reads, "This client measures up."

A do-do bird is about to stick a dollar into a can of lard for safe keeping. It says, "I'm no do-do when it comes to large dollars." The sign reads, "A dollar saved is a dollar earned."

Conjugation of "To Like"

The last important verb listing will be the conjugation for the irregular verb "to like," which is "gust**ar**." This is an "**ar**" or "**art**" verb, but the endings do not follow the normal "**ar**" conjugation pattern. **The subject pronouns are not used for this verb.**

English	Spanish	Phonetic Pronunciation
I like	Me gusta(n)	may – goose - tah(n)
You like	Le gusta(n)	lay – goose - tah(n)
We like	Nos gusta(n)	nohs – goose - tah(n)
He likes	Le gusta(n)	lay – goose - tah(n)
She likes	Le gusta(n)	lay – goose - tah(n)
They like	Les gusta(n)	lehs – goose - tah(n)

This verb has been saved for last, because it requires some special instruction for its use. When you examine this conjugation you will notice that the "you," "he" and "she" forms are all the same as always. **The Identifier Detective** pointed this out to you earlier. You will also notice that "we" and "they" do not follow the basic pattern you learned for regular verbs. As you can see in the above conjugation the verb form is always "gusta" or "gustan." The real difference with the conjugation of this verb is the word preceding the verb in each form. "Me" is used for "yo" and "le" is used for "you," "he" and "she." These three are always the same. "Nos" is used for "we" and "les" is used for "they." "Me" is pronounced "may." "Le" is pronounced "lay." "Nos" is pronounced "nohs," and "les" is pronounced "lace."

There are three important points that must be learned about this verb before you begin to practice with it. First you must understand the **direct object** concept. It was mentioned briefly earlier, but with this verb you need more detail. Whatever is the object of someone's like becomes the subject in Spanish. For instance, look at this sample sentence in English and Spanish. The words have been spread out, so the Spanish words come under the corresponding English words.

I   like   the flower.
Me   gusta   la   flor.

The singular word "**flower**" is the **direct object** in this sentence, because it is the object of my like or it is what I like. The first point Dr. Memory™ wants you to understand is that the number of **the direct object determines the verb form to be used**. It is backwards from English in this instance, because in English the subject normally determines the verb. In this case the word "flower" is **singular in number**, so **the verb has the singular ending** of "a." So then, the **direct object acts like the subject** in determining the verb form with the verb "to like" or "gustar."

Look at this sample sentence in English and Spanish. The words have been spread out, so the Spanish words come under the corresponding English words.

I   like   flowers.
Me   gustan   las flores.

The plural word "**flowers**" is the **direct object** in this sentence, because it is the object of my like or it is what I like. The number of **the direct object determines the**

verb form to be used. It is still backwards, because in English the subject normally determines the verb. In this case the word "**flowers**" is **plural in number**, so **the verb has the plural ending** of "**an**." So then, as has already been stated, the **direct object acts like the subject** in determining the verb form with the verb "to like" or "gustar."

Dr. Memory™ has a picture to help you better understand this concept. In the picture below you see the same two sample sentences that were just discussed. Unusual looking **sub**marines are above the direct objects in both sentences. Notice that the **sub**marine looks like an in**ject**ion syringe. This is Dr. Memory's™ picture for the word **subject**. The bold letters in the words "**sub**marine" and "in**ject**ion" spell out the word "**subject**." These special submarines are above the direct object in each sentence, because the direct object acts like the subject in determining the number of the verb.

You see only **one sub** above the **singular Spanish subject**. The serum in that sub is being squirted on the ending of the verb in the sample sentence with the **singular Spanish subject**. Only **one sub** is needed to squirt **one drop** from the **singular Spanish subject** on the **singular verb** ending, because it ends with a **single letter** "**a**." Only one sub and one drop signify a **singular Spanish subject** and a singular verb ending.

You see **two subs** above the **plural Spanish subject**. The serum in those subs is being squirted on the ending of the verb in the sample sentence with the **plural Spanish subject**. **Two subs** are needed to squirt **two drops** from the **plural Spanish subject** on the **plural verb** ending, because it ends with **two letters** which are "**an**." Two subs and two drops signify a **plural Spanish subject** and a plural verb ending.

Study the picture until you are sure you know this first important principle for the verb "gustar."

Direct Object
in English

Subject in Spanish

Me gusta la flor.

Direct Object
in English

Subject in Spanish

Me gustan las flores.

The second important point you must understand is the use of the **indirect object pronoun**. "Me," "le," "nos" and "les" are the **indirect object pronouns** that are used with "gustar." Indirect object pronouns are used all the time in Spanish, but you cannot always put your finger on them. In this case you can. You must use one of these **indirect object pronouns** when using the verb "gustar." It always precedes the verb in a sentence. Examine the upcoming sample English and Spanish sentences that show several uses of **indirect object pronouns.** The words have been spread out, so the Spanish words come under the corresponding English words.

What person you are talking about determines if you use "me," "le," "nos" or "les." The listing below shows the uses again. The **indirect object pronouns** are in red to make them stand out, and they have been separated from the verb form for even more emphasis.

English	Spanish	
I like	**Me**	gusta(**n**)
You like	**Le**	gusta(**n**)
We like	**Nos**	gusta(**n**)
He likes	**Le**	gusta(**n**)
She likes	**Le**	gusta(**n**)
They like	**Les**	gusta(**n**)

Examine this sample sentence. You have already seen it before, but it will be used to help teach this second important principle for the verb "gustar."

I	like	the flower.
Me	gusta	la flor.

Since this is the "yo" form of the verb "gustar" many students say, "Yo gusto la flor." This is a special verb, so the **indirect object pronoun** "me" must be used instead of "yo." The normal "o" ending for the "yo" form is not used with the verb "gustar." The ending is "**a**."

I	like	flowers.
Me	gus**tan**	las flores.

In this sample sentence "me" is still used instead of "yo." The verb ending is **"an"** in this case, because the **Spanish subject is plural**. You have already learned that unique principle for the verb "gustar" when you studied Dr. Memory's™ special submarines. In English this would be equivalent of saying, "Flowers like me," but the verb usage is correct in Spanish. "Gustar" is not the only verb in Spanish with these unique principles. But it is the only one you will use for survival Spanish.

We	like	the flower.		We	like	the flowers.
Nos	gus**ta**	la flor.		Nos	gus**tan**	las flores.

In these sample sentences "nos" is used instead of "nosostros." "Nos" is the **indirect object pronoun** for the "we" form of the verb "gustar." The verb ending is **"a"** with the **singular Spanish subject** and **"an"** with the **plural Spanish subject**. This principle never changes no matter what indirect object pronoun is being used in a sentence.

They	like	the flower.		They	like	the flowers.
Les	gus**ta**	la flor.		Les	gus**tan**	las flores.

In these sample sentences "les" is used instead of "ellas or ellos." "Les" is the **indirect object pronoun** for the "they" form of the verb "gustar." The verb ending is **"a"** with the **singular Spanish subject** and **"an"** with the **plural Spanish subject**.

Gustar Identifier

She	likes	the flower.		She	likes	the flowers.
A ella	le gus**ta**	la flor.		A ella	le gus**tan**	las flores.

In these sample sentences "le" is used instead of "ella." "Le" is the **indirect object pronoun** for the "you," "he" and "she" forms of the verb "gustar." It is also used with the "you" and "he" forms of the verb. The verb ending is **"a"** with the **singular Spanish subject** and **"an"** with the **plural Spanish subject**. This principle never changes no matter what indirect object pronoun is being used in a sentence.

There is one more important principle you must learn about the "le" forms of the verb "gustar." A **"clarifier,"** or what Dr. memory™ calls an **"identifier,"** must be used with the "le" forms of the verb "gustar."

Dr. Memory™ introduced you to the **Identifier Detective** earlier. He was examining the endings of the "you," "he" and "she" forms of the verb "visitar" at the time. He had to try to identify whether "you," "he" and "she" was the person being discussed.

With the verb "gustar" "A" is used at the beginning of the sentence to **"clarify"** or **"identify"** the person being discussed. The "A" must be used as an "identifier" with the verb "gustar" with the "you," "he" and "she" forms of the verb. It comes before "usted," "él" or "ella" when these forms are being used.

In the picture below you see the **Identifier Detective** examining the "A" that comes before "ella" in the sample sentence. He is also examining the "A" in two other similar sentences using the "you" and "he" forms. The **Identifier Detective** examining these three sentences will remind you that the "identifier" "A" must always be used with these three verb forms for the verb "gustar."

The Identifier "A"

A ella le gusta la flor.

A él le gusta la flor.

A usted le gusta la flor.

Now that you understand these three important principles for the verb "gustar" it is time to practice forming some sentences with "gustar." Although you have already practiced the "yo" form of "me gusta" with other infinitives, it will still be included in the upcoming drills. You have not practiced using it with full sentences yet.

When you are sure you know these verb forms you can practice using them with Spanish infinitives in the upcoming drills. In the first drill you should first speak compound verb phrases as you did before with the other verb forms. You will then be able to speak complete sentences that begin with the verb phrases and end with the words from the "vehicles," "travel" and "elements and environment" categories. You won't be able to use all of the infinitives with each form, because they won't make sense, but use as many as you can in this very important practice drill.

The various forms will be represented by boxes on the left side of the page as before. You will select a verb form on the left and say it with an infinitive on the first door. For instance, you could say, "A él le gusta viajar en un tren." This is, "He likes to travel in a train," in English. You might also say, "Nos gusta caminar con un mapa." This is, "We like to walk with a map," in English. After you have practiced with the infinitives on the door expand your practice by using the infinitives listed above and below the door. You can also skip a door and not use the words on it if you so desire.

Use as many of these words as possible during your practice. If you are not sure of all of the words go back and review them briefly until you know them well. You will continue to have to use "**el**" or "**la**" and "**un**" and "**una**" depending on whether the noun is **masculine** or **feminine**. It would also be good practice for you to use "**los**" or "**las**" and make the words **plural**. You could use some more practice using the plural form of the definite article. Practice using all forms of the verb "can" with as many words as possible. You can never practice too much.

As has already been stated several times, these practice drills are vital for your progress and success. You must participate in all of them to advance your skills. Practice makes perfect. You will be able to hear several of these sentences spoken by a Spanish-speaking person on Dr. Memory's™ web site. By listening to a Spanish-speaking person you will better understand Spanish vocal tendencies. Remember that "in" and "at" are "en" in Spanish, and "to" is "a".

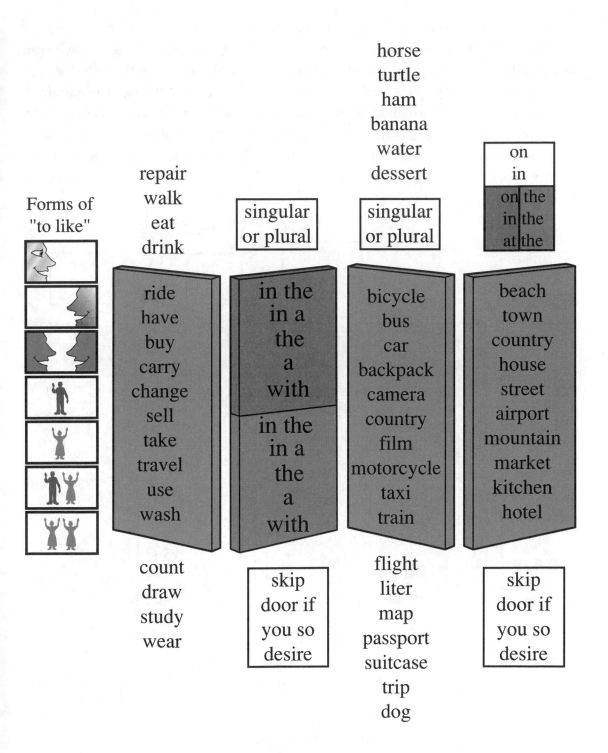

Forms of
"to like"

repair
walk
eat
drink

horse
turtle
ham
banana
water
dessert

singular
or plural

singular
or plural

on
in

on the
in the
at the

ride
have
buy
carry
change
sell
take
travel
use
wash

in the
in a
the
a
with

in the
in a
the
a
with

bicycle
bus
car
backpack
camera
country
film
motorcycle
taxi
train

beach
town
country
house
street
airport
mountain
market
kitchen
hotel

count
draw
study
wear

skip
door if
you so
desire

flight
liter
map
passport
suitcase
trip
dog

skip
door if
you so
desire

Dr. Memory™ has created another practice drill for the verb "gustar." The various forms will be represented by boxes on the left side of the page as before. Once again, you will select a verb form on the left and say it with an infinitive on the first door. For instance, you could say, "Nos gusta nadar en el mar." This is, "We like to swim in the ocean," in English. You might also say, "Me gusta caminar en la playa." This is, "I like to walk on the beach," in English. After you have practiced with the infinitives on the door expand your practice by using the infinitives listed above and below the door. You can also skip a door and not use the words on it if you so desire. Remember that "on" with days of the week is "el" or "los."

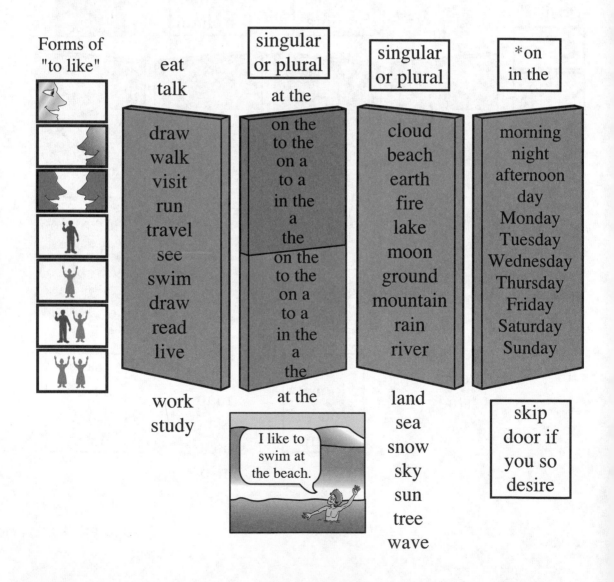

Forms of "to like"	eat talk	singular or plural / at the	singular or plural	*on in the
	draw walk visit run travel see swim draw read live	on the / to the / on a / to a / in the / a / the / on the / to the / on a / to a / in the / a / the	cloud beach earth fire lake moon ground mountain rain river	morning night afternoon day Monday Tuesday Wednesday Thursday Friday Saturday Sunday
	work study	at the	land sea snow sky sun tree wave	

I like to swim at the beach.

skip door if you so desire

The Verb "To Be"

The verb "to be" in English has only one conjugation and form of expression, but it has two forms and two conjugations in Spanish. The two Spanish verbs that mean "to be" in Spanish are "ser" and "estar." "To be" means to exist or have being. The conjugation of the "to be" verb in English looks like this.

I –	am
you –	are
we –	are
he –	is
she –	is
they -	are

The conjugations of the Spanish verbs "ser" and "estar" can be seen below. You have already practiced with "es," which means "is" in English.

		ser	**estar**
I –	yo	soy	estoy
you –	usted	es	está
we –	nosotros, nosotras	somos	estamos
he –	él	es	está
she –	ella	es	está
they –	ellos, ellas	son	están

Take plenty of time to study these two conjugations, so you know them well. After you know them Dr. memory™ will conduct some more adjective drills, but don't go on until you know these conjugations very well.

CHAPTER 17

More Adjectives

You will now learn two more categories of adjectives. The first are adjectives that describe "what people and things are like." These adjectives are used with the verb "ser," as you will discover in an upcoming drill. The next category of adjectives describes "how we look or feel." These adjectives are used with the verb "estar" as you will discover in an upcoming drill. There are 35 words in these two categories. Study and review the pictures on the next six pages to make sure you know all 35 adjectives before continuing. Make it a habit to review all of the words in a particular grouping each time you learn eight new words.

The words "better" and "worse" will be taught in this grouping even though they are not used in a drill until page 344. This is the logical place to learn them.

bad & mean - malo
mah - low

Ma, I've been mean, but I'll slow down and not be bad.

You're a mean, bad little mop.

Mops bow low.

A little mop slinks down very low, because a big, mean, bad mop is scolding it. The mean mop says, "You're a mean, bad little mop." The little mop says, "Ma, I've been mean, but I'll slow down and not be bad."

difficult & hard - difícil
dee - fee -seal

This demon paid its fee, and this seal's trick better be difficult.

Don't be hard headed.

A demon paid a fee to see a seal perform a difficult trick. The sign reads, "Don't be hard headed."

dumb & foolish- tonto
tone - toe

A foolish tone a day keeps the toe away.

He's too dumb to know what a great tone this toe makes.

Dumb and Dumber

A foolish boy hit a toe with a tuning fork. The toe says, "He's too dumb to know what a great tone this toe makes." The boy says, "A foolish tone a day keeps the toe away." The sign reads, "Dumb and Dumber."

easy - fácil
fah - seal

Take It Easy

Mr. Fox, that is too easy for this seal.

A fox holds a hoop above the water, so a seal can jump through it. The seal says, "Mr. Fox, that is too easy for this seal." They are at the Take It Easy Water Park.

fast - rápido
rah - pea - doe

He's too fast!

Rah! That peanut don't have a chance against Fast Freddy.

Fast Freddy pitches today.

A fast ball was thrown by a baseball pitcher named Fast Freddy. A cheer of, "Rah," was heard as a peanut misses the ball. A donut umpire calls a strike and says, "He's too fast."

funny - divertido
dee - vair - tea - doe

Dee's varicose veins need tea and donuts, and I hit my funny bone.

That funny bone business is funny.

Dee

A girl named Dee with varicose veins is having tea and donuts. She hit her funny bone on the counter. The funny clown says, "That funny bone business is funny."

important - importante
eem - pour - tahn - tay

Medicine is important in these cases.

It is important for cream to pour tonic on dog's tails.

Tonic

Cream

Try to look important.

A carton of cream is pouring tonic on the tail of a dog. The dog's tail needed the tonic, because it got burned. The dog says, "Medicine is important in these cases." The sign reads, "Try to look important."

intelligent - inteligente
een - tehl - ee - hen - tay

This teenager could tell you more than the intelligent legal eagle and the hen at that table.

I am intelligent.

An intelligent teenager uses a telephone to call an eagle and a hen standing on a table. Her comment shows that she believes she is more intelligent than they are. The sign reads, "I am intelligent."

interesting - interesante
een - tay- ray - sahn - tay

A bean was thrown on a table by a manta ray in a sauna. That tape should be interesting.

Sauna

Interesting Stories

A green bean was thrown on a table by a manta ray while it was in a sauna. The manta ray is recording interesting information into a tape recorder. Notice that the cover of the book reads, "Interesting Stories."

kind - amable
ah - mah - blay

Ah, ma, why in the blazes do you have to be so kind?

KIND

KIND

Always be kind.

A kind hearted mother puts a large tongue depressor in her son's mouth and he says, "Ah." A mop in the corner has a blazer hanging from it. The emblem on the blazer has the word "kind" on it. The sign reads, "Always be kind."

lazy - perezoso
pair - ay - sew - sew

This pear and ape are just so, so lazy.

Lazy Bums

A lazy pear is lying down. A lazy ape is seated next to the pear. The pear is holding a strawberry soda, and the ape is holding a chocolate soda while lazing around. The sign reads, "Lazy bums."

likeable, nice & pleasant - simpático
seam - pah - tea - co

It seems that polygraph tests are distorted by tea and cocoa. I'm always so pleasant, nice and likeable.

Wanted
Dead or Alive
Likeable Lil
A Very
Pleasant
Criminal
$1,000,000
Reward

Likable Lil

Co-coa

**Seamstress
Polygraph Station**

A seamstress, Likeable Lil, is taking a polygraph test. She was on the most wanted list before her arrest. Tea and cocoa are on the desk as well. She comments in a pleasant way about the test.

angry - enojado
ehn - oh - hah - doe

This engineer is angry at old ha-ha Dobermans.

He's an angry man.

Ha-ha!

A train engineer bending over to pick up a pair of overalls is getting angry. "Ha-ha" comes out of the angry Doberman dog. The dog wants to keep the overalls away from him. The engineer makes an angry **comment**. The sign reads, "He's an angry man."

bored - aburrido
ah - boo - ree - doe

Say ah, not boo, and stop reading about donuts. Are you that bored?

I'm bored.

BOO

A bored wild boar doctor says, "Say ah, not boo, and stop reading about donuts. Are you that bored?" The booing ghost is reading about a donut on skates, rolling "R's."

busy - ocupado
oh - coo - pah - doe

My old coonskin, busy bee cap warms me when pot holing with donuts.

Busy as a Bee

A busy bee in overalls is wearing a coonskin cap while plugging up a pothole in a road with a donut. The sign reads, "Busy as a bee."

comfortable - cómodo
co - moe - doe

Comfortable Furniture

Cobras with Mohawks and doe **deer** love comfortable furniture.

The World's Most Comfortable Sofas

A cobra with a Mohawk haircut and a doe deer examine a very comfortable love seat in front of a furniture store. The sign reads, "The world's most comfortable sofas."

crazy - loco
low - co

Crazy Freddy is loco as coconuts. His prices are crazy.

He's really crazy.

Crazy Freddy, the furniture salesman, has his ad on a billboard. A locomotive full of coconuts passes by the billboard. The engineer says, "He's really crazy."

drunk - borracho
boar - ah - cho

The Drunken Skate

Ah

This drunk boar might, ah, choke.

A drunk wild boar is on roller skates, (rolling "r's"). A tongue depressor (ah) is trying to keep it from falling. A choke chain is around the boar's neck. The name of the roller rink is, "The Drunken Skate."

happy - feliz
fay - lease

Fay is so happy with this lease.

Happy birthday to you, happy -

Fay

LEASE
Paid

She's happy go lucky.

Fay is presented a paid up lease as a present at a birthday party. She says, "Fay is so so happy with this lease." One guest is singing happy birthday to her.

sad & unhappy - triste
trees - tay

Treats on a table that you can't eat. How sad!

I'm unhappy!

Sad at Heart

Treats are lying on a table. The boy's mother won't let him eat them, so he is very unhappy. She says, "Treats on a table that you can't eat. How sad." The plaque reads, "Sad at heart."

sick & ill - enfermo
ehn - fair - moe

I got ill from the big engine fair motorcycle ride

I'm sick of this.

A big engine at a fair is in front of a motorcycle. The boy says, "I got ill from the big engine fair motorcycle ride." The sign reads, "I'm sick of this."

tired - cansado
cahn - sah - doe

Convicts get tired playing soccer, but do-dos don't.

I'm tired of all of this.

A convict playing soccer with a do-do bird can't understand why it doesn't get tired. The sign reads, "I'm tired of all this."

uncomfortable - incómodo
een - co - moe - doe

I'm a teenage cobra that won't mow, even for a donut.

We are about to have an uncomfortable discussion.

Don't make life uncomfortable for anyone.

A rebellious teenage cobra refuses to mow the grass. His father, who is on a very uncomfortable bed of nails that is on a donut said, "We are about to have an uncomfortable discussion." The sign reads, "Don't make life uncomfortable for anyone."

worried - preocupado
pre - oh - coo - pah - doe

Worried Preacher

This preacher is, Oh, so worried, coo, that my torn pocket will distract you, Mr. Donut.

I'm not worried.

The worried preacher is a dove wearing overalls. It coos about its torn pocket to a donut. It says, "This preacher is, Oh, so worried, coo, that my torn pocket will distract you, Mr. Donut."

Some adjectives are only used with "ser," while other adjectives are only used with "estar." "Ser" is used with adjectives that describe **characteristics**, **inherent qualities** or **classification**. A characteristic, for example, could be "difficult" or "slow." An inherent quality could be "intelligent" or "lazy." A classification could be "expensive" or "cheap."

"Estar" is used with adjectives that describe **mental and physical states**. A **mental state**, for example, could be "happy" or "angry." A **physical state**, for example, could be "broken" or "dirty."

In the upcoming drill the verbs "ser" and "estar" will be on a door together. You will begin your practice sentences with a pronoun of your choice. A person of your choice will follow the pronoun. You will then choose to use the verb "ser" or "estar." The form of the verb you use will depend on the pronoun you chose. "Ser" is on the upper part of the door, and "estar" is on the lower part of the door. Adjectives that are used with "ser" are on the upper door that follows, and adjectives that are used with "estar" are on the lower door that follows.

For instance you might say, "Nuestro primo es difícil." In English this is, "Our cousin is difficult." You might also say, "Mucha gente está loca." In English this means, "Many people are crazy." You would have to use the "a" ending on "loca," because "gente" is a **feminine** noun.

Remember that a plural noun requires a plural adjective, because the adjective must agree with the noun it describes in gender and number. Have fun!

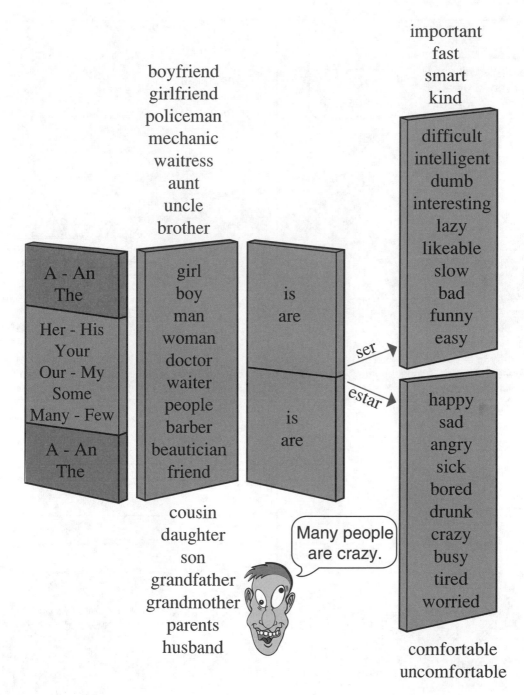

important
fast
smart
kind

boyfriend
girlfriend
policeman
mechanic
waitress
aunt
uncle
brother

difficult
intelligent
dumb
interesting
lazy
likeable
slow
bad
funny
easy

A - An
The

Her - His
Your
Our - My
Some
Many - Few

A - An
The

girl
boy
man
woman
doctor
waiter
people
barber
beautician
friend

is
are

is
are

ser

estar

happy
sad
angry
sick
bored
drunk
crazy
busy
tired
worried

Many people
are crazy.

cousin
daughter
son
grandfather
grandmother
parents
husband

comfortable
uncomfortable

You will now learn 10 new adjectives. These adjectives describe "which one or what kind." Some of these adjectives are used with the verb "ser" and some are used with the verb "estar," as you will discover in an upcoming drill. Study and review the pictures on the next three pages to make sure you know all 11 adjectives before continuing.

old - viejo
vee - ay - hoe

On V-day, Abe, my hobo friend, we weren't so old.

We've grown old gracefully, my old friend.

Abe

Old Folks

Old Testament

An old timer is standing on an Old Testament while holding up a "Vee" for victory sign. Abe, the old hobo, is his friend. Abe says, "We've grown old gracefully, my old friend." The sign reads, "Old Folks."

broken - roto
row - toe

Row, toe row!

Broken oars and broken Spanish.

A broken row boat is trying to be rowed by a big toe. The toe has also broken its oars and isn't getting any place. The toe says, "Broken oars and broken Spanish."

clean - limpio
leam - pea - oh

It gleams because this peanut in overalls cleaned it.

Clean it up.

A clean sink is gleaming. A peanut in overalls cleaned the sink. The peanut is proud of what it has done. The sign reads, "Clean it up."

closed - cerrado
sair - ah - doe

Donut Shop

CLOSED

Sarah says, ah, this donut shop is always closed.

A girl named Sarah and an Amish man want to enter the donut shop, but it is closed. The girl comments on the closed shop.

dirty - sucio
sue - sea - oh

Sue see**saws, but,** Oh, what a dirty mess.

Oh!

Seesaw

Sue

Dirty Deeds Equal Dirty Consequences

A girl named Sue is on a seesaw with an orangutan. She came down in a mud puddle, and got very dirty. The orangutan says, "Sue see**saws, but,** Oh, what a dirty mess."

open - abierto
ah - bee - air - toe

Ah, bees love air sprayed into an open mouth by a toad.

Open up.

Ah

Toad

Open for Business

Air

A tongue depressor, ah, is used to hold the mouth of a bee open. Air from an air compressor is being sprayed into the bee's mouth by the toad dentist who says, "Open up." The sign reads, "Open for business."

In the next drill the verbs "ser" and "estar" will be practiced again with a new group of nouns and the new adjectives you just learned. As with the last drill, you will begin your practice sentences with a pronoun of your choice. An item of your choice will follow the pronoun. You will then choose to use the verb "ser" or "estar." The form of the verb you use will depend on the pronoun your chose. "Ser" is on the upper part of the door, and "estar" is on the lower part of the door. Adjectives that are used with "ser" are on the upper door that follows, and adjectives that are used with "estar" are on the lower door that follows.

For instance you might say, "Su plato está roto." In English this is, "Her plate is broken." You might also say, "Su plato es caro." In English this is, "Her plate is expensive." You might also say, "Nuestros dormitorios están sucios." In English this means, "Our rooms are dirty." Remember that a plural noun requires a plural adjective, because the adjective must agree with the noun it describes in gender and number.

"Listo" has two different meanings according to which verb it is used with. When it is used with a form of "ser" it means "smart." When it is used with a form of "estar" it means "ready," and that is the meaning that will be used with "estar" in this drill.

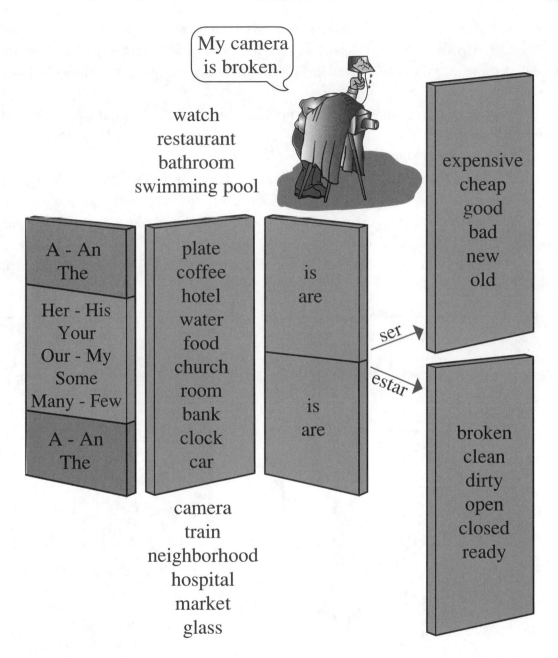

watch
restaurant
bathroom
swimming pool

My camera is broken.

A - An
The

Her - His
Your
Our - My
Some
Many - Few

A - An
The

plate
coffee
hotel
water
food
church
room
bank
clock
car

is
are

is
are

ser

estar

expensive
cheap
good
bad
new
old

broken
clean
dirty
open
closed
ready

camera
train
neighborhood
hospital
market
glass

In the upcoming drill the verb "tener" will be with a group of nouns. You will begin your practice sentences with a pronoun of your choice. A person of your choice will follow the pronoun. You will then to use the verb "tener." The form of the verb you use will depend on the pronoun you chose. "Tener" is on the door. Nouns that are used with "tener" are on the door that follows. Spanish expresses concepts like "I am cold" or "I am thirsty" with the verb "tener" and the nouns "cold" and "thirst." For example, "Tengo frio" and "Tengo sed." In English we use the adjectives "cold" and "thirsty" in these sentences. As a result, these adjectives in English are nouns in Spanish. "Hungry" in this case is "hunger" in Spanish.

For instance you might say, "Mi novio tiene miedo." In English this is, "My boyfriend is afraid." You might also say, "El barbero tiene hambre." In English this means, "The barber is hungry."

You must learn four new words before participating in this drill. You will use "tener" with these words. In addition to the four new words you must also use the word "calor" for hot in this usage. The four new words include a phrase. They are "afraid," "hungry," "thirsty" and "in a hurry."

Make sure you know these words well before participating in the upcoming drill. Remember to use "calor" for "hot" in this drill. Have fun!

afraid - miedo
me - ay - doe

Meteors make apes and does afraid.

A meteor landed next to an ape and a doe. Others are on the way, and they are afraid. The ape says, "Meteors make apes and does afraid."

cold - frío
free - o

I'm getting cold feet. This freezer is, oh, so cold.

Cold Storage

A Cold Hearted Person

A freezer full of cold cuts also has a shivering man in it. The man is wearing a pair of overalls. He is obviously very cold. He says, "I'm getting cold feet. This freezer is, oh, so cold." The sign reads, "A cold hearted person."

"Calor" actually means "heat" in this usage, but in English it is translated as "hot." "Frio" is used as both a noun and an adjective, but in the case of "tener frio" it is used as a noun.

hot (heat) - calor
cah - lohr

Cah, there sure is a lot of heat on this lorry.

A cahing crow is getting all heated up with a hot foot on a lorry. The crow says, "Cah, there sure is a lot of heat on this lorry." A lorry is a long, flat wagon.

hungry - hambre
ahm - bray

I'm Amish, and I'm hungry, Mr. Braydey.

Bray

Feed the hungry.

An Amish man is so hungry he is on his knees asking a braying donkey for some of its food. The Amish man says, "I'm Amish, and I'm hungry, Mr. Braydey." The sign reads, "Feed the hungry." The letters "Am" in "Amish" had to be used to duplicate this sound.

thirsty - sed
sehd

I'm thirsty, but this water is full of sediment.

A thirsty man walked up to a water fountain and said, "I'm thirsty, but this water is full of sediment."

in a hurry - prisa
pre - sah

This preacher is in a hurry to get to the soccer match.

A preacher is in a hurry. He finished his sermon and said, "This preacher is in a hurry to get to the soccer match."

In the next drill the verb "es" for "it is" will be practiced with a group of adjectives, an infinitive, a pronoun and another group of nouns. You will begin your practice sentences with "es" which will be followed by an adjective of your choice. An infinitive of your choice will follow the adjective. You will then choose a pronoun, a descriptive word, or words which will be followed by your choice of a noun.

For instance, you might say, "Es importante visitar el centro." In English this is,

"It is important to visit the downtown." You might also say, "Es difícil caminar a la playa." In English this means, "It is difficult to walk to the beach." Remember that a plural noun requires a plural adjective, because the adjective must agree with the noun it describes in gender and number.

A red asterisk is in front of "*to the" to remind you to use "**al**" if it will be used with a **masculine** noun. You can skip a door if the sentence will make sense. Have fun!

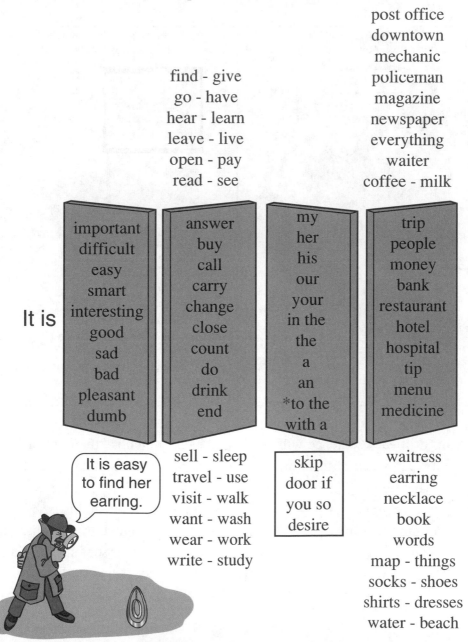

post office
downtown
mechanic
policeman
magazine
newspaper
everything
waiter
coffee - milk

find - give
go - have
hear - learn
leave - live
open - pay
read - see

It is

important	answer	my	trip
difficult	buy	her	people
easy	call	his	money
smart	carry	our	bank
interesting	change	your	restaurant
good	close	in the	hotel
sad	count	the	hospital
bad	do	a	tip
pleasant	drink	an	menu
dumb	end	*to the	medicine
		with a	

It is easy to find her earring.

sell - sleep
travel - use
visit - walk
want - wash
wear - work
write - study

skip door if you so desire

waitress
earring
necklace
book
words
map - things
socks - shoes
shirts - dresses
water - beach

By learning a few more adjectives to be used with the very useful "hay," you will be able to describe how many of something there is. There are four new words you will learn in this grouping. One of them is another meaning for the word "little." You have learned that "little" means "pequeño" when referring to size. "Little" also means "poco" when referring to an amount of something.   These four words are taught in two pictures. Study the pictures and know the words before participating in the upcoming drill.

little & few - poco & pocos
poe - co & poe - coas

There is too little snow.

Only a few polar bears can coast like this.

A polar bear coasting down a road on a sled says, "Only a few polar bears can coast like this." The sign reads, "Few and far between."

many, much & a lot of - muchos & mucho
moo - chos & moo - cho

How many is too much, or how much is too many?

This is too much, Mini.

Moo, these chokes choke.

That's a lot of bull.

A mooing cow has many choke chains around its neck. The other cow says, "This is too much, Mini." The sign reads, "How many is too much, or how much is too many?" Many means muchos, and much and a lot of mean mucho.

In this drill each sentence will start with "hay," which is "there is" or "there are." It will be followed by one of the words you just learned. You will complete the sentence with a quantifying noun.

For instance you might say, "Hay mucha agua." In English this is, "There is a lot of water." You might also say, "Hay pocos hoteles." In English this means, "There are few hotels." Remember to match the gender and number of your sentences. You can complete the sentence with many other nouns you have learned. Have fun!

people
cats
cows
horses
shirts

There are a lot of cats.

There is

There are

a lot of

few

many

little

hotels
apples
butter
sugar
salt
pepper
water
paper
bananas
dogs

choose
another
noun

fruit
coffee
chairs
forks
cheese

You have just practiced expressing a limited amount of something. When you learn the word for "all" and "everything" you will be to express an entire amount of something. Study this picture and know it before participating in the upcoming drill. The picture for "all" and "everything" that you learned in the "pronoun" category is on the top of the next page as a review for the upcoming drill.

all & everything - todo
toe - doe

What a disgrace, a totem pole carved by a do-do.

I carved it all, everything, the whole enchilada.

Money isn't everything.

All or Nothing at All

A totem pole has a do-do bird standing next to it. The do-do says, "I carved it all, everything, the whole enchilada." One sign reads, "Money isn't everything." Another sign reads, "All or nothing at all." The totem pole says, "What a disgrace, a totem pole carved by a do-do."

This drill is divided into two parts. In the upper part you will express all of something with the verb "are." You might say, "Todos los muchachos son altos." In English this is, "All the boys are tall." Notice that the gender and number of the words in this sample sentence match up. In the lower part of the drill you might also say, "Todo es azul." In English this is, "Everything is blue." Each sentence will be completed with an adjective that goes with "es." Have fun!

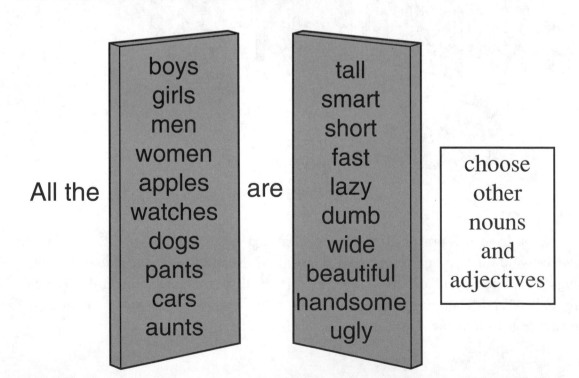

All the

boys
girls
men
women
apples
watches
dogs
pants
cars
aunts

are

tall
smart
short
fast
lazy
dumb
wide
beautiful
handsome
ugly

choose
other
nouns
and
adjectives

You may need to express the position of something. To do that you must learn four position words. Study these pictures and know them before participating in the upcoming drill.

first - primero
pre - mair - oh

A priest is the first to say Merry Christmas to old Santa.

Merry Christmas.

I'm a first sergeant.

First come, first served.

A priest is first in line to see Santa Clause. He said, "Merry Christmas." A little boy wearing short overalls is behind the priest. A first sergeant is in line behind the boy. The sign reads, "First come, first served."

last - último
ool - tea - mo

The Last Frontier

This fool is teed off. That motor should be last.

He won't last.

Tea

A fool, a court jester, is last in a line at a movie theater. A tea bag and a motor are just in front of him. The tea bag says, "He won't last." The movie that is playing is "The Last Frontier."

middle - medio
may - dee - oh

Month

MAY

Month

May this decoy always be in the middle of old roads.

Decoy

A month of May is in the middle of a road in the middle of two other months. A decoy duck sitting on overalls is in front of the middle month. The decoy says, "May this decoy always be in the middle of old roads." You must say, "En medio de," which means "in the middle of," when using this word.

next - próximo
prohk - sea - moe

Who's next?

K

Moe

A pro "K" can't out sea Moe. I'm the next great quarterback.

SEA

A pro quarterback with a letter "K" on his jersey threw a football through a tire. The ball landed in a sea. The next quarterback, who is named Moe, yells, "A pro "K" can't out sea Moe. I'm the next great quarterback." The sign reads, "Who's next?"

This drill is also divided into two parts. In the upper part you will express the positions first, last and next. You might say, "La última casa es blanca." In English this is, "The last house is white." Notice that the gender and number of the words in this sample sentence match up. You might also say, "La primera mujer es Maria." In English this is, "The first woman is Maria." "Primero" always becomes "primer" before a singular masculine noun. Thus "The first Man" would be "El primer hombre." In the lower part of the drill you might say, "En medio de la calle hay un carro." In English this is, "In the middle of the street there is a car." You will skip "a" or "an" for plural words that end a sentence. Have fun!

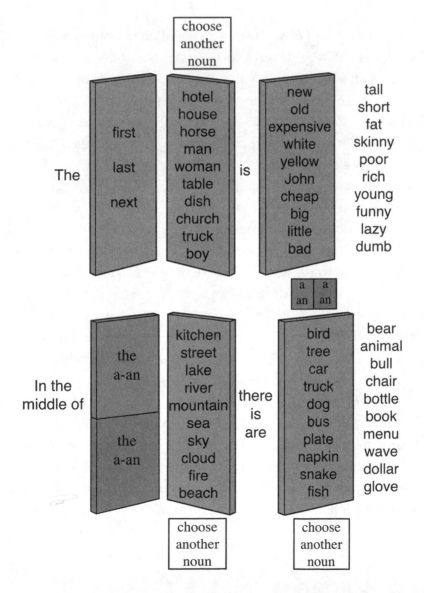

CHAPTER 18

Regular Verb Practice

Now that you have had plenty of practice and understand Spanish conjugation, it is time to come back to the regular verbs for a little more practice. There will never be a substitute for practice in any activity if you want to become accomplished. Great athletes became great, because they were willing to work longer and harder than others who participated in their sport . People who become successful in business have likewise generally worked harder and longer than their competitors. Your continued practice will assure your own success in speaking Spanish.

You will recall that verbs are classified as verbs of the first, second or third conjugation according to the ending of the infinitive. First conjugation verbs end in "**ar**," second conjugation verbs end in "**er**" and third conjugation verbs end in "**ir**." You will also recall how Dr. Memory™ pictured those endings. The letters "**ar**" in Spanish sound like the beginning letters in the word "**ar**t," so Dr. Memory™ calls these the "**ar**t" conjugation verbs. The letters "**er**" in Spanish sound exactly like the English word "**air**," so Dr. Memory™ calls these the "**air**" conjugation verbs. The letters "**ir**" in Spanish sound exactly like the English word "**ear**," so Dr. Memory™ calls these the "**ear**" conjugation verbs. The infinitive endings of "ar," "er" or "ir" are dropped and other endings are added to the stem as the verb is used in various conjugation forms.

A listing of three verbs from the three classes appears on the next page. Those three verbs are "to visit," "to drink" and "to write." You will also recall the three models representing the endings for Dr. Memory™. Because these are all regular verbs the **bold**, **black** letters in the infinitive form of the verbs will not change. As you already know, this is the stem, or main part of regular verbs. This stem does not change during conjugation. However, the **bold**, **red** letters in the infinitive form of the verbs will change as the verbs are conjugated in its various forms.

	visitar	**beber**	**escribir**
I	visito	bebo	escribo
you	visita	bebe	escribe
we	visitamos	bebemos	escribimos
he	visita	bebe	escribe
she	visita	bebe	escribe
they	visitan	beben	escriben

The regular verbs that you have learned are listed below in two groups. The first group is made up of "ar" or "art" verbs. They are all conjugated the same way. The second group is made up of "er" or "air" verbs and "ir" or "ear" verbs. They are all conjugated the same way except for the "e" or "I" with "emos" and "imos." There are 36 regular verbs in these two groups. Both lists are in alphabetical order.

"Ar" Verbs

Answer	Buy	Call	Carry & Wear	
Change & Exchange		Draw	End & Finish	Help
Need	Pay	Repair	Send	Study
Take	Talk & Speak		Travel	Use
Visit	Walk	Wash	Work	

"Er" and "Ir" Verbs

Drink	Eat	Learn	Live	Read
Receive	Run	Sell	Understand	Write

In the next drill you will practice with only "ar" regular verbs. These verbs are easier than the irregular verbs you have practiced with so far, because the stem of the verbs never change when they are conjugated. The various "ar" verb forms will be represented by boxes on the left side of the page as before. You will select a verb form on the left and say it with a regular verb on the first door. For instance, you could say, "Ud. estudia con el muchacho en la tarde." This is, "You study with the boy in the afternoon," in English. After you have practiced with the regular verbs on the door expand your practice by using the regular verbs listed above and below the door.

This practice drill uses words from a variety of categories that you should have already learned. If you have had **a little bit of discipline** to review on a regular basis as Dr. Memory™ has asked you to do you will not have any problem remembering the words used in this drill. If you haven't had **a little bit of discipline** to review, you won't be as successful as you would like. Never stop reviewing!

Below you see the conjugations of the verb "visitar" as a reminder of the endings for "ar" verbs.

visitar

I	**visito**
you	**visita**
we	**visitamos**
he	**visita**
she	**visita**
they	**visitan**

The personal "a" may be needed in the next two drills. For example, in the first drill "I help the boy," would be "Yo ayudo <u>al</u> muchacho." "We call the children" would be "Llamamas <u>a</u> los niños." In the second drill "She understands the man" would be "Ella comprende <u>al</u> hombre." A red asterisk * is above the singular or plural box in both drills to remind you to use "a" or "**al**" if needed.

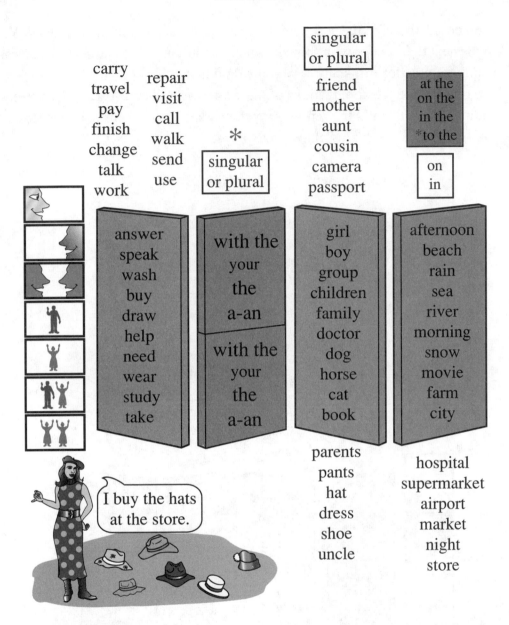

carry
travel
pay
finish
change
talk
work

repair
visit
call
walk
send
use

*

singular
or plural

singular
or plural

friend
mother
aunt
cousin
camera
passport

at the
on the
in the
*to the

on
in

answer
speak
wash
buy
draw
help
need
wear
study
take

with the
your
the
a-an

with the
your
the
a-an

girl
boy
group
children
family
doctor
dog
horse
cat
book

afternoon
beach
rain
sea
river
morning
snow
movie
farm
city

parents
pants
hat
dress
shoe
uncle

hospital
supermarket
airport
market
night
store

I buy the hats at the store.

In the next drill you will practice with only "er" and "ir" regular verbs. These verbs are also easier than the irregular verbs you have practiced with, because the stem of the verbs never change when they are conjugated.

The various "er" or "ir" verb forms will be represented by boxes on the left side of the page as before. You will select a verb form on the left and say it with a regular verb on the first door. For instance, you could say, "Ellos aprenden la Biblia in la iglesia." This is, "They learn the Bible in the church," in English.

You could also skip the second door and say, "I eat food in the kitchen." You can also skip the next to last door with some sentences and they will make sense. You can mix and match these practice drills any way you would like.

Below you see the conjugations of the verbs "beber" and "escribir" as a reminder of the endings for "er" and "ir" verbs. As you can see they are all conjugated the same way except for the "e" or "i" in "emos" and "imos."

beber	escribir
bebo	escribo
bebe	escribe
bebemos	escribimos
bebe	escribe
bebe	escribe
beben	escriben

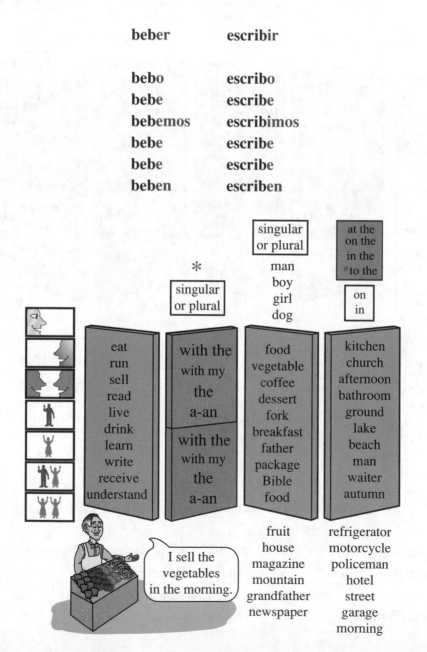

CHAPTER 19

Question Words

The next category of words you will learn is **question words**. You would use these words to find information that might be important to you. There are 9 words in this category.

You will use them over and over again, as you learn what you need to know. There will be many fun and helpful make-up drills associated with these words, and they are essential for your survival in the Spanish language. You will notice that all question words in Spanish have an accent mark in them.

Make sure to study each vocabulary word picture until you can easily recreate it in your mind and say the Spanish equivalent while thinking of the English word before moving to the next word. The reward far surpasses the small investment of time required for these reviews.

"How much" was taught in the adverb category earlier. The picture is reproduced in this question words category for your review.

how - ¿cómo?
co - moe

How, how do you expect to win against **me** you coconut Mohawk?

A wrestling **match** is **about** to take place. An Indian named How is going to wrestle a coconut with a Mohawk haircut. The Indian says, "How, how do you expect to win against **me** you coconut Mohawk?

---

how many - ¿cuántos?
coo - ahn - tos

kwan

How many ways can toast be made?

How many can you make?

I kwan **make four** pieces of toast at a time? **How many** do you want?

A cooing dove flips on a four-piece toaster. The man asks, "How many can you make?" The dove answers, " I kwan make four pieces of toast at a time. How many do you want?"

---

how much - ¿cuánto?
coo - ahn - toe

kwahn

This dove kwahns to buy the stone, Mr. Toe. **For** how much?

For how much?

Onyx

A cooing dove wants to buy an onyx stone. The salesman is a toe. The dove says, "This dove kwahns to buy the stone, Mr. Toe. For how much?" The toe repeats, "For how much," as though it is trying to arrive at a price. The only difference between " cu nto?" and " cu ntos?" is that one is singular and one is plural.

---

what - ¿qué?
kay

Kay can't remember what I was doing.

Kay

Know what's hot and what's not.

A "What" is a letter "W" that is very "hot." The "What" watches a girl named Kay scratch her head. She forgot something and said, "Kay can't remember what I was doing." The sign reads, "Know what's hot and what's not."

when - ¿cuándo?
coo - ahn - doe

kwahn

When shall we unload this large quantity of donuts?

W-hen? How about now.

Quantity of Donuts

A "When" is a "W" shaped "hen." The man asks the When, "When shall we unload this large quantity of donuts?"

where - ¿dónde?
dohn - day

Where? In you "W-hair."

Where are you going to put those Doan's pills, Miss Daisy?

Extra Strength **DOAN'S** PAIN RELIEVER RELIEVES BACKACHE PAIN 24 ANALGESIC CAPLETS

A "Where" is a letter "W" with "hair." The "Where" says, "Where are you going to put those Doan's pills, Miss Daisy?" The daisy answers, "Where? In your "W-hair."

which - ¿cuál?
kwahl

Mr. Kwahl, which letter is the big one?

I can't tell which is which.

K WALL

A "Which" is a letter "W" with an "itch." The "Which" looks at a letter "K" on a wall. It is trying to learn to read and asks, "Mr. Kwahl, which letter is the big one?" The "K" says, "I can't tell which is which."

who - ¿quién?
key - ehn

Key
Encyclopedia

Who are you looking for?

Who's Who

A "Who," a letter "W" that "hoots" like an owl when it sleeps, is dreaming about a key to unlock knowledge in an encyclopedia. A Who's Who book is under the "Who." The sign reads, "Who are you looking for?"

A "Why" is a letter "W" saying "hi." The "Why" watches a porcupine named Kay cross the road. The "Why" asked, "Why did the porcupine named Kay cross the road?" The sign reads, "Why ask why?"

How

"How" is the first question word that you will use in drills. You will use "how" when asking about a person's **mental or physical state**, and, as a result, you must use the verb "estar." For instance you might ask "¿Cómo está Juan?" In English this is, "How is John?" You might also ask, "¿Cómo están ellas?" In English this is, "How are they?"

You see a box to the right of the door to the right at the top of the next page. The words "choose another person" are in the box. That means you could insert any name you might choose to use to complete the sentence. This procedure will be used throughout the rest of the drills. Since you are expanding your vocabulary as you proceed through Dr. Memory's™ learning pictures, there is no reason to limit the vocabulary words you can use in drill practices. Simply choose words and use them as you please. Of course, this means that you must know the vocabulary, and you will if you have followed the advice of having a little bit of discipline to review the vocabulary lists in the back of the book on a regular basis.

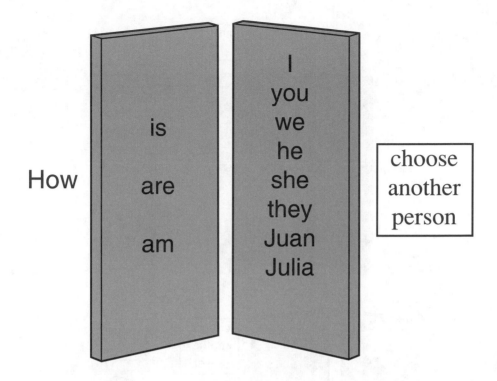

In the first of the two drills to follow you will use "how" to tell what a place is like. You are interested in knowing the **characteristics or essential qualities** of airports, apartments, etc. As a result, you must use the verb "ser." For instance you might ask "¿Cómo son las farmacias?" In English this is, "What are the pharmacies like?" A typical answer could be, "Las farmacias son interesantes." (The pharmacies are interesting.)

In the second of these two drills you will use "how" to tell what a person is like. You are interested in knowing the **characteristics or essential qualities** of a person. As a result, you must use the verb "ser." In English we would say, "What is she like?" This drill uses, "How is she?" which is the literal translation of "¿Cómo es ella?" A typical answer could be, "Ella es alta y simpática." (She is tall and nice.)

You see boxes encouraging you to insert other names or nouns you might choose to use to complete the sentence.

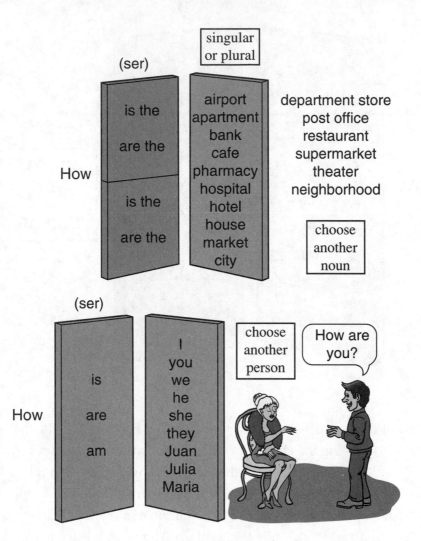

How Many

"How many" is the next question word that you will use in drills. You will ask "how many" of something there are. For instance you might ask "¿Cuántos hombres hay?" In English this is, "How many men are there?" You will start every made-up sentence with "Cuántos" and end every sentence with "hay."

In this drill you must match the gender of the question word with the gender of the noun in the question. You will use "¿cuántos?" with **masculine** nouns and "¿cuántas?" with **feminine** nouns.

You see the box encouraging you to insert other plural nouns you might choose to use to complete the sentence.

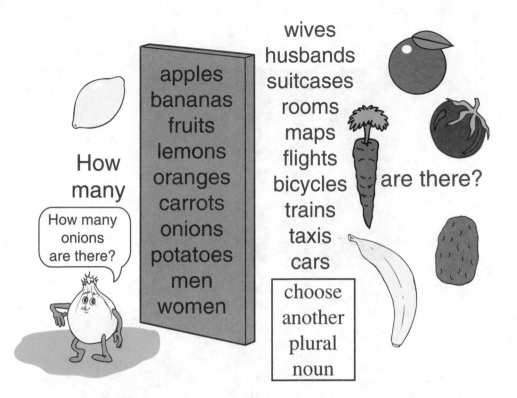

In this drill you will be asking "how many" items "does" a person have, need etc. In English "do" or "does" in a question are markers to tell us it is a question. These markers don't exist in Spanish, so you will not need a Spanish equivalent. In the drill the words "do" and "does" are in brackets to show you that they will not be used in the questions. The Spanish word order for these questions do not follow the English word order. Here is an English question, "How much fish does the waiter need?" In this sentence the word order is – how much – of what – subject – verb. The verb follows the subject in English. The verb and subject are reversed in Spanish, so the verb comes before the subject. The word order in Spanish is – how much – of what – verb – subject.

You might ask "¿Cuántas zanahorias necesita el camarero?" In English this is, "How many carrots does the waiter need?" You will notice that the verb "necesita" came before the subject "camarero." That will be the order for every question you make up in this drill. You might also ask, "¿Cuántos taxis lavan ellos?" In English that is, "How many taxis do they wash?"

In this drill you must also match the gender of the question word with the gender of the noun in the question. You will continue to use use "¿cuántos?" with **masculine** nouns and "¿cuántas?" with **feminine** nouns.

How Much

"How much" is the next question word that you will use in a drill. You will ask "how much" of something people have, need, etc. For instance, you might ask "¿Cuánto pescado necesita el camarero?" In English this is, "How much fish does the waiter need?" You might also ask, "¿Cuánta sal tenemos nosotros?" In English that is, "How much salt do we have?" In the drill the words "do" and "does" are also in brackets to show you that they will not be used in the questions. There is no Spanish equivalent.

In this drill you must match the gender of the question word with the gender of the noun in the question. You will use "¿cuánto?" with **masculine** nouns and "¿cuánta?" with **feminine** nouns. The plural was used with "how many," and the singular is used with "how much." Have fun! The drill is at the top of the next page.

What

"What" is the next question word that you will use in drills. You will ask "what" does someone speak, eat, etc. For instance, you might ask "¿Qué necesita el camarero?" In English this is, "What does the waiter need?" You might also ask, "¿Qué estudia su esposo?" In English that is, "What does your husband study?"

In the second part of the drill you will ask "what" with English "ing" words. This time the words "am," "is" and "are" will be in brackets, because they are not used in this Spanish application. Word usage in Spanish is not always word for word as it relates to English. In this drill you might ask, "Qué estudio yo?" In English that is, "What am I studying?" "Qué yo estudio?" is wrong, because a subject pronoun never follows a question word in Spanish.

The words to the right of each door actually should be on the door if there was enough room. They just provide more choices of nouns to use. The boxes suggest that you choose even more nouns for your practice. Have fun!

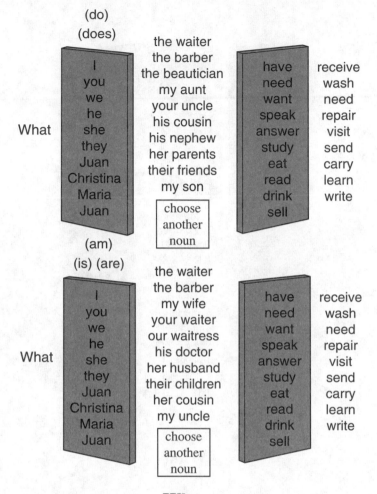

When

"When" is the next question word that you will use in drills. In the first drill you will ask "when" is something. For instance, you might ask, "¿Cuándo es la fiesta?" In English this is, "When is the party?" You might also ask, "¿Cuándo son los viajes?" In English that is, "When are the trips?" You "must" use the definite article when asking these simple questions, and it must be singular or plural depending on the number of the noun. You must also use the verb "es" or "son" in these questions.

In the second part of the drill you will ask "when" does someone do something. This time the words "do" or "does" will be in brackets, because they are not used in this Spanish application. In this drill you might ask, "¿Cuándo viajamos nosotros?" In English that is, "When do we travel?" You might also ask, "¿Cuándo come su esposo?" In English that is, "When does her husband eat?" Have fun!

Where

"Where" is the next question word that you will use in a drill. You will ask "where" is something. For instance, you might ask, "¿Dónde están los hospitales?" In English this is, "Where are the hospitals?" You might also ask, "¿Dónde estamos?" In English that is, "Where are we?" You would need to skip the first door to ask this question. You "must" use the correct form of the verb "estar" when asking these simple questions. If you choose to use an article it must match the gender of the noun you will be using. You will notice the **blue** and **pink** sections of the door. Have fun!

326

PICTURE PERFECT SPANISH

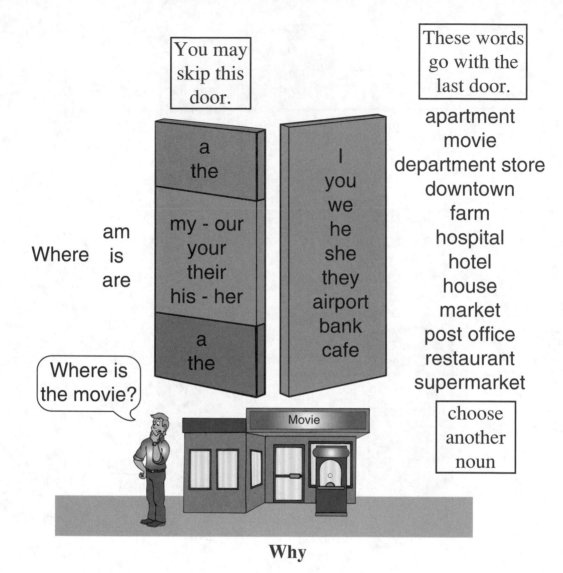

Why

"Why" is the next question word that you will use in a drill. You will ask "why" about something and will be able to add adjectives to your questions. You need to learn a new and simple adverb for this drill. The English word "so" is "tan" in Spanish. It is pronounced "tahn." "So" will be in brackets, because you can choose whether you want to use it or not use it. For instance, you might ask, "¿Por qué es el hotel tan caro?" In English this is, "Why is the hotel so expensive?" You might also ask, "¿Por qué es su amigo rico?" In English that is, "Why is your friend rich?" The word "so" was skipped with this example. If you choose to use an article it must match the gender of the noun you will be using. You will notice the **blue** and **pink** sections of the door. Have fun!

Which

"Which" is the next question word that you will use in a drill. You will ask "which" about something. For instance, you might ask, "¿Cuál mapa necesita ella?" In English this is, "Which map does she need?" You might also ask, "¿Cuáles zapatos quiero yo?" In English this is, "Which shoes do I want?" If you choose to use an article it must match the gender of the noun you will be using. You will notice the **blue** and **pink** sections of the door.

With this drill you will choose a word from one of the two doors under the words "do" and "does." If you choose to use one of the subject pronouns on the bottom, small door, you will skip the next door and go to the last door as demonstrated by the red arrow.

You must read page 334 to learn the meanings of "this" and "these" before participating in the next two drills.

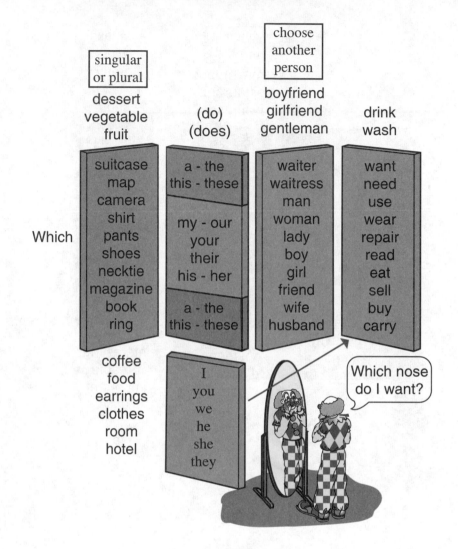

Who

"Who" is the next question word that you will use in a drill. You will ask "who" about someone. For instance, you might ask, "¿Quién es el mecánico?" In English this is, "Who is the mechanic?" You might also ask, "¿Quiénes son las señoras?" In English this is, "Who are the ladies?" You might also ask, "Quién es ella?" In English this is, "Who is she?" With this sentence and others like it you would not use the words on the last door. You will notice the word "stop" in red type to alert you to not use the last door from the small door.

If you choose to use an article it must match the gender and number of the noun you will be using. You will notice the **blue** and **pink** sections of the door. Have fun!

Possession

The next practice drill involves possession with people, clothing and colors. With this drill you could say, "The doctor's pants are white." In Spanish that sentence is, "Los pantalones del médico son blancos." Two observations must be made about this sentence. First of all, in Spanish the words "doctor" and "pants" are reversed from the English word order. This will be the case with all of your Spanish practice sentences. Secondly, in Spanish this means "the pants of the doctor." You have learned that "of the" forms the contraction "**del**" in Spanish when used with a **masculine** noun. Remember that there is no contraction for the plural form. You will use "de" with a feminine noun.

You could also say, "Las camisas de los camareros son negras." In English this is, "The waiters' shirts are black." These are plural waiters with plural shirts, and all words must match the plural number.

If you choose to use an article it must match the gender and number of the noun you will be using. You will notice the **blue** and **pink** sections of the door. Have fun!

| | singular or plural | is are |

A The	barber's beautician's mechanic's waiter's doctor's aunt's brother's daughter's father's boy's	necktie pants shirt suit T-shirt clothes blouse dress skirt coat	black blue brown green orange red white yellow
My - Our Your Their His - Her			
A The			

grandfather's
grandmother's
husband's
wife's
friend's
boyfriend's
girlfriend's
man's
woman's

glove
hat
jacket
shoe
sock

long
short
big
small

| choose another adjective |

Clock Time

The next practice drill will teach you how to use time, and time deadlines, with the days of the week. With this drill you could say, "We have to be at the hotel by 4:15 today." In Spanish that sentence is, "Tenemos que estar en el hotel para las cuatro y quince hoy." Two observations must be made about this sentence. First of all "para" will be used for the deadline "by," and at is "a la" or "a las" depending on whether it is singular or plural. "A la" will only be used with one o'clock. All other times are plural.

Forms of the verb "tener" will be used with a form of "estar," which is "to be," with each sentence.

You could also say, "Mi hija tiene que estar aquí a la una el sábado." In English this is, "My daughter has to be here at 1:00 on Saturday." "There" and "here" are above the second door to point out that these words will not be used with "in the" or "at the" as the rest of the words on and below the second door. "**El**" will be used with all of the days, since they are all **masculine**.

A new word for "half past" the hour is used in this drill. The word is "media." It is very similar to the word "middle" taught on page 308. Turn back to that page and look the picture for "middle." The only difference between these two words is the ending letter. For example, "It is four thirty" would be "Son las cuatro y media." Have fun!

Duration of Time

The next practice drill will teach you how to express duration of time. With this drill you will be able to express how long you want to do something or how long you want to be someplace. This drill will be divided into three sections. The key word in this drill is the preposition "por" which is "for" in English. This word expresses duration of time. In the first section you will use "ing" forms of regular verbs for a duration of time. You might say, "Leo por dos horas." In English this is, "I'm reading for two hours" or "I read for two hours."

In the second section you will use "going to" with regular verbs for a duration of time. You could say, "Ellos van a visitar por un día." In English this is, "They're going to visit for one day."

In the third section you will express that you are going to a particular place for a duration of time. You might say, "Juan va a la playa por dos horas." In English this is, "John's going to the beach for two hours."

Make sure to remember that anytime you use **"to the"** before a **masculine** noun it becomes "al." A red asterisk mark follows the words "to the*" in the practice drill to remind you to use "**al**" with **masculine** nouns. The drill is at the top of the next page. Have fun!

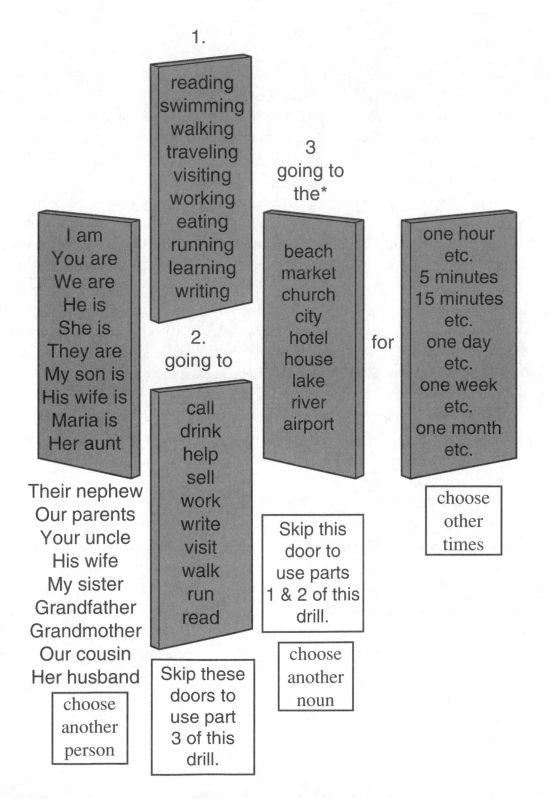

1.
reading
swimming
walking
traveling
visiting
working
eating
running
learning
writing

3
going to the*

beach
market
church
city
hotel
house
lake
river
airport

I am
You are
We are
He is
She is
They are
My son is
His wife is
Maria is
Her aunt

Their nephew
Our parents
Your uncle
His wife
My sister
Grandfather
Grandmother
Our cousin
Her husband

2.
going to

call
drink
help
sell
work
write
visit
walk
run
read

one hour
etc.
5 minutes
15 minutes
etc.
one day
etc.
one week
etc.
one month
etc.

for

choose
other
times

Skip this
door to
use parts
1 & 2 of this
drill.

choose
another
noun

Skip these
doors to
use part
3 of this
drill.

choose
another
person

Use of "For" as in "Intended For"

The next practice drill will teach you how to use the preposition "for" to express "as intended for." With this drill you will be able to express that something is "for" or "intended for" someone. You will use the preposition "para" which also means "for" in English with this drill. "Por" expressed duration of time, but "para" expresses that something is "intended for" for someone or something. You might say, "La ropa es para mi esposa." In English this is, "The clothes are for my wife."

Before you can participate in this drill you must learn the words for "this" and "these" in Spanish. "**This**" is known as a demonstrative adjective, because it points out, or demonstrates, which one. Someone might ask, "Which dog." The response could be, "This dog." The Spanish word for "this" is "este." "Este" may be **masculine** or **feminine** like the definite article "the" depending on the gender of the noun it precedes or points out. "Este" is **masculine**, and "esta" is **feminine**. Notice that the vowel endings of the demonstrative adjectives, "**e**" and "a," are the same as the vowels in the definite articles, "**el**" and "la." As a result, "this dog" in Spanish would be "est**e** perr**o**" or "esta perra." The first example is a **masculine** dog, and the second example is a **feminine** dog.

The difference between the demonstrative adjective "esta" and the verb "está" must be pointed out. The accent mark over the letter "a" in "está" causes the last syllable to be stressed. The stress for the demonstrative adjective "esta" is on the first syllable. Though they are spelled the same except for the accent mark, they are different in meaning and pronunciation.

"Este" can also be **singular** or **plural** depending on the number of the noun it precedes or points out. When it is plural it represents the word "**these**" in English. Est**os**" is **masculine**, and "estas" is **feminine**. Notice that the endings of the demonstrative adjectives, "est**os**" and "estas," are the same as the vowels in the definite articles, "l**os**" and "las." The masculine ending is "**os**," and the feminine ending is "as." As a result, "these dogs" in Spanish would be "est**os** perr**os**" or "estas perras." The first example are **masculine** dogs, and the second example are **feminine** dogs.

Make sure you know the words for "this" and "these" before participating in the upcoming drill. The verbs used in this drill are "is" and "are," and they will be "es" or "son" in Spanish.

You might also say, "Estas flores son pars la señora." In English this is, "These flowers are for the lady." Have fun!

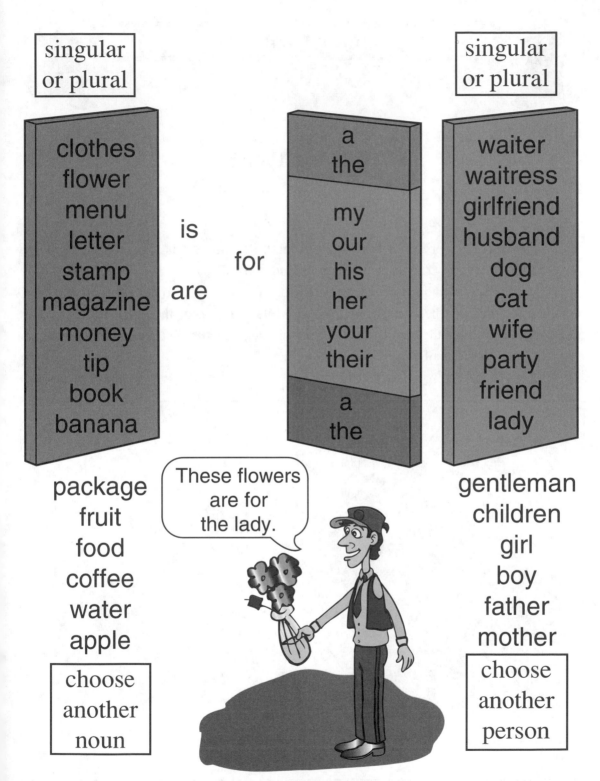

CHAPTER 20

The Last Words

The next category of words you will learn is **mail** words. There are only 6 new words in this category. You have already learned "post office."

Make sure to study each vocabulary word picture until you can easily recreate it in your mind and say the Spanish equivalent while thinking of the English word before going on. There is another word you will learn in these pictures. It isn't a mail word, but it will be used in the mail drill. The word is "near."

letter - carta
cahr - tah

It will make a good car top cover letter.

This letter might make a great car top.

Letters Only

A man thought of using a letter as a car top for his convertible. The letter carrier placing a letter in a mailbox says, "It will make a good car top cover letter."

mail - correo
core - ay - oh

This apple core hit the ape and, Oh, I spilled his mail.

An apple core on skates, rolling "r's," is holding up its mail as it skates. It ran into an ape wearing overalls. The ape was just about to read its mail, but its mail flew everywhere.

mailbox - buzón
boo - sohn

Boo, his Sony almost went in the mailbox.

A man opened a mailbox, and a ghost flew out and said, "Boo." The man's Sony Walkman flew in the air when the ghost flew from the mailbox and scared him. The beginning of the second syllable of the word "Sony" along with the first had to be used to duplicate the "sohn" sound.

package - paquete
pah - kay - tay

This pottery was just what Kay expected in the table package.

Kay

The Package Place - We give you a package deal.

A piece of pottery is lifted up by a lady named Kay. It was in the opened package on the table. The sign reads, "The Package Place. We give you a package deal."

stamp - sello
say - yo

A sailor loves to stamp yo-yos.

USA 33

Yo-yo

The Stamp of Genius

A sailor is about to put a large stamp on a yo-yo to mail it. The sign reads, "The stamp of genius."

near - cerca de
sair - cah - day

I'm also near the **one I love.** Sarah, I will cah and give you this daisy.

Sarah loves to cah for daisies.

Near the One I Love

A female crow named Sarah is near the one she loves. She cahs and reaches for a daisy. The male crow says, "I'm also near the **one I love.** Sarah, I will cah and give you this daisy." The sign reads, "Near the one I love."

Now that you have learned the new vocabulary you can help Dr. Memory's™ clown create some sentences using mail words. You will make statements or ask questions with "hay" in the upcoming drill. You might ask, "¿Hay una carta para nosotros?" In English this is, "Is there a letter for us?" You could say, "Hay muchos correos en la ciudad." In English this is, "There are many post offices in the city."

You must know that you say "para mí" and not "para yo" to say "for me." You will use the normal subject pronouns for the rest of the subject pronouns. "You" will be "Ud.," "us" will be "nosotros," "him" will be "él," "her" will be "ella" and "them" will be "ellas" or "ellos." There will be a red asterisk as well as "mí" in brackets to remind you of this special situation. Have fun as you "deliver" the mail.

Temperature and Weather

The next category of words you will learn is **temperature and weather** words. You have already learned many of the words in this category. You learned **rain**, **sun**, **snow** and **cloud** in the "elements" category. You also learned **hot** and **cold** in an adjective grouping. Hot and cold are repeated for a quick review. Wind and temperature are the only new words you need to learn, and you will seldom ever have a need for the word "temperature" in survival Spanish.

The word "hot" when used as an adjective means "caliente." It is normally used with the verb "estar." "The water is hot," is "El agua está caliente" in Spanish. The learning picture for "caliente" is seen below. Caliente also means "warm."

Study these vocabulary pictures until you know them before going on. Make sure you know the six bold words in the previous paragraph before you begin the upcoming temperature and weather drill.

By now you should know hundreds of words. If you have had **a little bit of discipline** as you have progressed through this book, you will have a very extensive Spanish vocabulary by this time.

hot & warm - caliente
cah - lee - ehn -tay

Make him cah some more, Mr. Leech. This engineer wants a real hot tater.

That will warm him up.

A cahing crow got a hot foot from a leech. The leech says, "That will warm him up." A train engineer holds a tater over the hot foot fire to warm it up.

cold - frío
free - o

I'm getting cold feet. This freezer is, oh, so cold.

A Cold Hearted Person

Cold Storage

A freezer full of cold cuts also has a shivering man in it. The man is wearing a pair of overalls. He is obviously very cold. He says, "I'm getting cold feet. This freezer is, oh, so cold." The sign reads, "A cold hearted person."

hot - calor
cah - lohr

Cah, there sure is a lot of heat on this lorry.

A cahing crow is getting all heated up with a hot foot on a lorry. The crow says, "Cah, there sure is a lot of heat on this lorry." A lorry is a long, flat wagon.

temperature - temperatura
tehm - pair - ah - two - rah

My temperature is too high.

Two Rah!

My temper is uncomparable. Ah, that's good.

Ah

A temper tantrum is thrown by a pear standing on a tongue depressor, ah, because two cheerleaders cheered "Rah" too loudly. Tempers were hot, because the temperature was so high. Notice the hot thermometer. It says, "My temperature is too high."

wind - viento
vee - ehn - toe

I didn't find a "V" in the encyclopedia, because the wind blew a tomato at me.

Encyclopedia

There's something in the wind.

A letter "V" is used as a firm seat by a boy to brace himself against the wind. His encyclopedia blew away, and a tomato blew into his face. The sign reads, "There's something in the wind." The boy says, "I didn't find a "V" in the encyclopedia, because the wind blew a tomato at me."

Now that you have learned the new vocabulary words you can help Dr. Memory™ check out the weather. Perhaps you will be a good weather forecaster. You will make statements concerning the weather by month, by season and by time of day. You might say, "En la noche hace frío." In English this is, "In the (at) night it is cold." You could say, "En marzo hace viento." In English this is, "In March it is windy." You could also skip the first part of the drill and say, "Hay nieve." In English this is, "There is snow."

For this drill you must know a few different variations of some words that you have learned. "Llueve" pronounced "you – ay – vay" is "it is raining." "Nieva" pronounced "knee- ay – vah" is "it is snowing." By putting "hace," pronounced "ha – say," before a hot, cold, sun or wind, you can say, "It is cold," etc. "Hace" comes from the verb "hacer," and it literally means "it makes cold, or hot" or whatever. The word for "hot" in this drill is "calor." Have fun!

Doctor Visit (Health)

The next category of words you will learn contains words you might use if you have to **visit a doctor** with concerns about your **health**. There are only 4 new words in this category. You have already learned **doctor**, **ache** and **hurt**, and **ill** and **sick** in other categories.

Study the words on the next page until you know them well before going on. Make sure you know the five bold words in the previous paragraph before you begin the upcoming temperature and weather drill.

emergency - emergencia
ay - mare - hen - sea - ah

The ape on the mare, the hen and this C-clamp will all have to say, "Ah," in the emergency room.

Emergency Entrance

Ah

An ape on a mare horse, a hen and a C-clamp holding a tongue depressor (ah) are standing near the emergency entrance to a hospital. The C-clamp says, "The ape on the mare, the hen and this C-clamp will all have to say, "Ah," in the emergency room."

fever - fiebre
fee - ay - bray

Do you feed or starve a fever, Mr. Ape? Bray, bray?

I think you need some oats to get rid of this fever.

You give me fever.

A

An empty feed bag was placed around the neck of a donkey by an ape. the ape wanted to cheer the donkey up, because it has a fever as the thermometer registers. **The** braying donkey asks the ape its opinion about a fever.

medicine - medicina
may - dee - sea - nah

Hey maid Dee, my sea medicine will knock your cold.

Knock Knock

Preventive Medicine

Maid Dee

Sea

Med Med Med Med Med M

A maid named Dee is standing by a sea throwing medicine into it, because it didn't work. An Indian medicine man is knocking on a sign behind her to tell her his medicine works. The sign reads, "Preventive medicine."

prescription - receta
ray - say - tah

I can't find my prescription, in here anyplace.

Mr. Ray, this sailor has your prescription in tip top shape.

#8

#1 #2 #3 #4 #5 #6 #7

The Prescription for Health

A manta ray was given several prescriptions by a sailor standing in a large top hat. The manta ray says, "I can't find my prescription in here anyplace." The sailor says, "Mr. Ray, this sailor has your prescription in tip top shape." This word also means "recipe."

Now that you have learned the new vocabulary words you can help Dr. Memory™ with his health. Perhaps you will be a good nurse. In this drill you will be addressing a doctor. When you address a doctor you call him "doctor," which is pronounced "doak – tore." His profession is a "medico."

You will also be using a form of the verb "doler," which you know means "to hurt." "Doler" is conjugated like "gustar," so you will use "duele" when discussing singular words and "duelen" when discussing plural words. "Duele" is pronounced "dew - ay - lay," and "duelen" is pronounced "dew - ay - lehn." You might say, "Doctor, me duele la garganta." In English this is, "Doctor, my throat hurts." You could say, "Doctor, me duelen los ojos." In English this is, "Doctor, my eyes hurt." There are more body part words to choose from than will fill two doors, so make sure you know all of the body parts before beginning this drill.

Dr. Memory™ himself has an encouraging message for you in this drill. Have fun!

The next drill will help you if you need to see a doctor. You will be addressing a doctor in this drill just as you did in the last drill. You will also be using three different grouping of verbs. The "estar" verbs are grouped together, and the "tener" verbs are grouped together. The red arrows will help you know where to go from each group of verbs. You will start with the word "doctor" and move up or down as the arrows indicate in order to begin the drill. The ongoing flow of the drill is obvious.

In the upper right portion of the drill you might say, "Doctor, nosostros tenemos una receta." In English this is, "Doctor, we have a prescription." In the middle section of the drill you could say, "Doctor, estoy peor." In English this is, "Doctor, I am worse." In the lower right portion of the drill you might say, "Doctor, este hombre siempre tiene miedo." In English this is, "Doctor, this man is always afraid." Have fun!

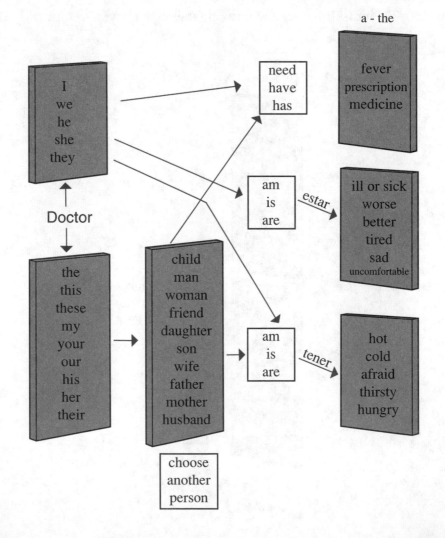

Additional Adverb Drill

The next drill is one of the most interesting of all the drills you have participated in. With this drill you will practice with some adverbs you have not yet used. Some sentences will begin with "generally" or "usually," or you can skip those two words and start with a word in the boxes above or below them. Simply follow the arrows and instructions and have fun. There are no new words to learn.

You might say, "Generalmente, yo siempre escribo muy rápido." In English this is, "Generally, I always write very quickly." You might also say, "Su esposa nunca come menos." In English this is, "Your wife never eats less."

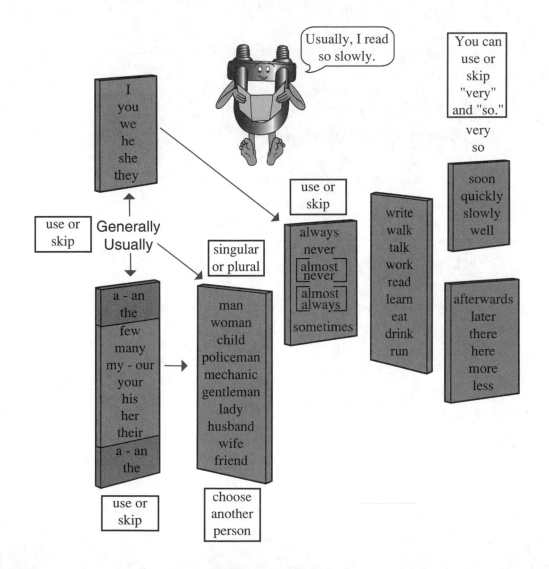

Vital Phrases

There are a few vital phrases you should know. They will help you in many situations. You have learned all of the necessary vocabulary to know all of these words. The phrases will be listed in English and Spanish, so you can practice them.

1.   What is this?   ¿Qué es esto?

2.   How do you say "this" in Spanish?

        ¿Cómo se dice "esto" en español?

        You could plug in any word that you want to learn.

3.   How do you write "book" in Spanish?

        ¿Cómo se escribe "libro" en español?

        You could plug in any word that you want to write.

        The answer would be, ""Libro" is written LIBRO.

        "Libro" es escribe l i b r o.

4.   More slowly, please.

        Más despacio, por favor.

5.   Call the police.

        ¡Llame Ud. a la policía!

6.   It's an emergency.

        ¡Es una emergencia!

Greetings, Introductions and Polite Words

This next drill is the last drill in this book. In most Spanish books readers are taught greetings, introductions and polite words very early in the course, but Dr. Memory™ does things a little differently. It won't do you any good to greet someone in the Spanish language if you can't carry on a conversation. Now that you have completed this book you will not have a problem carrying on a conversation. You may have to ask a Spanish speaker to speak more slowly, but you will understand and be understood. The more practice you can get speaking with Spanish-speaking people the more accomplished you will become with the Spanish language. Very soon Dr. Memory™ will show you how you can make-up your own practice drills, but let's finish this last drill first.

There are several new words you will need to learn for these expressions. Study the following pictures to prepare for the drill. There are 13 new words in this grouping. Some words in the drill will not be in these pictures. These words are simple enough to learn on your own.

excuse me & pardon - perdón
pair - dohn

please - por favor
poor - fah - vohr

Excuse me while I take a pair of Doan's pills.

I beg your pardon.

Please do this, please do that.

Would you please pour this fox a drink. I'm voracious.

My wish is to please.

A pear takes a pair of Doan's backache pills. The sign reads, "I beg your pardon." The pear says, "Excuse me while I take a pair of Doan's pills."

"Would you please pour this fox a drink. I'm voracious," the fox asked its mate. It has been eating everything in sight. No wonder it is thirsty. The female fox sarcastically says, "Please do this, please do that." The sign reads, "My wish is to please."

sorry (I'm sorry) - lo siento
low - sea - ehn - toe

My locomotive went into the sea, and this engineer is totally sorry.

Sorry Express

Sea

You'll be sorry.

A locomotive was driven into the sea by the train engineer after derailing and knocking down a totem pole. The engineer comments on how sorry he is. The sign reads, "You'll be sorry."

thanks & thank you - gracias
grah - sea - ahs

Grotto

My grotto was full of sea water, and this ocelot thanks you.

Sea

An ocelot was pulled out of its grotto by a zoo keeper. The sea had washed into the grotto. A grotto is a cave. The ocelot expressed its thanks. The letters "o" and "c" in the word "ocelot" are actually in two different syllables, but they are pronounced together for our purposes.

goodbye - adiós
ah - dee - ohs

Goodbye!

Ah, Dee, I'm a friendly ghost. Don't say good-bye.

Ah

Dee

Goodbye forever.

A tongue depressor (ah) is held very tightly by a girl named Dee as she runs away from a ghost. She yells, "Goodbye," as she runs. The sign reads, "Goodbye forever."

good morning - buenos dias
boo - ay - nos - dee - ahs

bway

It is not a good morning. This demon is getting the ostrich out of here.

Oh, bwaby with notes, and good morning.

Good morning to you.

A "boo" ghost greets an ape with music notes around it. It says, "Oh, bwaby with notes, it's a good morning." The ghost scared a demon that is riding away on an ostrich. The song playing on the radio is, "Good morning to you."

good afternoon- buenas tardes
boo - ay - nahs - tar - dace

It was a good afternoon for a card game. A "boo" ghost had been playing with an an ape. The ghost has knots on his head. The ghost yells, "Oh, bwaby, I have knots, and this tar has my D-ace." His wife yells, "Good afternoon you bum." A letter "D" is on the ghost's ace for this sound.

good night - buenas noches
boo - ay - nahs - no - chase

It is a good looking night. A "boo" ghost scared an ape. The ghost has knots on his head. The ghost yells, "Oh, bwaby, I have knots. Good night and no chase me," as his wife keeps chasing him and throwing dishes at him. She yells, "Good night I guess." This ghost is still in trouble. Please excuse the bad grammar.

hello & hi - hola
oh - lah

A man wearing overalls says, "Oh, hi, Mr. Llama" to a llama. The llama says, "Hello," back to the man. The sign reads, "If you can't say hello at least say hi."

you're welcome - de nada
day - nah - dah

A daisy knocked a doctor down. The doctor said, "You're welcome." The daisy said, "This daisy knocks docs down, and you're welcome to do the same to me."

This drill is not like the ones you have been using so far to create sentences. The greetings, introductions and polite words will be listed with their Spanish translations, so you can see them side by side. You could say, "Buenos días, señor," which is, "Good morning, sir," in English. You can add any name after these greetings, introductions and polite words.

Good morning, _____.   Buenos días, _____.

Good afternoon, _____.   Buenas tardes, _____.

Good night, _____.   Buenas noches, _____.

How's everything, _____.   ¿Qué tal, _____?

How are you, _____.   ¿Cómo está Ud. _____?

I'm very well, thank you.   Estoy muy bien, gracias.

I'm so so.   Estoy así así.

I'm not very well, thank you.   No estoy muy bien, gracias.

Hello, _____.   Hola, _____.

Thank you, _____.   Gracias, _____.

You're welcome, _____.   De nada, _____.

What is your name?   ¿Cómo se llama Ud.?
                                       This literally means,
                                       "How do you call yourself?"

My name is _____.   Me llamo _____.

Glad to meet you.   Mucho gusto.

The pleasure is mine.	Igualmente.
Goodbye, _____.	Adiós, _____.
Until then, _____.	Hasta luego, _____.
With your permission, _____.	Con permiso, _____.
I beg your pardon, _____.	Perdón, _____.
I'm sorry, _____.	Lo siento, _____.

Make-up Practice

Now that you have learned over 600 Spanish words, how to conjugate verbs and how to form the words you have learned into sentences, you can make up your own practice drills. You can go to Dr. Memory's™ web site where you will find a complete listing of all of the categories of words you have learned as well as a variety of practice drill door formats. You can download them and develop your own practice drills. You can form thousands of combinations for more practice. Simply select the words you wish to practice and the drill format you want to use and place the words on the doors and in the boxes in the appropriate places. You might want extra practice with adjectives, for instance, so you could develop several practice procedures for that category. As you develop these practice formats keep them for future reference. As Dr. Memory™ has stated many times by having **a little bit of discipline** you can be as successful as you want to be.

Now that you have had a lot of practice with Dr. memory's™ practice drills you could also go back to each of his drills and practice with them again plugging in different words to become even more successful. The ways in which to practice are limitless. Use your imagination and create other practice methods.

You have been very successful if you have followed the simple and fun procedures in this book and have had **a little bit of discipline** as Dr. Memory™ has suggested. There will be an opportunity for you to expand your Spanish knowledge and become a fully fluent Spanish speaker when Dr. Memory's™ comprehensive Spanish course is published. Until that time you will be very successful with what you have already learned. Never stop practicing. That is the key to success in any endeavor. It's a great day to remember.

Review List

Body Parts – 42 Words (Pages 68 - 73)

Body Parts from the Neck Up - 17 Words

Beard	Chin	Ear	Eye	Eyebrow
Eyelash	Face	Forehead	Hair	Head
Lip	Mouth	Neck	Nose	Teeth
Throat	Tongue			

Body Parts from the Neck Down - 19 Words

Ankle	Arm	Back	Biceps	Body
Breast	Chest	Elbow	Finger	Fingernail
Fist	Foot	Forearm	Hand	Knee
Leg	Shoulder	Toe	Wrist	

Hand is an exception to the rule. It is feminine even though it ends with a letter "o."

Skin and Internal Body Parts – 6 Words

Blood	Bone	Heart	Muscle	Skin
Stomach				

Animals and Insects – 34 Words - Total Words 76 (Pages 90 - 97)

Animals – 28 Words

Animal	Bear	Bird	Bull	Cat
Chicken	Cow	Deer	Dog	Duck
Elephant	Fish	Fox	Goat	Hen
Horse	Lamb	Lion	Monkey	Pig
Rabbit	Rooster	Sheep	Snake	Tiger
Turkey	Turtle	Wolf		

Insects – 6 Words

Ant	Bee	Bug	Fly	Insect
Spider				

People – 41 Words - Total Words 117 (Pages 112 - 118)

People – General – 5 Words

Friend	Boyfriend	Girlfriend	Man	Woman

People by Vocation – 7 Words

Barber	Beautician	Doctor	Mechanic

Policeman (La policía is used for police in general and el policía is used for a male policeman.)   Waiter   Waitress

People – Relatives – 17 Words

Aunt	Brother	Cousin (2)	Daughter	Father
Grandfather	Grandmother	Husband	Mother	Nephew
Niece	Parents	Sister	Son	Uncle
Wife				

Young & Multiple People & Titles – 12 Words

Baby	Boy	Children	Family	Girl
Group	Lady	Miss	Mister	Mrs.
People	Sir			

Adjectives – 23 Words - Total Words 140 (Pages 112 - 125)

Description by Size - 10 Words

Big & Large	High & Tall	Little & Small	Long

Short (As to things)   Short (As to stature of a person)   Wide

Appearance of People (How People Look) - 13 Words

Bald	Beautiful	Fat	Handsome & Good Looking
Poor	Pretty	Rich	Skinny & Thin
Strong	Ugly	Young	

Pronouns – 18 Words - Total Words 158 (Pages 128 -138)

All, Everything & Whole		He	I	Nobody & No one
Our	Some & Any	She		They We
You	Your, His, Her & Their			

Verbs – Action Words – 34 Words - Total Words 192 (Pages 143 - 147)

Ache & Hurt	Buy	Call	Can & Be Able To	
Carry & Wear	Change & Exchange		Close & Shut	
Do & Make	Drink	Eat	End & Finish	
Find	Give	Go	Have	Hear
Help	Know	Learn	Leave	Like
Live	Need	Open	Talk & Speak	Want

Buildings and Places – 26 Words - Total Words 218 (Pages 152 - 157)

Buildings – 18 Words

Airport	Apartment	Bank	Cafe
Church	Department Store	Drugstore & Pharmacy	
Hospital	Hotel	House & Home	Market
Post Office	Restaurant	Store	Street
Supermarket			

Places – 8 Words

Center & Downtown	City	Corner
District & Neighborhood	Farm	Movie

More Verbs - 24 Words - Total Words 242 (Pages 177 - 182)

Pay	Place	Put	Receive	
Repair	Ride	Run	Say & Tell	See
Sell	Send	Sleep	Take	Travel
Understand	Use	Visit	Walk	Wash
Work	Write	There is	There are	
I want	I'm going	I can	I know how	
I have	I like	I need		

There are a few other verbs taught in the school category.

Clothing – 18 Words - Total Words 260 (Pages 192 - 195)

Male – 7 Words

Necktie & Tie	Pants	Shirt	Suit	T-shirt & Undershirt

Female – 3 Words

Blouse	Dress	Skirt

General – 8 Words

Coat	Clothes & Clothing	Glove	Hat	Jacket
Shoe	Sock			

Colors – 10 Words - Total Words 270 (Pages 196 - 198)

Black	Blonde	Blue	Brown	Brunette
Green	Orange	Red	White	Yellow

Food – 43 Words - Total Words 313 (Pages 200 - 210)

General – 9 Words

Beans	Bread	Burrito	Cheese	Food & Meal
French Fries		Hamburger	Taco	

Vegetables – 7 Words

Carrot	Lettuce	Onion	Potato
Salad	Tomato	Vegetable	

Meats – 6 Words

Meat	Fish	Ham	Pork
Seafood	Turkey		

Drinks – 5 Words

Coffee	Juice	Milk	Soda	Water

(Although "water" has a masculine article (el agua) the word is feminine. "La agua" does not sound good to a Spanish speaker's ears. The plural is "las aguas.")

Desserts – 3 Words

Chocolate	Dessert	Ice Cream

Fruit – 5 Words

Apple	Banana	Fruit	Lemon	Orange

Spices & Condiments – 4 Words

Butter	Pepper	Salt	Sugar

Meals – 4 Words

Breakfast   Lunch   Dinner & Supper

Vehicles – 7 Words - Total Words 320 (Pages 216 - 217)

Bicycle   Bus   Car   Motorcycle
Taxi   Train   Truck

Travel – 10 Words - Total Words 330 (Pages 218 - 220)

Backpack   Camera   Country   Film   Flight
Liter   Map   Passport   Suitcase   Trip

Elements and Environment – 18 Words - Total Words 348
(Pages 221 - 224)

Beach   Cloud   Earth, Ground & Land   Fire
Lake   Moon   Mountain   Rain   River
Sea   Sky   Snow   Star   Sun
Tree   Wave

School Words – 12 Words - Total Words 360 (Pages 228 - 230)

Learn & Write – **Already Taught**   Answer   Count   Draw
Letter (Of the alphabet)   Paper   Pen   Pencil
Read   School   Study   Teacher   Word

Jewelry – 4 Words - Total Words 364 (Pages 231 - 232)

Bracelet   Earring   Necklace   Ring

Days of Week – 7 Words - Total Words 371 (Pages 233 - 234)

Sunday	Monday	Tuesday	Wednesday	Thursday
Friday	Saturday			

Months – 13 Words - Total Words 384 (Pages 235 - 238)

January	February	March	April	May
June	July	August	September	October
November	December	Month		

Printed Material – 3 Words - Total Words 387 (Page 239)

Bible   Book   Magazine (This word has already been taught and is not counted in word total of this category.)
Newspaper

Home - 27 Words - Total Words 414 (Pages 243 - 250)

Rooms – 8 Words

Bathroom	Bedroom	Dining Room	Garage
Kitchen	Living Room	Room	*Swimming Pool

Appliances & Things around the Home - 19 Words

Bed	Bottle	Chair	Clock	Cup
Dish	Fork	Glass	Knife	Magazine
Napkin	Party	Radio	Refrigerator	
Spoon	Stove	Table	Television	Thing

Seasons – 4 Words - Total Words 418 (Page 251)

Autumn	Spring	Summer	Winter

Directions – 9 Words - Total Words 427 (Pages 252 - 253)

Above, Up & Upstairs	Down, Below & Downstairs	
Left	Right	Straight

Numbers – 30 Words - Total Words 457 (Pages 257 - 263)

1	2	3	4	5	6	7	8	9	10
11	12	13	14	15	16	17	18	19	20
30	40	50	60	70	80	90	100	1,000	Dozen

Time of Day – 12 Words - Total Words 469 (Pages 264 - 266)

Afternoon & Late	Day	Evening & Night
Hour	Minute	Morning & Tomorrow
(Note: La manaña" is "morning, and "el manaña" is "tomorrow.")		
Today	Tonight	Yesterday

Adverbs – 23 Words - Total Words 492 (Pages 267 - 269)

Afterwards & Later	Almost	Always & Forever		During
Generally	Here	How Much		Less
More	Never	Now	Quickly, Rapidly & Fast	
Slowly	Sometimes	Soon	There	Usually
Very	Well			

Restaurant – 5 Words - Total Words 497 (Pages 273 - 274)

Bill & Check	Booth	Menu
Restaurant – Already Taught	Tip (Gratuity)	

Shopping – 8 Words - Total Words 505 (Pages 275 - 276)

Cash & Money	Cent	Coin
Cost	Client & Customer	Dollar

More Adjectives - 60 Words - Total Words 565

Appearance of People and Things - 22 Words (Pages 287 - 290)

Bad & Mean	Difficult & Hard	Dumb & Foolish	Easy
Fast	Funny	Important	Intelligent	Interesting
Kind	Lazy	Likeable, Nice & Pleasant	Slow
Smart & Ready		Better	Worse

Description of How People Look or Feel - 14 Words (Pages 292 - 293)

Angry	Bored	Busy	Comfortable	Crazy
Drunk	Happy	Sad & Unhappy		Sick & Ill
Tired	Uncomfortable		Worried	

Description of Which One or What Kind - 10 Words (Pages 296 - 298)

Cheap	Expensive	Good	New	Old
Broken	Clean	Closed	Dirty	Open

Description by Condition - 5 Words (Pages 300 - 301)

Afraid	Cold	Hot & Warm	Hungry	Thirsty
In a Hurry	(The word for "cold" was taught elsewhere."			

Description by How Many - 5 Words (Page 304)

Little & Few   Many, Much & A Lot Of
(All and everything were taught elsewhere.)

Description by Position - 4 Words (Page 308)

First	Last	Middle	Next

Question Words – 8 Words - Total Words 573 (Pages 316 - 318)

"How Much" was taught in adverbs and is not counted in the word total.

How?	How Many?	How Much?	What?	When?
Where?	Which?	Who?	Why?	

Mail – 5 Words - Total Words 578 (Pages 336 - 337)

Letter	Mail	Mailbox	**Package**
Post Office – Already Taught		**Stamp**	Near

Temperature & Weather – 4 Words - Total Words 582 (Pages 339 - 340)

Cold	Hot & Warm	Temperature	**Wind**

Doctor Visit (Health) – 4 Words - Total Words 586 (Page 342)

Ache & Hurt (This verb was taught in the "verb" category)

Doctor (This word was taught in the "people" category)

Emergency	Fever	Medicine	Prescription

Ill & Sick (This word was taught in the "adjective" category)

Vital Phrases – 6 Phrases - Total Words 592 (Page 346)

What is this?	How do you say "this" in Spanish?
How do you write "book" in Spanish?	More slowly, please.
Call the police.	It's an emergency.

Greetings, Introductions and Polite Words – 13 Words

Total Words 605 (Pages 347 - 349)

Plus the additional small words taught in the text.

Excuse Me & Pardon	Please	I'm Sorry
Thanks & Thank You	Goodbye	Good Morning
Good Afternoon	Good Evening	Hello & Hi
You're Welcome		

Doctor Memory™ Web Site

To enter the Doctor Memory™ web site go to:

http://www.doctormemory.com

The auxiliary code for *Picture Perfect Spanish* is PPS001DM.

Doctor Memory™ Products

All Dr. Memory™ products use the Lucas Learning System™ where visually reinforced association models make learning fun and easy. Dr. Memory™ teaches Learning That Lasts™. Please visit the web site at www.doctormemory.com for up-to-date information on the complete product line. Included are descriptions of the complete Learning That Lasts™ product line, as well as actual demonstrations. Excerpts of many of the products are available free of charge also. These revolutionary products available at doctormemory.com include the following:

Adult - Young Adult General Interest

Doctor Memory's™
Picture Perfect Spanish
A Survival Guide to Speaking Spanish

Doctor Memory's™ Learning That Lasts™ methodology is adapted to learn more than 600 "Survival" words required for basic communication of the Spanish language. Careful attention has been paid to insure that the most critical words are taught and that each word is associated with the English equivalent in a way that guarantees accurate pronunciation. In this course, the Spanish language is explored primarily through commonly used words. The addition of basic sentence structure, common phrases and sentences complete the materials; which are designed to prepare the reader to speak the Spanish language more thoroughly than that which is typically covered in a one-year Spanish foreign language course. In addition to teaching over 600 words this book teaches phrases, sentences and basic rules of sentence structure required to speak Spanish.

Doctor Memory's™
Comprehensive Picture Perfect Spanish
Your Reference to the Spanish Language

Doctor Memory's™ Learning That Lasts™ methodology is adapted to aid in the memorization of over 1,600 of the most commonly used Spanish words in this four-volume set. Careful attention has been paid to insure that each word is associated with the English equivalent in a way that guarantees accurate pronunciation. This comprehensive reference teaches words, more detailed grammar, basic sentence structure, conjugation of verbs and more while also exploring common phrases and sentences typical of the Spanish language.

Doctor Memory's™
Names and Faces Made Easy
The Fun and Easy Way to Remember People

The Jerry Lucas technique for remembering names and faces revealed! This unique product tailors Doctor Memory's™ Learning That Lasts™ methodology to aid in remembering the first and last names of those you meet. This method has enabled Mr. Lucas to meet, remember, and correctly pronounce the names of more than 500 people at a time in live studio audience environments. The technique has been successfully taught to hundreds of thousands of people, including numerous Fortune 500 companies. While based on teachings in the best selling The Memory Book, the material covered here is far more detailed and comprehensive. Previously available only through exclusive guest appearances and live seminars, this fun and easy technique can now be purchased in either a book or videotape format.

Doctor Memory's™
Learning How to Learn

Doctor Memory's™ unique learning methodology is taught in detail in this comprehensive follow-up to the best selling The Memory Book that was co-authored by Mr. Lucas in 1973. Learning How to Learn teaches the reader how to apply the Learning That Lasts™ methodology to any subject matter. All eight tools of learning developed by Jerry Lucas are taught in detail. Hundreds of applications are discussed and illustrated. Taking almost 30 years to compile, this is the most innovative and comprehensive learning instruction book ever written!

Childrens' Educational Products

Doctor Memory's™
Ready Set Remember
States & Capitals and The Presidents

Doctor Memory's™ unique Learning That Lasts™ methodology is adapted to children's social studies to instruct the memorization of the states, their capitals, and the presidents of the United States. This book with accompanying audio cassettes will guide the learning process and is ideal for either self-directed students or for use in a more traditional classroom environment. An interactive computer based training version is currently under development and will include animation to assist in learning the geographic location of each state as well.

Doctor Memory's™
Grammar Graphics & Picture Perfect
Punctuation - Volume I

Designed for students, teachers, and adults, this first in an eight volume series includes fun and unique pictures that "lock in" the application and usage of the fundamental rules of grammar and punctuation. Doctor Memory's™ revolutionary learning methodology makes even grammar and punctuation fun and easy to learn!

Doctor Memory's™
Ready Set Remember The Times Tables

Doctor Memory's™ unique learning methodology is adapted to assist in the memorization of the times tables from 2x2 to 12x12. This book teaches a simple and fun method of seeing numbers tangibly. Each problem is then pictured in a unique way in order to differentiate it from the others.

For Families that Wish to Study the Bible Together

Doctor Memory's™
Bible Memory Made Easy

Doctor Memory's™ unique Learning That Lasts™ methodology is adapted to help students of any age to better understand and remember Bible facts in this eight volume video tape series. Students learn the Books of the Bible, the Ten Commandments, the Fruit of the Spirit, selected Bible verses, Gifts of the Spirit, and much more. Just by watching and listening you will learn and remember many of the important teachings of the Bible!

Doctor Memory's™
Bible Basics

A fun and easy way for the whole family to learn together! Doctor Memory's™ unique Learning That Lasts™ methodology is adapted to help students of any age to better understand and remember Bible facts. Students learn the Books of the Bible, the Ten Commandments, the Fruit of the Spirit, Gifts of the Spirit, and much more as they discover how fun and easy learning can be with this book and two accompanying audio cassettes.

Doctor Memory's™
View-A-Verse™
Bible Verse Learning Program

Doctor Memory's™ unique Learning That Lasts™ methodology has been adapted to help students of all ages memorize Bible verses simply and easily by seeing the verses tangibly on learning cards that can be reviewed much like everyday flash cards. However, since the verses are pictured and associated with common everyday objects, two amazing things will happen. First, the verses are easily learned and memorized. Second, when the commonly used everyday objects are seen in real life, the verses will be automatically remembered bringing the Word of God to mind throughout the day! Learning Bible verses has never been so easy or fun.

Soon to be Released Products for Reading and Writing

Doctor Memory's™
Alphabet Friends™

Doctor Memory's™ unique Learning That Lasts™ methodology is adapted to children's reading and writing in this alphabet and phonetic sound recognition program. Each letter is pictured graphically so as to guarantee the student learns to recognize and write upper and lower case shapes. All possible sounds made by each letter are pictured tangibly, so the student can see and never forget them. This revolutionary product is the first ever published that allows students to actually see all of the sounds tangibly. The student also learns how to read words that include the basic sounds. An interactive computer based training version will be available as well as traditional workbooks with instruction manuals.

Doctor Memory's
See and Know Picture Words™ Reading Program

Doctor Memory's™ unique Learning That Lasts™ methodology is adapted to children's reading in this sight word recognition program.. Two hundred twenty words (220) make up 75% of what students will read through the sixth grade and 50% of all words an adult will read throughout their lifetime. All of these "sight" words are pictured graphically to guarantee the student learns the words permanently. Recognition of all significant sounds made within the English language are also taught, including silent letters, letters that change sounds, and the common consonant sound combinations such as "ch" and "th". After completing this course the student will tangibly see and know every sound in the English language while being able to read and pronounce new words. Doctor Memory's™ Alphabet Friends™ is a pre-requisite to this program which will be available in a computer based training version or a more traditional workbook with accompanying instruction.

Give the gift of Learning That Lasts™
to your family, friends, and colleagues.

Check with your favorite bookstore or place your order
by logging onto our website.

www.doctormemory.com

FOR MAIL ORDERS, PLEASE COMPLETE THIS ORDER FORM:

☐ **YES**, I want _____ copies of **Picture Perfect Spanish** at $24.95 each, plus $5.95 shipping and handling for U.S. orders (or $9.70 shipping and handling for foreign orders). Non-U.S. orders must be accompanied by a postal money order in U.S. funds. Please allow 3-4 weeks for delivery within the United States and 6 weeks for delivery elsewhere.

**Call the toll-free phone number noted below
for assistance with completing this order form.**
(Please note: We cannot accept cash, personal checks or C.O.D.'s.)

Check One:
☐ Money Order or ☐ Cashier's Check (payable to Lucas Educational Systems, Inc.)
☐ Visa   ☐ Master Card   ☐ Discover   ☐ American Express

Picture Perfect Spanish @ $24.95 per book	= $_____
Add appropriate shipping charge (as noted above)	= $_____
Add applicable sales tax*	= $_____
TOTAL PAYMENT	= $_____

Include sales tax where required.

Ship to: (please print)

Name_____

Organization_____

Street Address_____

City/State/Zip_____

Phone_____E-Mail_____

Credit Card #_____Exp. Date_____

Signature_____

*For mailing instructions call our
toll free order hot line:*
1-877-479-6463

1-930853-00-9